Approaching Ottoman History
An Introduction to the Sources.

Suraiya Faroqhi is one of the most imp ___ ᴊ**ᴏ**ᴄıaı nistor-
ians of the pre-modern Ottoman empire writing today. Her scholarly
contribution to the field has been prodigious. Her latest book, *Approaching
Ottoman History: An Introduction to the Sources*, represents a summation of
that scholarship, an introduction to the state-of-the-art in Ottoman history, or as the author herself describes it, 'a sharing' of her own fascination
with the field. In a compelling and lucid exploration of the ways that
primary and secondary sources can be used to interpret history, the author
reaches out to students and researchers in the field and in related disciplines
to help familiarise them with these documents. By considering both
archival and narrative sources, she explains to what ends they were
prepared, encouraging her readers to adopt a critical approach to their
findings, and disabusing them of the notion that everything recorded in
official documents is necessarily accurate or even true. Her critique of the
handbook treatments of Ottoman history, quite often the sources students
rely on most frequently during their undergraduate years, provides insights
into the broader historical context. While the book is essentially a guide to
a rich and complex discipline for those about to embark upon their
research, the experienced Ottomanist can expect to find much that is new
and provocative in this candid and sophisticated interpretation of the field.

SURAIYA FAROQHI is Professor of Ottoman Studies in the
Department of Near Eastern Studies at Ludwig Maximilians Universität in
Munich. Her many publications include *Pilgrims and Sultans* (1994) and
Kultur and Alltag im Osmanischen Reich (1995). She is a contributor to Halil
Inalcik (with Donald Quataert), *An Economic and Social History of the
Ottoman Empire, 1300–1914* (1994).

Approaching Ottoman History

AN INTRODUCTION TO THE SOURCES

SURAIYA FAROQHI

Ludwig Maximilians Universität

CAMBRIDGE
UNIVERSITY PRESS

PUBLISHED BY THE PRESS SYNDICATE OF THE UNIVERSITY OF CAMBRIDGE
The Pitt Building, Trumpington Street, Cambridge, United Kingdom

CAMBRIDGE UNIVERSITY PRESS
The Edinburgh Building, Cambridge, CB2 2RU, United Kingdom
http://www.cup.cam.ac.uk
40 West 20th Street, New York, NY 10011–4211, USA   http://www.cup.org
10 Stamford Road, Oakleigh, Melbourne 3166, Australia

First published 1999

Printed in the United Kingdom at the University Press, Cambridge

Typeset in Bembo 10/13pt [VN]

A catalogue record for this book is available from the British Library

Library of Congress cataloguing in publication data

Faroqhi, Suraiya, 1941–
Approaching Ottoman history: an introduction to the sources / Suraiya Faroqhi.
    p.   cm.
ISBN 0 521 66168 4 (hardback). – ISBN 0 521 66648 1 (paperback)
1. Turkey – History – Ottoman Empire, 1288–1918 – Sources.
I. Title.
DR486.F36   1999
956.1'015–dc21   55156   CIP

ISBN 0 521 66168 4 hardback
ISBN 0 521 66648 1 paperback

To Tülay Artan and Halil Berktay,
pursuing a common project of knowledge . . .

CONTENTS

ILLUSTRATIONS

ACKNOWLEDGEMENTS

Every scholar accumulates debts to his/her colleagues. This applies more specially to the present book, which is so largely dependent upon secondary literature. I am grateful to my friends and colleagues Marigold Acland, Virginia Aksan, Arzu Batmaz, Halil Berktay, Palmira Brummett, Eleni Gara, Erica Greber, Huricihan Islamoğlu, Barbara Kellner-Heinkele, Markus Koller, Sabine Prätor, Donald Quataert, Richard Saumarez Smith and Maria Todorova for the time they have taken to improve the finished product. Some of them have read chapters and commented on them, others have provided bibliographical references and much appreciated moral support. Special thanks are due to Ekmeleddin Ihsanoğlu, who allowed me to reproduce the photograph of the Süleymaniye by B. Kargopulo, from the IRSICA collection. The four anonymous readers of Cambridge University Press have caused much soul-searching, which hopefully has improved the quality of the final product. Special thanks are due to Christoph Neumann, who not only read the whole manuscript but even put up with different drafts, and to Christl Catanzaro, whose attention, patience and skill with the computer made life a great deal easier than it would otherwise have been.

If I had been able to follow the guidance so generously given to me, this book would have been much closer to perfection. As things stand, it would be churlish in the extreme to make my friends responsible for the many imperfections which doubtlessly remain.

NOTE ON TRANSLITERATION
Modern Turkish spelling has been used whenever the place, institution or person in question belonged to the Ottoman realm or pre-Ottoman Anatolia, albeit in a marginal way. Only when dealing with Arab or Iranian contexts has the EI's transliteration been adopted; this concerns primarily

the names of modern archives and sections of archives. The Turkish letter (İ) has been retained, except in personal names and geographic terms occurring in isolation, (thus: Inalcik, Izmir). The titles of journals contain the (İ) where appropriate.

1

INTRODUCTION

In this book I hope to share with my readers the fascination with Ottoman sources, both archival and literary in the wider sense of the word, which have become accessible in growing numbers during the last decade or so. The cataloguing of the Prime Minister's Archives in Istanbul advances rapidly, and various instructive library catalogues have appeared, both in Turkey and abroad. On the basis of this source material it has become possible to question, thoroughly revise, and at times totally abandon, the conventional images of Ottoman history which populated the secondary literature as little as thirty years ago. We no longer regard Ottoman officials as incapable of appreciating the complexities of urban economies, nor do we assume that Ottoman peasants lived merely by bartering essential services and without contact to the money economy. We have come to realise that European trade in the Ottoman Empire, while not insignificant both from an economic and a political point of view, was yet dwarfed by interregional and local commerce, to say nothing of the importation of spices, drugs and fine cottons from India.

Not that our methodological sophistication has at all times corresponded to the promises held out by these new sources, far from it. But some stimulating novelties are visible, such as the growing interface between art history and political history of the Ottoman realm, and an awakening interest in comparative projects shared with Indianists or Europeanists. Many Ottomanist historians now seem less parochially fixated on their particular speciality and willing to share the results of their research with representatives of other fields. Paradoxically, the recent growth in the number of available sources has led to a decline in the previously rather notable tendency of Ottomanists to identify with 'their' texts and the points of view incorporated in them. Many of us indeed have become aware of the

1

dangers of 'document fetishism'. By this exotic-sounding term we mean the tendency to reproduce more or less verbatim the statements of our primary sources and the associated unwillingness to use logic and/or experience of the relevant milieu to interpret them (Berktay, 1991). More Ottomanist scholars appear to follow research going on in related disciplines – even though we still have a long way to go before Ottoman history becomes a branch of world history *à part entière*.

In certain instances, Europeanists or Indianists have responded to these developments by showing a degree of interest in Ottoman society. International projects treating trade guilds, the business of war or the movements of gold and silver will now often include an Ottomanist histor-ian, even if the latter may still play the role of the odd man/woman out. Collective volumes treating European economic history will not rarely contain contributions by Ottomanist historians, while until quite recently, chapters on the pre- and/or post-Ottoman histories of certain Balkan territories would have been considered sufficient. Hopefully, the present volume will increase this kind of give and take between Ottomanists and historians of Europe, India or even China, by emphasising some of the methodologically most interesting approaches to Ottoman history.

PRIMARY AND SECONDARY SOURCES

The present book deals with the archival and narrative sources available to the Ottomanist historian, and to a degree, with the historiogra-phy which scholars have constructed on the basis of this material. Primary sources constitute the first priority, a choice which is obviously open to challenge. For while the available primary sources condition the kinds of questions an historian may usefully ask, it is also true that we read secondary sources, including non-scholarly ones such as newspapers and magazines, long before we ever embark on specialised training. One might therefore argue, with some justification, that our view of the primary sources is conditioned by the secondary material we have read, often without even being conscious of the fact. As a result, it has taken European historians studying Ottoman–Habsburg or Ottoman–Polish relations a long time to get away from the glorification of the Austro-Hungarian Empire or Poland as *antemurale Christianitatis*, and there are some who have not managed this act of distancing down to the recent past (Barker, 1967). Conversely the celebration of *sefer ve zafer* (campaigns and victories) for a long time has been part of Turkish historiography, and scholars who attempt to demolish this paradigm are not having an easy time either. Less obviously, our knowledge of the secondary literature will often condition the primary sources we seek and find. Materials that nobody believed to exist even a decade or two ago have been located, once an overriding historiographical concern has caused scholars to look for them. As a recent example, we might mention the case of Ottoman women's history, even though the documents unearthed to date still leave many important questions unanswered.[1]

A case could thus be made for discussing current and not so current secondary studies before embarking on a discussion of primary sources. This would also involve a recapitulation of the 'basic features' of Ottoman state and society, on a level of abstraction more or less acceptable to social scientists. Or else one might decide to integrate an introduction to primary sources into a discussion of secondary research. Stephen Humphreys' work on Middle Eastern history of the pre-Ottoman period constitutes a particularly successful example of this approach (Humphreys, revised edn 1995). But in the present book the opposite approach has been taken, namely to proceed from primary to secondary sources. As long as we do not pretend that we approach our primary material 'without preconceptions', it seems equally reasonable to start research into Ottoman history by examining chronicles and sultans' orders, coins and accounts of pious foundations. And since the explosion of available sources during the last few decades has constituted one of the main reasons for writing this book at all, primary sources will form the starting point of our quest.

There is also a subjective reason for thus stressing archival records and chronicles. Throughout my work in the archives, I have been fascinated by the unexpected documents that will crop up, either suggesting new answers to old questions, or more likely, leading the researcher on to a new track altogether. This is particularly true of the eighteenth century, but any period will offer its own lot of surprises. As a corollary, carefully elaborated dissertation proposals may turn out to be unworkable in the archives; but usually the researcher will find documents suggesting new approaches, not envisaged when the proposal was written. Under such conditions, the historian may stick to the old plan against increased odds, or else abandon him/herself to the drift of the sources. But for the sake of mental stability, it is good to expect the unexpected, and to regard the unpredictable as part of our common human destiny.

From a postmodernist viewpoint, the approach taken in this book will be considered very conservative. In Europeanist historiography, the last twenty years or so have seen a lively debate on the very foundations of

---

[1] For examples see Jennings (1975) and Tucker (1985). Their work, which deals with non-elite women, would have been considered impossible forty or fifty years ago.

historical research. It has been proposed that the personal, social or political bias of any writer trying to recover what happened in the past is overwhelmingly strong. Thus it is impossible to relate the divergent stories about any historical event to things 'as they really happened'. As a background for this claim, the historian of historiography may propose a number of factors: as a new generation of scholars has emerged, economic and social history, which formed the cutting edge of historical research in the 1960s and 1970s, was bound to come under attack sooner or later. Moreover while social and economic history certainly is not practised only by Marxists, this field has traditionally attracted socialists, social-democrats and left liberals. As a result, the revival of the Cold War in the early 1980s, economic deregulation and globalisation, in addition to the collapse of 'bureaucratic socialism' in the past decade have left this branch of study wide open to attack. And while certain representatives of the postmodernist paradigm, such as Michel Foucault, have shown a profound interest in history and a social concern for the rights of deviants and handicapped people, many postmodernists were and are specialists of literature with little interest in social phenomena. These scholars are inclined to enlarge the field of their studies by claiming that social conflict and stratification are of scant importance, while annexing both primary and secondary historical sources to the mass of literary material already within their purview. In the perspective of the more extreme postmodernists, the distinction between primary and secondary sources is in itself an illusion. All that remains is a corpus of texts which can refer to each other but never to a reality outside of them (on this debate, see Evans, 1997).

However in the Ottomanist context, this fundamental debate about the legitimacy of history has not so far left any traces. Whether this situation should be taken as yet another sign of the immaturity of our discipline is open to debate. If any Ottomanist historian were to claim that we should limit ourselves to 'stories' without concerning ourselves overmuch with the degree of truth they contain, doubtlessly this approach would be decried on moral and political grounds. Let us consider an example from a different field: extreme historical relativism makes it impossible for Europeanist historians to counter the claims of those who, for instance, propound that the crimes of the Nazis were invented by the latter's opponents (Evans, 1997, pp. 241–2). In a very similar vein, many Ottomanist historians, and that includes the present author, would be very much dismayed by the notion that one cannot argue against the different varieties of nationalist and other mythmaking which all too often beset our discipline. Maybe the immaturity of our field has some hidden virtues after all . . .

SCANNING THE HORIZON: OTTOMAN AND EUROPEAN HISTORY

The undertakings of both Ottomans and Ottomanists only make sense when we relate them to the wider world. We will therefore begin our *tour d'horizon* with the histories of different regions in which the Ottomans were active, both inside and outside the Empire, or which seem especially instructive for comparative purposes. Many students of Ottoman history outside of Turkey have to some extent been trained in European history. Some non-Turkish Ottomanists may first have turned to Ottoman materials in order to obtain a better understanding of historical problems encountered when studying the history of Spain, Russia or the Netherlands. Thus a researcher dealing with sixteenth-century Dutch history may observe that the Spanish armies attempting to conquer the country after its several rebellions (1565–68, 1569–76, 1576–81) behaved in a rather strange manner. Although they were victorious many times, Spanish commanders typically did not follow up their victories but withdrew, and in the end, the Spanish king lost the war. One eminent specialist has tried to explain this enigmatic behaviour by the Spanish crown's Mediterranean wars with the Ottomans (Parker, 1979, pp. 22–35). Whenever the Spanish conquest of the Netherlands appeared imminent, the Ottoman sultans, who were not particularly anxious to see all the resources of the Spanish Empire deployed against them, stepped up the war in the Mediterranean. The Spanish crown, whose supplies of bullion were great but not inexhaustible, saw no alternative but to draw off some of its resources from the Netherlands. As a result, the Dutch rebels were able to maintain themselves. We may feel intrigued enough by this thesis to explore the relations between the Ottoman and Spanish world empires. Remarkably enough, not many scholars have done so, and the 'forgotten frontier' which separated the two empires still largely remains a *terra incognita* (Hess, 1978).

Another example of Ottoman history's allowing us to place European developments into perspective concerns the question of royal absolutism in the sixteenth century through to the early nineteenth. Conventional wisdom has it that sultanic rule was different in kind from European absolutism, if only because in the Ottoman Empire there existed no private property in agricultural lands and no nobility controlling the countryside, which rulers needed to subdue and pacify (Anderson. 1979, pp. 365–366). But recent research has cast doubt on this clear-cut opposition. We have come to understand that particularly seventeenth- and eighteenth-century sultans operated within the constraints of a high-level bureaucracy whose members possessed well-entrenched households. In spite of their apparent power, these sultans were not nearly as free in their decisions as official ideology postulated (Abou-El-Haj, 1991, p. 44). Remarkably enough, sultanic absolutism really reached its apogee in the nineteenth century, when several sultans sought out the support of European powers to strengthen their rule against rebellious subjects in the capital and provinces (Akarlı, 1988). Under these circumstances, the old question of how early modern European absolutism and sultanic rule compared to one another can be viewed in a new light.

At first, students with a background in European history thus may feel challenged by questions concerning the relations between the Ottoman Empire and the European world. But in time, emphasis may shift. Earlier historians who studied the rich documentation of the English Levant Company or the Marseilles Chamber of Commerce were concerned with European establishments in Syria, Izmir or Egypt. But more recent work has concentrated on the way in which the masses of numerical data provided by European commercial records can be used to shed light upon the surrounding Ottoman society. Daniel Panzac has thus employed the documentation on ships arriving in Marseilles from the Levant (Panzac, 1985). In the eighteenth century such vessels were permitted to enter this port only after presenting a certificate from the French consul resident in the locality from which the voyage had originated. This certificate informed the authorities of the presence or absence of plague in Izmir, Istanbul or Sayda. As a result, a mass of data has come together in Marseilles from all the major ports of the eastern Mediterranean, and Panzac has used this documentation to reconstruct the course of plague epidemics.

But not only epidemic disease in the Ottoman Empire can be studied by a close analysis of French archival records. By examining the many shipping contracts which have survived in the archives of the former French consulate of Alexandria (Egypt), Panzac has demonstrated that by the middle of the eighteenth century, Muslim merchants still constituted the vast majority of all traders freighting French ships in this port. Older historians had believed that by this late date, Muslim merchants had long since vanished from the scene, allowing Christians to take their places (Panzac, 1992). Tunisian historians equally have made good use of the Marseilles records to reconstruct the commercial history of their country, which in the eighteenth century was still an Ottoman province (Sadok, 1987).

In a sense this use of European archives to elucidate Ottoman history is more demanding than the conventional studies of European–Ottoman relations, since one needs to know a great deal about

Ottoman state and society in order to ask the right questions of Levant Company or Chambre de Commerce records. But the results are rewarding, as these kinds of studies allow new insights often unsuspected until quite recently. And once the indispensable background knowledge of Ottoman history is acquired, some students may feel that they might as well specialise in Ottoman history pure and simple.

THE BYZANTINE–OTTOMAN TRANSITION

Western European history apart, one of the fields most closely connected to Ottoman history is its Byzantine conterpart. The special status of this field is in part due to the fact that Byzantine history has benefited from the centuries-old traditions of classicism, so that a large number of the extant sources are available in high-quality editions. Ottoman historians used to working from manuscripts or less than reliable editions will often regard this situation with more than a bit of envy. On the other hand, Byzantine history in the narrow sense of the word came to an end in the fifteenth century, while Ottoman history continued into the twentieth. As a result Ottoman documentation, in which archival materials play a prominent role, can be considered as a variant of early modern and modern recording practices. By contrast Byzantine documentation, which requires the historian to deal with large chunks of narrative history and small archives, fits well into the 'medieval' pattern.

But the difficulties Ottomanists and Byzantinists have experienced in relating to one another stem less from the differences in source bases than from the fact that the relevant fields have been 'adopted' by Turkish and Greek nationalist historiography respectively. There is nothing inevitable in this. I remember the pipedreams of a Turkish archaeologist working on Anatolia, who once wished that Turkish republican ideology had decided to regard Byzantine civilisation as one of the many 'autochthonous' civilisations which had flourished in the Anatolian homeland before the immigration of the Turks. For if that had been the case, money for Byzantinist excavations would have been much more abundant . . . European philhellenism, with its tendency to search for Byzantine 'influence' everywhere, has further complicated matters. For as a defensive reaction, ever since Fuat Köprülü's article of 1931, Turkish historians and, in their wake, foreign Ottomanists have tended to play down links between Byzantines and Ottomans (Köprülü, 1931, reprint 1981).

It is only during the past twenty years or so that a certain number of scholars have made serious efforts to circumnavigate these particular shoals. It may not be entirely due to chance that many of the people involved have at one time or another been linked to institutions on 'neutral' ground, namely the Dumbarton Oaks Center in Washington DC and the Centre for Byzantine, Ottoman and Modern Greek Studies in Birmingham, England. One means of 'defusing' the conflict at least on the linguistic level has been the ample use of Venetian and Genoese sources. Neither Byzantine nor Ottoman, notarial records and commercial correspondences provide information on economic matters, not amply covered by either the Ottoman or the Byzantine documentation of the fifteenth century. A separate field of 'transition studies' has thus come into existence, with its own conferences and edited volumes (Bryer, Lowry, 1986; concerning the historiography, an important article by Klaus-Peter Matschke to be expected soon, hopefully). A major scholar such as Elizabeth Zachariadou has even devoted her life's work to this topic (Zachariadou, 1985).

SCANNING THE HORIZON: OTTOMAN AND ASIAN HISTORY

The study of Ottoman involvement with its Asian neighbours, as well as comparative research into the major Asian empires, constitute relatively new branches of historical endeavour, and researchers concerned with them are still trying to find their feet. As long ago as 1948, Halil Inalcık drew attention to the sixteenth-century attempts of Ottoman governments to maintain liaison with the Central Asian khanates and impose themselves as protectors of the Sunni pilgrims to Mecca originating from that particular region (Inalcık, 1948). For the sixteenth century, Inalcık assumed that Ottoman sultans and their advisers had systematically designed a 'northern policy'. This suggestion did not find favour with the French Central Asianists Alexandre Benningsen and Chantal Lemercier-Quelquejay, who preferred to think in terms of *ad hoc* reactions to specific challenges (Benningsen and Lemercier–Quelquejay, 1976). On the other hand, the idea that sixteenth-century Ottoman sultans developed a coherent 'southern policy' has been adopted by many more scholars. From Cengiz Orhonlu to N. R. Farooqi and Palmira Brummett, historians have pointed out that the Ottoman struggle against the Portuguese in the Indian Ocean, the conquest of the Mamluk sultanate, the establishment of bases on the African coasts of the Red Sea as well as the Indian Ocean and last not least, the control of the Hijaz and Yemen were closely linked as part of a political 'grand design' (Orhonlu, 1974; Farooqi, 1986; Brummett, 1994). Under Süleyman the Magnificent (1520–66) the Ottoman state was apparently poised for the conquest of the coastlands of the Indian Ocean. However naval units sent against the Portuguese were lost and it proved difficult to secure long-term control of Yemen and the coasts of western India. Ottoman statesmen then retreated from the Indian Ocean, concentrating instead on aims closer at hand, such as the conquest of Cyprus and the struggle against the Habsburgs. This set of priorities was to involve the Ottomans in the political struggles of southeastern Europe, while the 'grand design' of controlling both the Mediterranean and the Indian Ocean receded into the background (Özbaran, 1994).

But more modest links between the Ottoman Empire and India endured none the less. In this context, evidence on the important trade between India and the Ottoman provinces of Syria and Egypt has attracted historiographical attention. André Raymond, K.N. Chaudhuri, Halil Inalcık, Halil Sahillioğlu and Katsumi Fukazawa have highlighted the importation of cotton textiles, rice and spices, and the imitation of Indian fabrics by local producers unwilling to relinquish their accustomed market shares (Raymond, 1973–74; Chaudhuri, 1985; Inalcık, 1960a and b; Sahillioğlu, 1985b; Fukazawa, 1987). These studies have also shown that even in the seventeenth and eighteenth centuries, the Indian Ocean trade was by no means a monopoly of the Dutch and English, but that Arab-Ottoman and Indian merchants continued to maintain direct contacts.

A long frontier was shared by the Ottomans and their rivals the Safavid rulers of Iran, which in spite of many wars and conquests, in its northern section corresponds roughly to the present-day frontier between Iran and Turkey. Yet even though Persian was a recognised medium of literary expression at the Ottoman court, and Turkish-speaking tribes played a major role in sixteenth-century Iran, studies of Ottoman–Iranian interactions have remained quite limited in number and scope. A major difficulty stems from the fact that the archives of the Iranian dynasties have for the most part been destroyed, so that it is much easier to reconstruct Ottoman views of Iran than Iranian views of the Ottoman Empire. Many scholars who have approached the topic therefore have studied Ottoman–Iranian relations within the Ottoman context. Bekir Kütükoğlu has discussed the wars and diplomatic crises of the later sixteenth century (Kütükoğlu, 1962). Cornell Fleischer has included an interesting discussion of Iranian immigrants in his path-breaking study of Mustafa Âli (Fleischer, 1986, p. 154). In a fascinating study of the inscriptions of the Süleymaniye, Gülru Necipoğlu has demonstrated how Süleyman the Magnificent had himself depicted as champion of Sunni Islam against Shi'ism (Necipoğlu, 1989). One of the few instances in which historians working on early modern Iran have branched out into the Ottoman Empire concerns the trade of the Armenians, whose far-flung network included Istanbul and Aleppo (Ferrier, 1973).

Even less is known about Ottoman links to China, which for the most part were not direct but mediated through ports in present-day India and Indonesia. While it has long been known that many Ottoman Sultans collected Chinese porcelain, only the recent excavations of Saraçhane/ Istanbul have demonstrated that at least by the seventeenth century, Chinese cups had become something of an item of mass consumption in the Ottoman capital. It has even been surmised that the decline of Iznik fayence owed something to the competition of this Chinese import (Atasoy and Raby, 1989, p. 285). By contrast, the mutual discovery of Ottomans and Japanese was very much a late nineteenth and early twentieth-century phenomenon, and thus belongs to the cultural history of the Hamidian and particularly the Young Turkish period. Through the work of Selçuk Esenbel and her colleagues, we have been allowed the first glimpses of this fascinating story (Esenbel, 1995).

While the study of Ottoman linkages to Asian empires is thus advancing, albeit haltingly, comparative ventures are still fraught with a great deal of difficulty. Again different source bases complicate matters. Ottomanist historians will place a probably exaggerated emphasis upon the archives of the Ottoman central government, while historians of the Safavid period deal mainly with chronicles and local archives. Indianist historians, when addressing economic concerns, have become very expert at extracting information from Portuguese, Dutch and British archives. When dealing with the eighteenth century, this material will be supplemented with information derived from local and even private archives.

Images culled from diverse sources by varying methods are notoriously difficult to compare. But a more serious barrier results from a widespread lack of information concerning 'the other side'. Many Ottomanist or Indianist historians have a reasonable background in European history. But an Ottomanist with even an amateurish interest in Indian history is still a rarity, and the same applies to Indianists knowing something of Ottoman history. Yet even though it may still be premature to study the Ottoman Empire in the context of Asian history, this seems promising in the long run (Togan, 1992).

OTTOMAN HISTORY AND THE SOCIAL SCIENCES

As our next step, we will take a brief look at the manner in which Ottomanists and social scientists have related – or refrained from relating – to one another. Ottomanist historians have almost never generated the paradigms with which they work. Thus a discussion of their relationship to social scientists will lead us to a short and simplistic overview of some of the debates concerning larger issues of historiography originally outside of the Ottomanist field, but in which Ottomanists have become involved. Occasionally we will encounter economists, social anthropologists and sociologists developing an interest in Ottoman history. This is not so common now as it was a decade or two ago, since presently the social sciences are less interested in regional peculiarities than they used to be, and the American tradition of area studies is under massive attack.

Among the generation of scholars active in Turkey today, many distinguished historians have a background in economics, sociology or regional planning. Students and scholars with a social science background will usually want to know about the processes which formed modern Turkish society, and Şevket Pamuk has published a book which attempts to answer these queries (Pamuk, 1988). Rural property relations, craftsmen inside and outside the guilds, monetary flows or the role of religion in politics will be of special interest to historians with a competence in development economics, business administration or sociology. The studies of Huri Islamoğlu, Murat Çızakça and Şerif Mardin constitute notable examples of this tendency, and Ilber Ortaylı's lively and sometimes sarcastic studies of Istanbul's urban history probably have been informed by this author's background in urban planning (Islamoğlu, 1994; Çızakça, 1996; Mardin, 1962; Ortaylı, 1986).

Social anthropologists doing fieldwork on villages and small towns of present-day Turkey will have somewhat different priorities. Rather than trying to make sense of Ottoman history from a social science point of view, they will be looking for historical background information on the places they study. Something similar applies to architectural historians, particularly those working on vernacular architecture. Anthropologists and architectural historians will often find that there are very few 'academic' studies on the places they are dealing with. They are therefore obliged to make extensive use of monographs written in the 1930s and 1940s by historical amateurs. Social anthropologists and architectural historians in this situation may turn to an Ottomanist in order to find out something about the reliability of such studies, and the possibility of locating hard-to-find primary sources. These questions are potentially enriching to the Ottomanist historian, who otherwise is in constant danger of losing him-/herself in the parochial concerns of our discipline.

Viewed from another angle, social anthropologists, whose primary concern is with the present and the recent past, are often charmed by the idea that the history of this or that village can be traced back all the way to the fifteenth or sixteenth century. Some of them have tried to mine oral history for accounts of nineteenth-century settlement processes. Or else the realisation that famous local specialities such as the fruit of Malatya or the hazelnuts of the eastern Black Sea coast have been cultivated in these places for several centuries may help to give field studies a sense of historical depth. Now that few social scientists would claim that 'history is bunk', there exists a real possibility of cooperation between Ottomanists and field anthropologists, which the former will ignore at their own peril (Benedict, 1974, pp. 74–90).

OTTOMAN STATE, OTTOMAN SOCIETY

In the 1980s, Europeanist historians and historical sociologists began to react against the historiography of the previous twenty years, during which economic and social history had held pride of place, by *Bringing the State Back In* (see Tilly, 1985). Ottomanists in due course also became interested in this historiographical current. Only in their case, the situation was somewhat paradoxical, as Ottomanist historiography had always been strongly state-centred, and at first glance, there seemed to be little reason for bringing 'in' what had never been 'out' in the first place. But here appearances are misleading, as 'traditional' Ottomanist state-centredness was overdetermined by the example of new-style Marxian historiography on the one hand, and non-Marxist theories of state formation on the other. Comparativists such as Perry Anderson emphasised that the locus of decisive class struggles was always the state (Anderson, 2nd edn 1979, p.11). For Ottomanist historians who, in Anderson's wake, grappled with the question of state structure in a Marxian sense, a major concern was the degree to which a given state bureaucracy was able to operate independently from the surrounding society (Haldon, 1993, pp. 140 ff.). In the European context, this question often had been phrased differently, namely the issue had been to what extent the state bureaucracy was independent from a landholding or mercantile ruling class.[2] Only in the Ottoman context landholding was closely controlled by the state, so that there existed no ruling class outside of the state apparatus, and this required a rephrasing of the *problématique*. Factionalism within the Ottoman bureaucracy being highly developed, one might usefully debate to what extent the state apparatus was independent of or else controlled by such factions within the ruling class (Kunt, 1974; Fleischer, 1986 pp. 159–161 and elsewhere).

Among Ottomanist historians outside the Marxian tradition and interested in state formation, the work of Charles Tilly has held special

---

[2] For a comparison, in these terms, between the Ottoman and Byzantine states see Haldon, 1993.

attraction (Tilly, 1992). This is in part due to his lively polemical style and his stress on the conflict between ordinary people and the states/ruling classes lording it over them. For scholars striving for a new understanding of the role of war in Ottoman politics, the major advantage is that Tilly has placed war-making along with capital accumulation at the centre of his theory of state formation. Moreover this historical sociologist has done concrete work on early modern France. As a large-scale kingdom with a ruling class strongly oriented toward the exploitation of rural society, France before 1789 also has exerted a special attraction on Ottomanists interested in comparative perspectives. Unfortunately, Tilly does not seem particularly interested in the Ottoman case, emphasising as he does urban capitalism as a variable determining the level of coercion exercised by a given state. This concern has led him to concentrate upon intra-European history, and where the present is concerned, on military régimes and US politics in the Third World.

NATIONALIST HISTORIOGRAPHY

Tilly's 'national state' is an organisation controlling a multiplicity of cities and regions, and possessing a strong bureaucratic armature with a degree of autonomy from the society governed (Tilly, 1992, pp. 2–3). It is thus not coterminous with the nation-state, which Tilly regards as a state whose people share a 'strong religious, linguistic and symbolic identity' (p. 3). According to this definition, France, Germany or England never could count as nation-states, even though it is likely that at least many French historians would disagree with Tilly's claim. The difficulty lies in the fact that the ruling classes of most states which are no nation states in Tilly's sense, still claim to govern a nation state, and a large part of the population tends to agree with them.

Most of the Ottoman successor states are certainly defined in their respective national ideologies as nation states, and have produced national historiographies in which the Ottoman period has been accommodated, often with a good deal of difficulty. Many studies could be written about the image of the Ottoman period in the scholarly and popular historiography of this or that present-day state. Yet reflection on different possibilities of conceptualising the Ottoman impact is a fairly new phenomenon. In part, this questioning is due to disillusion. Several rival ideologies and agendas have come to address the fact that in many instances, the establishment of national states and (would-be) nation states has not made life any easier for the populations involved. This challenge has encouraged reflection on the merits of the nation-state *per se*. In Turkey and the Arab states, some version of Islam has served as a common ground from which historians may question the 'national enmities' which seem to be an indispensable concomitant of the nation-state. Among secularists, the fate of national minorities at the hands of a would-be nation-state often has led to a degree of disillusionment with nationalist ideals, and the civil war in former Yugoslavia has strengthened this feeling.

On the positive side, historians disillusioned with the nation state model have discovered the advantages of plural societies. For a long time, the limited amount of interaction between different ethno-religious communities, or even just populations sharing the same urban space, was considered an irremediable defect of Ottoman society. But this evaluation has now changed. On the one hand, recent research has shown that intra-urban interaction was often more intensive than had been assumed earlier (Faroqhi, 1987, pp. 157 ff.). More importantly, the willingness with which empires such as the Ottoman down to the eighteenth century accommodated separate and unequal communities has gained in respectability. Or at least this is true when compared to the murderous attempts at 'national unification' which have been undertaken throughout the nineteenth and twentieth centuries.

In the Turkish context, historians critical of nationalist historiography have often aimed their darts at the presumed uniqueness of Ottoman society, for which Turkish possesses the pretty formulation *biz bize benzeriz*.[3] Of course the claim to the uniqueness of a 'pre-existing national essence' is common enough among nationalists the world around. Many of the various state formation theories recently developed, for all their obvious differences, aim at demonstrating the fallacy of nationalist essentialism, by showing the contingency both of national boundaries and of the consciousness associated with them (B. Anderson, 1983). Ottomanists attacking the nationalist notion of uniqueness often do so in the name of making Ottoman history accessible to international comparison (Berktay, 1991). For only when we acknowledge that an empire such as the Ottoman shared significant features with its neighbours, can we make sense of certain peculiarities which no one would wish to deny. The existence of a peasant base, consisting of individual peasant households running their own enterprises (as opposed to rural labourers working landholdings managed by outsiders)

---

[3] We resemble (no one but) ourselves.

constitutes the basic feature. All comparative work involving Ottoman society must begin from this point (Inalcık, 1994; Berktay, 1992).

THE ORIENTALIST TRAP

Apart from the dubious claims resulting from nationalism, orientalism constitutes the major trap into which, given prevailing cultural assumptions, many Ottomanist historians are likely to fall. The pervasiveness of orientalist assumptions in secondary studies down to the present day has been shown to us by the critical work of Edward Said and his students. Orientalism involves a persistent tendency to define the Islamic world as the eternal 'other' and an unwillingness to concede that Middle Eastern societies have a history and dynamic of their own. In some instances, such a dynamic may be conceded, but then it is assumed that Middle Eastern history is something *sui generis* and not amenable to historical comparison. It has often been claimed that 'original observation' as opposed to reliance on authority characterised European high culture since the Renaissance. Yet orientalism also involves an excessive reliance on literary sources from long bygone times, so that ancient prejudices get carried over from one generation to the next without much regard for historical realities (Said, 1978, pp. 202 ff.). When discussing the European sources on Ottoman history, this problem must never be left out of sight.

Many elements of the later orientalist world view were originally formulated by seventeenth and eighteenth-century travellers, among whom Jean-Baptiste Tavernier is probably one of the best known (Tavernier, ed. Yérasimos, 1981). This was an enormously enterprising merchant and jeweller, who traversed the Ottoman Empire several times on his way to India.[4] His travelogue contains a rather dubious account of what he considered 'oriental despotism', a concept which ever since has continued to bedevil European political thought. But his work is still indispensible, for he has produced an extensive account of life on the seventeenth-century Ottoman roads which complements the work of his Ottoman contemporary and fellow traveller Evliya Çelebi (Evliya Çelebi, 1896 to 1938).

Political conceptions apart, a further problem posed by European travellers of the period is the fact that they normally had read their predecessors' work. In some instances, maybe when they had lost their own notes, they might even piece together their accounts out of unacknowledged quotes. This way of proceeding may cause the modern user some disagreeable surprises: when working on Eriwan (Revan), in the seventeenth

---

[4] He was to leave France after the toleration of the Protestants had been revoked in 1685 and die, over eighty years old, in the attempt to reach India by way of Russia.

century an Ottoman–Iranian border town, it took me a while to find out that Joseph Pitton de Tournefort, a highly respected French botanist who visited Anatolia and the Caucasus around 1700, had bodily 'lifted' his account from the works of Jean Chardin and Tavernier. To be sure, Pitton de Tournefort mentions the work of these authors; but there is no indication that practically *all* his statements on Revan were derived from his predecessors (Tournefort, ed. Yérasimos, 1982, vol. II, pp. 221–4; Tavernier, ed. Yérasimos, 1981, vol. I, pp. 82–6; Chardin, 1711, vol. II, p. 218ff). This tendency to copy 'ancient authorities' is far from dead today, even though today's scholars are more careful about acknowledging their sources. Of course the inclination to accept travellers' claims at face value reinforces the ahistorical tendency of much European writing on the Middle East, which Edward Said has justly attacked. Given these circumstances, it is tempting to disregard the testimony of European travellers altogether. But since many kinds of information that we urgently need have been preserved only by these authors, we will have to learn to use their work, albeit with a great deal of caution.

As we have seen, there exists a degree of continuity between the travellers of the seventeenth, eighteenth and nineteenth centuries on the one hand, and the nineteenth-century orientalists on the other. Certain scholars, such the Prussian A. J. Mordtmann Sen. (1811–1879) or later the Czech Alois Musil (1868–1944) were in fact both academics and travellers (Mordtmann, ed. Babinger, 1925). Some of these people might combine scholarly and diplomatic roles, the latter of which in some cases shaded off into espionage activity. Thus the famous Dutch Islamicist Christian Snouck Hurgronje at the end of the nineteenth century, even managed to stay in Mecca for a while as the guest of the reigning Sherif. He had been sent by his government to unearth information about the Javanese and other Dutch subjects of present-day Indonesia who went on pilgrimage to Mecca in increasing numbers at the end of the nineteenth century. It was assumed that there they might become imbued with Pan-islamic sentiments, and upon their return, constitute a danger to the Dutch administration of the islands (Snouck Hurgonje, 1931, pp. 290–2). Obviously it is not possible in a short introductory volume to discuss the political ramifications of the work of all Ottomanists of the recent past. But the examples mentioned here and there should at least make us sensitive to the issue.

MODES OF PRODUCTION AND WORLD SYSTEMS THEORY

Paradigms of present-day scholarship are even more difficult to fairly describe than those of the past; as the owl of Minerva flies in the dark, the main lines of a paradigm usually become visible only when it is already on the way out. However we will at least briefly refer to the role of Ottoman studies in the discussion concerning the 'Asian Mode of Production' (AMP). This Marxian concept, which in the 1960s regained relevance particularly among French anthropologists, also found adherents among Turkish economists and social scientists (Divitçioğlu, 1967). At the same time, another group of political intellectuals explored the possibilities of the concept of 'feudalism'. Certain Ottoman economic historians, some of whom had also used the AMP as a framework for their research, equally involved themselves with the 'world systems' paradigm put forward by Immanuel Wallerstein and his school (Islamoğlu-Inan, 1987).

The debate concerning the relative merits of the 'Asian Mode of Production' and 'feudalism' has been marred by numerous complications and misunderstandings. Extraneous considerations of left-wing political strategy tended to get mixed up in the debate to the great disadvantage of its intellectual content. Apart from that, the fate of AMP in international discussion, outside the Ottoman context, has also caused difficulties for Ottomanists. The concept had originally gained favour as a means of counteracting a notion of history which assumed that all societies necessarily would have to pass through the same sequence of 'stages'. This idea of historical stages had been widespread in nineteenth and early twentieth-century social theory, both within Marxism and outside of it. By assuming that certain societies were neither 'primitive', 'feudal' nor 'capitalist', social theory of a Marxian bent regained a degree of flexibility which had been lost during the Stalinist period. However after about 1980, the AMP was sharply attacked by many scholars as eurocentric, and as a result, most Turkish adherents of AMP gave up or at least strongly modified their views.[5]

As to the 'feudalism' side of the debate, many participants have been unaware that two different meanings can be attached to this particular term. One of them is inapplicable to Ottoman history because it involves things such as vassalage and feudal homage, which never existed in the Ottoman world. But the other usage simply refers to a society of peasants managing their own farms, and thus having direct access to their means of livelihood. Such peasants, who can directly reproduce themselves with the products of their own labour, can be made to hand over part of their produce only by non-economic coercion (Berktay, 1985). This broad use of the term 'feudal' is applicable to a great many human societies of the pre-industrial age.

---

[5] Compare Abou-El-Haj's criticism of Anderson: Abou-El-Haj (1991), pp. 105–6; Anderson (1979), pp. 361–94. Keyder (1987) contains an interesting development on continuity between the Byzantine, Ottoman and early Republican periods which appears to result from the author's previous espousal of AMP.

Debate therefore has centred upon the question whether peasants yielding part of their produce to a central state in the shape of taxes, and not as rent to a feudal lord, can properly be included in the 'feudal' category. For the specialist Ottomanist historian, the main advantage of this debate is probably the stimulus it has given to comparative history.

While the 'feudalism debate' has during the last few years lost many of its political implications, this does not apply to the discussion connected with the concept of a world system, associated primarily with the name of Immanuel Wallerstein (Wallerstein, 1974, 1980, 1989). The manner in which the Ottoman Empire was 'incorporated' into a world system, dominated by a capitalist Europe and later by the United States, continues to be of political relevance. As a result, this linkage of Ottoman history with the debate on world systems theory as an explanatory model continues to make many historians uncomfortable. But from a professional point of view, the links of certain Ottomanist historians to the Wallersteinian school also have had very positive consequences. While Ottoman history in the past few decades was often an arcane endeavour of little interest to anybody but its practitioners, the debate on world systems theory has made it much easier for Ottomanists to enter a broader historical discussion. And that should be an appreciable advantage to students now entering the field.[6]

DESIGNING RESEARCH IN OTTOMAN HISTORY: SOME PRELIMINARY REFLECTIONS

As has become apparent from the preceding paragraphs, working as an historian implies questioning our own motives. This is easier said than done, for usually we need a certain distance before motivations, our own or those of our predecessors, will become visible to us. Political changes in the world we inhabit are often a precondition for changes of scholarly orientation; but these changes constitute merely a necessary and not a sufficient condition. Only the anticolonial struggles of the post-World War II period have made it possible for us to question the views of many European and American practitioners of orientalism in the nineteenth century and early twentieth. It has taken quite some time and intellectual effort to acknowledge the simple fact that many of these people were either colonial administrators themselves or else trained such officials, and that these political concerns had an impact on their scholarship (Said, 1978). Obviously the generation presently active in Ottoman history has its own political agendas, and will in its turn be questioned by its successors, in all likelihood with

---

[6] Among the historians with a strong interest in the Wallersteinian paradigm, one might name Murat Çizakça, Huricihan Islamoğlu-Inan, Reşat Kasaba, Çağlar Keyder and Donald Quataert.

unflattering results. But an even worse thing is also 'on the cards' – our work may be considered too insignificant to be worth demolishing . . .

Reflection on our activities as historians will start where the student planning a paper or thesis normally begins. During the first stage of his/ her work, the prospective author may have only a very vague notion of the topic to be covered. Certain people will be fascinated with a given primary source and decide to make it the basis of their study. Thus the correspondence of a vizier or sultan's mother, or else the diary of a dervish, may become the basis for a combined historical and philological examination. The text is edited, translated, or if that is not feasible, summarised and annotated. At a later stage, this explicated text will serve as a means of understanding processes of communication within the Ottoman Palace, the prerogatives of royal women, or the process of education within a dervish convent. This type of study is perfectly legitimate; however it involves a good deal of philology, and many ambitious researchers prefer to look for something 'more theoretical'. This will generally involve a *problématique* derived from current research as reflected in the secondary literature, both Ottomanist and non-Ottomanist. A student may recognise that Ottoman notables of the eighteenth century, even though they wished to govern the localities they controlled with as little outside interference as possible, for the most part did not attempt to set up independent states. Starting from this observation, he/she may launch an inquiry into the mechanisms, such as tax-farming, which integrated provincial notables into the fabric of the Ottoman state (Salzmann, 1993). Moreover a student may first familiarise him/herself with the problem-oriented historiography practised by the more respected representatives of the profession today. But as a second step, he/she may decide to return to the interpretation of a given primary source with questions derived from sophisticated *problématiques*. Cemal Kafadar's work on Ottoman diaries and letters springs to mind in this context (Kafadar, 1989, 1992).

TIME, SPACE AND TOPICS

As an introductory volume, the present text makes no claim to comprehensiveness. Even less do I aim to recreate the all-knowing impartiality and invisibility so typical of narrators in certain nineteenth-century novels. My own competences, and even more, blind spots, have had a visible impact upon the composition of this book. Many more examples come from the sixteenth, seventeenth and early eighteenth centuries than from the periods before and afterward. For in my own work I have concentrated upon this particular period, which we will often call 'early modern'. Where the nineteenth century is concerned, more is said about the

Tanzimat than about the Hamidian period, and more about the latter than about the early twentieth century. I apologise to the reader on this account. But given the enormous amounts of material which have become available on especially the latest periods of Ottoman history, this topic should be dealt with by a specialist on Abdülhamid II and the Young Turks.

Less of an apology is due, I think, for the focus on Istanbul and Anatolia, and for concentration upon the Muslim rather than the non-Muslim section of the Ottoman population. To begin with, the documentation available in Istanbul and Ankara does accord pride of place to these groups; and I have decided to follow the drift of the sources. Yet in spite of an abundance of source material, it would seem that Anatolia constitutes one of the former Ottoman provinces most neglected by historians, and I hope to contribute toward correcting this imbalance. Moreover there exists a flourishing secondary literature on the former Arab, Greek, Serbian, Bosnian and Bulgarian provinces of the Ottoman Empire in the languages of the relevant modern nations. Unfortunately I do not read any of these, and my discussion remains confined to works in Ottoman and modern Turkish, English, French and German. As to the historiographical discussion in Syria, Egypt or Greece, it can be accessed only imperfectly through the more or less rapid summaries available in western languages. After writing brief overviews over these discussions for an earlier version of this book, I have become aware of all the aspects closed to me because of my linguistic limitations. I have therefore consigned my drafts to the wastepaper-basket without too much regret.

In certain chapters or sections of chapters, a more or less limited topic will be covered by way of example, such as rural history in chapter 4. Hopefully, current methodological discussion of particular kinds of sources thereby will become accessible to the non-specialist. However in chapters 2, 3 and 6 this arrangement, when first attempted, resulted in a rather artificial text, and these chapters have been rewritten as ordinary surveys. Topics have been selected according to my own interests and areas of competence, and I must stress once again that there is no claim to exhaustiveness. Political nd military history have been downplayed, obviously not because they lack importance. But personal competence apart, I have tried to provide a counterweight to the still rather widespread notion of the Ottoman Empire as a perfect war machine governed by an upper class totally uninterested in economic problems. This aim can probably not be pursued without weighting the balance in the opposite direction. In any case, the rediscovery of Ottoman political history is well underway (Har-El 1995, Hickok 1997), and it will not be difficult for the reader to fill in the gaps of this rather selective account.

Two kinds of users have been envisaged for the present book. On the one hand, there are the students of Ottoman history, and on the other, beginning researchers or specialists in other historical disciplines who need information on the use of a particular source category. These readers will hopefully use the present book as a kind of map, which indicates opportunities for further research, and also, on occasion, dead ends and road blocks best avoided. Moreover it is hoped that people involved in Middle East survey courses, either as teachers or as students, will find some supplementary readings here. The needs of these different categories of readers overlap only to a limited degree, and some sections will seem elementary to one type of reader and rather complicated to another. Writing two separate books for beginning and advanced audiences would have resulted in a more unified text in both instances. But given the relatively small number of students and teachers concerned by our discipline, this solution would not have been feasible from a practical point of view. Yet most chapters can stand on their own to some extent; it is therefore possible to select individual chapters according to current needs. In addition, the reading lists at the end of each chapter will hopefully make life easier for the beginner. Given their brevity, these lists cannot avoid being highly subjective, and the comments in parentheses even more so. I trust, their usefulness to the reader will outweigh the critical asperities which the author will doubtlessly suffer on their account.

THE SCOPE OF THIS BOOK: SEARCHING FOR PRIMARY SOURCES

As it is one of the aims of this book to help students newly entering the field, the next chapter (chapter 2) will contain information which mature researchers may decide to skip. The section 'Works of Reference' at the end of this book will introduce the major dictionaries and bibliographies. Chapter 3 is devoted to libraries and archives, along with the publications which give the researcher an idea of the holdings of these institutions. Building on this information, Chapter 4 introduces a few frequently consulted document types, and also discusses the uses to which these sources can be put. As an example, we will survey the documents which can provide information on Ottoman rural society, a choice motivated by two considerations. On the one hand, the vast majority of Ottoman subjects were peasants and nomads. We tend to forget this basic fact of life in our absorption with the documents, in which members of the ruling groups and townsmen in general are vastly overrepresented. On the other hand, this discussion will allow us to introduce the fifteenth- and sixteenth-century tax registers (*tahrir*), arguably the best known and most intensively studied among Ottoman primary sources.

THE SCOPE OF THIS BOOK: PROBLEMS OF GENRE

Both primary and secondary sources are not products of nature but were written by people. In order to critically evaluate them, we must know something about the manner in which they were composed. Most insidious, because most easily overlooked, are the conventions of genre. Everything we say or write, and everything that was said or written in the past, belongs either to an established genre or to a 'mixed' type combining the properties of several genres. Every genre has its own rules, and the impact of such rules on historical writing will be examined for the European context in chapter 5, and for the Ottomanist context in chapter 6.

In the European context we will pay special attention to travel accounts. For apart from a very few histories and archival documents, travelogues constitute the main genre in which Europeans of the sixteenth and seventeenth centuries expressed their views of the Middle East. The most widespread type was the pilgrimage account, which recorded a visit to Jerusalem and other biblical sites in Palestine. Unfortunately, the 'genre rules' of the pilgrimage account did not include individual observations made on the trip. With a few exceptions proving the rule and which we will discuss, the historian of the Middle East will find this genre singularly unrewarding. Among other travel accounts, one must mention the reports on diplomatic missions, which were composed according to their own well-established rules. As we have already seen, using travel accounts of any kind means coming to terms with the inclination of many writers to copy their predecessors. It is therefore necessary to form some notion of what claims to authorial originality meant in practice, when made by different authors of the sixteenth, seventeenth or eighteenth century.

On the Ottoman side, genre conventions equally constrained what a given author might be able to say. Thus many Ottoman chroniclers used the reigns of sultans as a means of organising their material, a preference more or less comparable to our use of the concept of 'century', and of course equally arbitrary. When a chronicler for one reason or another departed from this format, we are confronted with a major change in style of thinking, and we have to investigate the reasons which may have prompted this decision (Neumann, 1994, pp. 53f). Moreover, even the authors of archival documents had to cope with the literary conventions of their genre. An Ottoman petitioner normally began his missive with a variation of 'it is the submission of this slave that . . .' and ended with the phrase 'and it is my lord's prerogative to command.' Or to mention a less straightforward example, it was common for sixteenth-century sultans' commands to include what looked like verbatim statements on the part of complainant or accused, people whose activities had originally motivated state officials to lay down the law in the name of the Sultan. These 'quotations' were couched in a non-literary language, probably close to actual speech. It is tempting to regard these phrases as actual quotations, and some of them may have been just that. But it is equally probable that these so-called quotations were included primarily for stylistic reasons, to provide a contrast between the rough language of mercenaries or robbers and the more or less polished writing of the bureaucrats composing the documents. As a result, it would be incautious to take these 'quotations' at face value (Veinstein, 1996).

Historical writing such as it is practised today, equally constitutes a 'literary' genre of its own, even though the literary talents of many historians may be quite limited. This means that when we read secondary literature, we also have to look for conventions of style, which limit what can legitimately be said in a history text of a given period. When I started to read historical secondary literature as a teenager in the late 1950s and early 1960s, I used to think how strange it was that family relations, which in my own experience constituted the determining factor of life, were never treated in the history books I encountered. This was of course quite correct as an observation; the studies I had access to at the time did not allow for the treatment of the 'private' lives of ordinary people. Family studies of the kind which are being written today, even by some Ottomanist historians, could only be accommodated by the genre of 'history writing' after the rules of this genre had been 'bent' somewhat (Duben, Behar, 1991). Or to give another example of the constraining force of genre conventions, present-day publishing practices, as well as the rules of academic promotion, often oblige the author of a manuscript presented for publication to comply with specifications made by anonymous readers. In order to get their books published, authors may well find themselves making statements which they may personally endorse only to a limited degree. Our critique of our contemporaries' output must therefore include an appreciation of the more or less rapid change, or else the stubborn inflexibility, of genre conventions.

TOWARD A NEW STYLE IN OTTOMANIST HISTORY-WRITING

Ottoman history presently finds itself in a situation in which basic assumptions, which had been accepted more or less tranquilly for several decades, are being questioned (Abou-El-Haj, 1991; Berktay, 1991). Therefore it is appropriate to include a short history of Ottomanist historiography (chapter 7). This is really a topic for a separate study. Chapter 7 will therefore limit itself to the syntheses which students normally encounter during their studies, and from which researchers gather their first impressions of Ottomanist research.

This procedure may be considered somewhat unfair to the field, because here as anywhere else, manuals tend to lag behind scholarly discussions. Articles forty or fifty years old are consulted only by specialists, with due regard for the fact that further research has been undertaken in the meantime. But manuals seventy years old and older, such as Lybyer's account of Ottoman administration in the age of Süleyman the Magnificent (Lybyer, 1913), will often be used by non-specialists as if they reflected the state of the art. On the other hand, a chapter focusing on manuals as opposed to monographs or articles may warn the reader against their uncritical use.

Manuals are intended to convey information, both on 'the facts of the case' and, in the more sophisticated works, on conceptual developments as well. The sheer accumulation of information which has taken place in the past years probably forms a necessary though not a sufficient precondition for the questioning of *problématiques* we are presently experiencing. People who wish to challenge the ruling paradigms now can obtain the data with which to do this, which was not usually true even twenty years ago. More importantly, changes in political climate have permitted some scholars to doubt the national state as a suitable yardstick by which to measure the performance of non-national empires, including the Ottoman. Current scepticism toward notions implying any kind of 'progress' also has contributed toward current revisions of Ottoman history. For it has become meaningless to claim that the Ottoman state and others of its kind were somehow inferior because 'not modern'.[7] Hopefully, the ongoing revisions of social and political concepts will make possible a different kind of

---

[7] However, scepticism about progress, while permitting us to get rid of some stultifying stereotypes, is not without its pitfalls. Not a few Ottomanist historians have a tendency to set themselves up as *laudatores temporis acti*, idealising the reign of Sultan Mehmed II, Süleyman I or Abdülhamid II. Intellectual respectability is often maintained by emphasising normative texts, which can then be interpreted in such a way that they appear as descriptions of actual conditions. That this idealisation of the past is often a response to the wholesale denigration of the Middle East by Orientalists is not in doubt; but even so, it can lead to some rather dubious historiography.

Ottoman history, which a growing number of scholars are now trying to achieve.

SUGGESTED READING

Abou-El-Haj, Rifa'at A. (1991). *Formation of the Modern State, The Ottoman Empire, Sixteenth to Eighteenth Centuries* (Albany NY: SUNY Press) (controversial, thought-provoking).

Anderson, Benedict (1983). *Imagined Communities, Reflections on the Origin and Spread of Nationalism* (London, New York: Verso) (based on southeast Asian evidence, the author explains how national communities are not natural phenomena, but have been created by people, often in very recent periods).

Anderson, Perry (1979). *Lineages of the Absolutist State* (London: Verso) (comparative history in a Marxian framework).

Bayly, Christopher A. (1983). *Rulers, Townsmen and Bazaars, North Indian society in the age of British expansion, 1770–1870* (Cambridge: Cambridge University Press) (great ideas concerning the impact of centralisation/decentralisation on commercial life).

Braudel, Fernand (2nd edn, 1966). *La Méditerranée et le monde méditerranéen à l'époque de Philippe II*, 2 vols. (Paris: Librairie Armand Colin) (1st edn in one volume, 1949) (More than any other, this work has placed Ottoman history on the world historical map).

(1979) *Civilisation matérielle, économie et capitalisme*, 3 vols. (Paris: Armand Colin) (fundamental for the history of trade and commercial agriculture, a 'five-star' book).

Esenbel, Selçuk (1995). 'İslam Dünyasında Japon İmgesi: Abdürreşid İbrahim ve Geç Meiji Dönemi Japonları', *Toplumsal Tarih*, 19, 18–26.

Evans, Richard (1997). *In Defense of History* (London: Granta Books).

Haldon, John (1993). *The State and the Tributary Mode of Production* (London: Verso) (comparative history, by a Marx-inspired Byzantinist).

Hess, Andrew (1978). *The Forgotten Frontier, A History of the Sixteenth-century Ibero-African Frontier* (Chicago, London: Chicago University Press) (brilliant; has unfortunately remained an isolated phenomenon).

Humphreys, R. Stephen (revised edn 1995). *Islamic History, a Framework for Inquiry* (London, New York: I. B. Tauris) (focus on the mediaeval Middle East, many ideas on research projects).

Inalcık, Halil (1969). 'Capital Formation in the Ottoman Empire', *The Journal of Economic History*, XXIX, 1, 97–140 (a classic; one of the texts which made the author into *the* major figure in Ottoman history).

İslamoğlu-İnan, Huri (1987). 'Oriental Despotism in World System Perspective', in *The Ottoman Empire and the World Economy*, ed. Huri İslamoğlu-İnan (Cambridge, Paris: Cambridge University Press and Maison des Sciences de l'Homme), pp. 1–26 (important discussion of the *problématique*).

Rodinson, Maxime (1987). *Europe and the Mystique of Islam*, tr. by Roger Veinus (Seattle, London: University of Washington Press) (thoughtful and informative).

Said, Edward W. (1978). *Orientalism* (New York: Vintage Books) (the book which changed the course of Middle Eastern studies; 'required reading', even though the Ottoman world is marginal to the author's interests).

Wallerstein, Immanuel (1974, 1980, 1989). *The Modern World-System*, 3 vols. (New York etc: Academic Press) (another 'paradigm creator' for many Ottomanist historians, including the present author).

2

ENTERING THE FIELD

PRELIMINARIES: LANGUAGE AND CULTURAL SKILLS

The present chapter being directed at the student entering the field, a few words should be said about the languages which the future Ottoman historian will need for his/her research. Here it is important to be realistic, and we will need to distinguish scholarly ideals from what can be realised with the practical possibilities at hand. Indispensable for everyone are Ottoman and modern Turkish, along with English as the major means of access to the international scholarly community. Ottoman is easier to learn if one already knows some Turkish; but experience with Turkish undergraduates has shown that the task is not easy even for them. Speakers of Arabic sometimes acquire access to Ottoman by learning the basic rules of Turkish grammar and using their knowledge of the script and large chunks of vocabulary. In this case, it must be remembered that the meanings Ottomans attached to Arabic loanwords are often different from those which the same words bear in the language of origin.

What other languages will be learnt depends on the questions the historian proposes to study. Alternatively, certain scholars may select their future fields according to the languages they already know. It is a truism, that anybody with more than a casual interest in early modern Balkan history should learn Ottoman in addition to Greek, Serbian, Bulgarian or whatever language is relevant. But in real life, this rule is often violated. Arabic is an absolute necessity for those people wishing to study not only the Arab provinces of the empire, but also the history of Ottoman science or law. French is an urgent need for those interested in the eighteenth and nineteenth centuries, when this language was used among educated Europeans as a *lingua franca*. Moreover, by the second half of the nineteenth century, the category 'educated Europeans' included quite a few members of the Ottoman upper class. This list obviously could be continued, but it is important to not make language into a fetish. Certain scholars have been known to spend so much energy on the acquisition of languages that they had little to say in any of the multitude of languages they knew. It is possible to write articles or even books as a cooperative venture between two or three scholars. This procedure allows the combination of language skills as required by the project to be undertaken. However, coauthoring does presuppose that the participants possess both social skills and a willingness to share their experiences. But then team spirit, in this day and age, is a virtue acquired and practised by many people.

More problematic is the question of what we may call 'cultural literacy', because it is not usually possible to make up for this deficiency by cooperation. Ottoman civilisation is no longer with us, even though its impact is. Tracing continuities is a favourite game among historians, and some modern authorities choose to place the'great divide' between Ottoman and modern Turkish society at some fairly late point in time (both Keyder, 1987 and Zürcher, 1993 seem to favour 1945–50). But whatever date is adopted, we must come to terms with the fact that Ottoman civilisation, especially in the shape it possessed before 1850 or so, is very different from its modern Turkish counterpart. This applies even to that version of present-day Turkish civilisation typical of circles who think of themselves as conservative. Given these circumstances, appreciating a piece from an eighteenth-century collection of poetry (*divan*) is an arduous skill to learn. This applies even to a Turkish student knowing Ottoman, to say nothing of anyone else.

Acquiring cultural literacy is thus a long-term process, which takes much longer than the acquisition of a working knowledge of most languages. Things are not made any easier by the fact that Ottomanist history is a relatively new discipline, practiced by a limited number of scholars. As a result, our field does not possess the multitude of books, films or videos which permit a curious spectator to initiate him/herself, for instance, to French cathedrals or Mozart's music. This is a problem which some scholars are now beginning to tackle, for instance the art historians currently working on Islamic ornament. But it is unlikely to be solved within the present generation.

HOW TO START?

In principle, one could start any historical research by locating, comparing and interpreting primary sources, and the organisation of this book might seem to invite this procedure. But in practice, this is rather a difficult undertaking. The relevant materials are for the most part not available in print, and given their great number, the vast majority will probably remain unpublished. More importantly, a text of any kind will only make sense if it is placed in the context in which it was composed. We cannot hope to understand the intentions of a chronicler unless we know who he was. Or if that is not possible, we at least need to know something about the political and social environment in which the work in question was written. We also need to determine what literary conventions governed composition, and who the intended addressee was. Last but not least, we need to find out what practical purpose the author had in mind; for instance, he may have been hunting for promotion at court by interesting a patron in his fate. Or else he was trying to legitimise a dervish convent by linking up this establishment with a saintly founder. For the holiness of a given dervish lodge, if made credible by a suitable legend, was probably important for those who solicited gifts from pious donors. Most of this information will not be immediately obvious from the primary source in question, and we will need to search in the secondary literature – where often enough, we will not find satisfactory information either.

Therefore the reading of a document establishing a pious founda-tion in Istanbul or Damascus, or of a customs register enumerating the shops of Iskenderun, may give us an initial notion of the questions we may treat. But usually it is more practical to begin with the secondary literature, in the notes of which we will find references to the relevant primary sources. There is however a danger involved in this convenient approach: an opinion may be widespread in the secondary literature without having much of a basis in fact. It is quite amazing what will get transmitted from one author to another over the generations. Some errors may be just amusing, such as the story that the heads of the Ottoman religious-*cum*-legal hierarchy, the *şeyhülislam*s, if executed, were ground to death in a gigantic mortar and pestle (Majer, 1989). Others are more serious, and have much hampered research, such as the inclination to explain anything and everything by 'Ottoman decline' (for a challenge to this tendency, see Darling, 1996, pp. 1–21). Established scholars are likely to have ingested the relevant miscon-ceptions, so to speak, with their 'mother's milk'. By contrast, young re-searchers approaching the topic with a fresh eye have a better chance of spotting inconsistencies in the secondary literature if they first immerse themselves in the primary sources, never mind what our contemporaries and predecessors have said about them. There is no easy solution to this difficulty.

Moreover the decision to start with primary or secondary sources may have implications for the manner in which historical study is understood. According to a view widespread at the turn of the last century, and still held by some scholars, our historical research is supposed to reconstruct an image of 'how things really were'. In order to advance toward that goal, the careful analysis of primary sources constitutes the major precondition; the work of predecessors is useful only in so far as it aids this analysis. Scholars who see history writing in this fashion therefore may praise a colleague for referring exclusively to primary sources in his/her notes (Quirin, 1991, p. 39 claims that this should in principle be demanded of any historical study).

However, the experiences of the twentieth century have left many of us with a good deal of scepticism concerning our capacity to understand or depict 'how things really were'. Advancing source criticism has made it obvious that even a list of taxpayers is not the unmediated reflection of an 'objective' reality, but the product of the assumptions, often quite unconscious, of the people who put it together (Ludden, 1989, pp. 102–14 discusses the problem on the basis of an example from Indian history). If primary sources are full of biases the extent of which we can never fully measure, the same is obviously true of present-day historiography as well. A reader of Edward Said's work may well come away with the melancholy reflection that present-day western culture is so ingrainedly racist and full of prejudices vis-à-vis whatever has been defined as the 'other', that any attempt to produce Middle Eastern history is doomed from the outset (Said, 1978). Even if one is not willing to go that far, it is difficult to assume that we are getting anywhere near to 'objective reality', whatever that may be. At the very best, we can engage in a dialogue with our fellow scholars and our students, and occasionally with creative writers and film-makers as well. In the process of this dialogue, we may be able to eliminate a multitude of naivetés and misconceptions, even though we probably introduce others in our turn. According to such a conception of the historian's craft, the observation that a given researcher has based him/herself entirely on primary sources is not high praise. Rather it should be regarded as a matter-of-fact statement if there is little secondary literature available, a situation not unknown to Ottomanist historians. But in all other cases, the observation that the author of a given study has neglected to consult the secondary literature is not praise but rather the opposite. For it implies that the historian has neglected to engage in the methodical and principled dialogue which many of us today regard as the chief virtue of any historical study.

TRANSLITERATION

With all these caveats in mind, we will now turn to published Ottoman primary sources. Among the editions we will find in our libraries, four separate categories can be distinguished in terms of the transliteration employed. Most of the available texts will probably be transliterations into the Latin alphabet as used in Turkey today. This alphabet was adopted by the Turkish republican government in 1928, and since this time, the Arabic alphabet which had been in use throughout the Ottoman period has been relegated to scholarly and religious contexts. Turkish differs from Arabic by possessing both a broad range of vowels (which, if incorrectly pronounced, affect the meaning of the word) and, at least if compared to Arabic, a limited number of consonants. As a result, several consonant signs differentiated in Arabic are pronounced the same in Turkish, and the Turkish version of the Latin alphabet does not distinguish them either. This means that to transliterate a word back into the Arabic script, which we often need to do in order to consult the older dictionaries of Ottoman, we need a Turkish–Ottoman lexicon.

A second category of source editions will use one or another of the available scholarly transliterations. This means that the letters of the Latin alphabet are supplemented by diacritical marks which enable the reader to directly reconstitute the Arabic spelling. The different transliteration alphabets in existence are based on the experience of different language users. In Turkey, it is customary to use the transliteration system adopted by the *İA*, while the *EI*, 2nd edition and *The International Journal of Middle East Studies* employ variants based on the English language. French transliterations differ from this usage in a number of details. Differences between all current systems however are relatively minor, and a student attuned to one system usually will have no trouble adjusting to another. Transliterations will often convert the vowels, which for the most part are not written out in the Arabic script, according to some standard scheme, often nineteenth- or twentieth-century Istanbul Turkish. By contrast, transcriptions include the vowels which probably were in use at the time when the text was composed. Thus the student wishing to transcribe a text will have to familiarise him/herself with the vocalisation in use during the fifteenth, sixteenth or seventeenth century.

The third category among our source editions has been published in the Arabic alphabet. This includes the numerous editions of chronicles that were undertaken in the Ottoman Empire and the Republic of Turkey before 1928. Taken by itself, the Arabic alphabet is not really difficult to learn. But it does take some time before one can recognise the words even of a text in Ottoman-Turkish posing no linguistic problems when they appear in this unfamiliar guise. Many Middle Eastern Studies Departments teach this skill in special courses. Finally there are facsimile editions which reproduce manuscripts photomechanically. These may be read with relative ease if the texts in question are books or treatises, as the characters used by the scribes who wrote down literary texts are often similar to those encountered in printed works. But if the editions in question happen to concern archival documents, palaeographical skills are necessary. Many archival scripts look (and are) intimidating – but people do learn to deal with them all the time.

IN MEDIAS RES: WHAT PRIMARY SOURCES CAN TELL US

Let us assume that we have located some primary sources relevant to the topic we wish to study; the tools suggested in the reading list will help us here. Now we must try to make these texts intelligible to a reader living in the late twentieth century. An example will show how this can be done. Quite arbitrarily, we will select a list containing administered prices in 1640s Istanbul. The prices promulgated by the Ottoman government, especially with respect to the capital city, have intrigued scholars ever since the 1920s, and in 1983, Mübahat Kütükoğlu edited 'our' price register, along with extensive and very instructive notes (Kütükoğlu, 1983). Her introduction gives a great deal of information on the uses to which such price lists were put, and discusses the reasons for their promulgation: the more elaborate registers of this kind were frequently connected with changes in the coinage. New price lists were deemed particularly necessary in case the silver content of the coinage was increased, so as to ensure that all tradesmen adjusted their prices accordingly. To check whether official commands were in fact respected, it would be useful to locate prices paid in actual sales in the Istanbul area (this has become easier with the appearance of the series edited by Kal'a et al., 1997– , but merely for the eighteenth century, not for the years around 1640 which concern us here). Only since there are no published materials available, one would need to check the original kadi registers surviving from the relevant period. Cemal Kafadar has once surmised, sensibly I think, that administered prices were enforced mainly when the Ottoman Palace or other official bodies were the purchasers (Kafadar 1986, p. 128). Or we may scour the kadi registers of provincial Ottoman towns for price registers from approximately the same period, and we will find that currency changes often made themselves felt in the provinces after considerable delay (Ergenç, 1978–9).

Anyone using Ottoman sources in print will owe a debt to Şinasi Tekin who, at Harvard University, edits *The Journal of Turkish Studies*

(Cambridge MA). Often working together with his wife Gönül Alpay Tekin, he has published, among other things, a facsimile edition of Evliya Çelebi's description of Istanbul (with Fahir Iz, 1989). In addition, Şinasi Tekin acts as the editor of a series, in which Ottoman sources have been published along with notes and commentaries by historians, such as Rhoads Murphey (Murphey, 1985). A special highlight for the social historian is the edition, by Fahir Iz, of the *Saltuk-name*, a fifteenth-century collection of legends pertaining to the warrior dervish Sarı Saltuk (Ebu'l-Ḥayr Rumi, ed. Iz, 1974).

OTTOMAN SOURCES IN TRANSLATION

Last but not least: for those who are intrigued by Ottoman sources and wish to try some browsing, Ottoman sources in translation are a great boon. Moreover, even scholars will often use the available translations to advantage, for they provide explanations of difficult expressions, an index, biographical information on the author, and at times, references to the works from which the Ottoman author has derived his/her information. We will here introduce three individuals who have made major efforts to make Ottoman sources accessible in translation. To Andreas Tietze, who taught at UCLA for several decades, we owe translations into English of *Mustafa Âli's Counsel for Sultans of 1581* (Âli, ed. Tietze, 1979–82) and the same author's account of his visit to Cairo (Âli, ed. Tietze, 1975). Both these works also provide editions of the original texts. Another major editor of Ottoman sources in translation is Robert Dankoff, known especially for his work on Evliya Çelebi (Evliya Çelebi, 1990 and 1991). Due to Dankoff's translation, the splendour of the seventeenth-century court of Bitlis has become accessible to the English-speaking reader.

For those who read German, the older translations from Ottoman sources contained in the series 'Türkische Bibliothek' may be of value. Of more recent vintage is the series of translated texts edited by Richard Kreutel, which contains a superbly annotated German version of Evliya Çelebi's account of his visit to Vienna in 1665. Here we find, among other things, a discussion of the folklore, both Ottoman and Austrian, pertaining to the two sieges of Vienna (1529 and 1683). Kreutel has ranged widely, although quite a few of his translated texts focus on the Balkans. After the editor's death his work has been continued by Erich Prokosch and Karl Teply (Evliya Çelebi, tr. and annotated Kreutel, Prokosch and Teply, 1987). The series also contains one of the more exotic texts ever written in Ottoman, namely Evliya Çelebi's account of his search for the sources of the Nile (Evliya Çelebi, tr. Prokosch, 1994).

DESIGNING A PAPER

After having located primary and secondary sources, we will discuss some of the perspectives opening up in front of a person who begins to write a research paper. As an example, we will set ourselves the topic 'Dervish orders (*tarikat*) and the Ottoman state'. As a first step, we need to decide on what level of abstraction we want to treat the issue. Monographs covering the Nakşbendis (van Bruinessen, 1989), Halvetis (Clayer, 1994), Bektaşis (Faroqhi, 1981) or Mevlevis (Gölpınarlı, 1953) demonstrate that within the unified framework of Islamic religious law (*şeriat*) and the administrative practice sanctioned by the orders of the Sultans (*kanun*) there was scope for considerable variation.[1] We will therefore need to discuss problems of unity, variety and variability over time, with respect to the organisation and practice of different groups of dervishes.

Some orders, such as the Halvetis, were so closely linked to the Ottoman state that when the latter retreated from a given territory, the dervishes followed suit, even though a sizeable Muslim community might remain in the area (Clayer, 1994, pp. 273–306). Something similar applied to Mevlevis and Bektaşis, orders which rarely attracted Arab adherents. Lodges of these orders in Syria or Egypt were thus usually frequented by resident Ottoman Turks, more often than not associated with the state administration. By contrast, the Mudjaddidiya branch of the Nakşbendis was brought from India to the Ottoman Empire by *şeyh*s whose connections with officialdom were not particularly strong. However, this constellation, characteristic mainly of the eighteenth century, was to reverse itself in the nineteenth. The Bektaşi order was closed down in 1826, allegedly because of its links to the recently abolished janissaries. But possibly this was also intended as a kind of test case, in order to gauge the reaction of the *ulema* toward an Ottoman government confiscating pious foundations on a major scale. At the same time, the Nakşbendis basked in the favour of Sultan Mahmud II, and were able to take over some of the lodges taken away from the Bektaşis. State favour or indifference might thus be an important factor in determining the potential of a given order for expansion, but it was by no means the only one.

When discussing the history of dervish orders during the eighteenth or early nineteenth century, it makes sense to regard the different orders as more or less established organisations. Individual *şeyh*s occasionally might switch allegiance from one to another, and quite a few Ottoman gentlemen became members of more than one order. But the major dervish groups

---

[1] For a recent summary of French research on dervish orders compare Popovic and Veinstein (1996).

1. Mevlevi dervishes. Not much is known about the antecedents of this photograph, except that it was made in the second half of the nineteenth century. The authors of the volume in which it appears thank the American missionaries of Talas (near Kayseri) for 'many' of the pictures reproduced, but do not say whether the present image comes from this source. It was not unknown to photograph people, even foreign visitors, in 'picturesque' garments and poses considered typical of the Ottoman civilisation. Thus in the absence of specific information, the authenticity of this picture cannot be guaranteed.

themselves could look back on stable, lengthy traditions and derive legitimacy from them. However, once we go back into the sixteenth century, things are much more fluid. An early sixteenth-century text from the milieu of Celveti dervishes shows us that the Bektaşis of that period had not yet gathered in all the heterodox adherents which were to give them a bad name in *ulema* circles during the eighteenth century (Karamustafa, 1993). This evidence gives support to an idea first brought up by Fuat Köprülü and later elaborated by Irène Mélikoff. These two scholars have claimed that in the course of the great sixteenth-century persecution of real and suspected Anatolian adherents of Shah Ismā'īl, ruler of Iran, many people who saw their beliefs open to challenge sought refuge in the Bektaşi order. Up to that time, the Bektaşis had not been especially noted for heterodoxy, and the incorporation of suspected adherents of Shah Ismā'īl may have been regarded as the first step to their ultimate assimilation. But acculturation is a two-way street, and it seems that the Bektaşis took over many of the beliefs current among the people whom they had set out to integrate into the Ottoman religious establishment (Köprülü, 1935; Mélikoff, 1975). If we want to understand this process a little better, it may be worth our while to turn to the relevant ethnological literature for guidance.

When we move yet further back, into the early period of the Ottoman Empire, it becomes even more difficult to understand the role of dervishes in state formation. For this period, sources are very sparse, and elaborate interpretations therefore often have to base themselves on a few sentences in a chronicle or foundation charter. A major step forward has been the edition of a fourteenth-century saint's legend, which apart from being one of the earliest extant monuments of Anatolian Turkish, also sheds new light on the so-called Babai uprising (Elvan Çelebi, ed. Erünsal and Ocak, 1984, see also Ocak, 1989). At the present stage of our knowledge, it would seem that this rebellion of Anatolian nomads against their Seljuk overlords, put down decisively in 1240, has served as a catalyst in the formation of Anatolian dervish orders. This is especially remarkable because, as far as we know, the uprising may not have been mainly motivated by religious concerns. But Hacı Bektaş, the putative founder of the Bektaşi order, is believed to have escaped from the repression unleashed against the defeated rebels, and the same supposedly applied to Şeyh Edebalı, who possibly became the father-in-law of the first Ottoman Sultan. Dervish saints may well have played a role in legitimising the Ottoman rulers when they were still struggling to establish a principality in northwestern Anatolia. But exactly how this happened continues to escape us.

Thus even a very brief and superficial treatment of the relationship between the Ottoman state and the dervish orders flourishing on its territory has confronted us with a complex and constantly shifting reality. We have encountered dervishes securing newly conquered territories for the Ottoman ruler, and major campaigns of repression whose victims were some of the very same dervishes whom we might otherwise have regarded as pillars of the Ottoman state. While in the fourteenth or early fifteenth century, Sultans seem to have favoured holy men and helped along their establishment in newly conquered lands, in the sixteenth century Süleyman the Magnificent acted as the defender of Sunnism against dervishes and other folk now perceived as heretics. All this has become apparent through a cursory perusal of the secondary literature. This means that a student working on the base of this material can come to formulate stimulating questions; at a later time, they may lead up to original research.

Papers based upon secondary literature, if not intended to be purely student exercises, should in general be more explicit about the theoretical framework employed than is necessary in papers focusing on primary sources. To discuss theoretical frameworks at all is something of a novelty to many historians; among the scholars of past generations, it was usually taken for granted that history dealt with the unique, while sociology and later anthropology were concerned with the regularities of social and political behaviour. Under these circumstances it was usually considered unnecessary to discuss the framework within which the proposed topic was to be treated, and introductions dealt with more technical matters, such as the availability and limits of primary sources. But those scholars who would still uphold a rigid division between history and the social sciences have decreased both in number and influence, and many historians would today see history as a social science rather than a part of the humanities. Albeit on a modest level of abstraction, social theory has become relevant to historians, and scholarly papers should, to a degree, reflect this situation.

It is therefore essential to discuss what predecessors have done, why the secondary literature on the relevant subject is insufficient and which set of ideas has inspired the author to ask the questions he/she is planning to answer. Moreover, the conclusion is often a good place to discuss the extent to which hypotheses have been proved right or wrong, and what further studies might be in order. Here it becomes possible to tie in with the mental framework discussed in the introduction. These procedures are not always easy to follow. If a beginner's work comes out sounding somewhat pretentious as a result of the reflections attempted, that is not in itself a terrible thing. It is quite normal that at the beginning of one's career, one tries to show what one knows and why one is so much better than one's predecessors or peers. However it is important to not 'go overboard' on this matter, 'too much is too much'. It does not make much sense to fill the introduction with the extensive development of a *problématique* which is irrelevant to the topic treated empirically in the body of the study. Yet this is a common failing in masters' theses and dissertations. Not every good historian also possesses the talents of a social theoretician. But excursions into social theory resemble the much-maligned piano classes middle-class girls were subjected to at the beginning of the twentieth century: most of these young women may have inflicted mediocre playing on themselves and their contemporaries, but they still gained an appreciation of music impossible to acquire in any other fashion.

'DOCUMENT-ORIENTED' VERSUS 'PROBLEM-ORIENTED' STUDIES

Let us now draw a few broader conclusions from our attempts to design a research project. During the early stages of twentieth-century concern with the Ottoman Empire, many scholars wrote studies centred around a single document or a group of documents. These involved the transliteration of the text and often an account of the location in which it had been found. This latter information was important at a time when many documents had been removed from the places where they had originally been stored, and not yet come to rest in modern-style libraries and archives. If the study was at all extensive, the information spread out over often numerous pages of primary sources was summarised in graphs and tables. Later on, the information made available would be placed in the historical context known from previous studies. This proceeding was particularly favoured by Ömer Lütfi Barkan, who, among other things, made accessible Ottoman foundation accounts and inheritance inventories. His major works usually combine secondary studies with editions of texts in modern Turkish transliterations.

But when historical research has progressed beyond a certain stage, many historians will feel that the explication of texts cannot be their only aim in life. Now active practitioners of Ottoman history are not very numerous, perhaps a few hundred the world over, while especially archival documentation is enormous. Thus historians' dissatisfaction with 'document oriented' work does not mean that 'all' the important source texts have been made available, far from it. Some researchers do in fact believe that it is not legitimate to deal with broader questions before all the relevant tax registers, foundation accounts or whatever have been studied in their entirety. But this is a work of many generations. If researchers were to isolate themselves from what is happening in historiography as a whole, by purely concentrating on document explication, they would lower the quality of their own work. For the best studies of individual archival documents, such as the work by Halil İnalcık on the fifteenth-century tax register of Albania (Arvanid) (İnalcık, 1954a) or the studies by Barkan already referred to, were definitely inspired by historiographical questions current at the time of writing. As an example, one might mention the manner in which Ottoman power was established in the Balkans, a problem which, by the way, is a subject of debate down to the present day.

SELECTING A PROBLÉMATIQUE

It is therefore likely that relatively more document-oriented studies will continue to coexist with mainly problem-oriented work. This of course obliges us to ask where historians find the problems they study. If we are honest, we will acknowledge the role of contemporary concerns in this process. A decade or so after the Iranian revolution, the editor of a major American scholarly periodical asked potential contributors to for God's sake not send in any more manuscripts on this topic, as the journal had reached saturation point. Another possible source of historical *problématiques* lies in the social and political commitment of the historian. Thus the interest in 'history from below', which has been current among Europeanists and Indianists for some time and, somewhat belatedly, has also reached Ottomanists, is linked to a democratic world view. For it is based on the assumption that the needs and aspirations of ordinary people matter in history. Rapid paradigm changes, even with respect to topics – such as the French Revolution – which seem to have been exhaustively studied, now characterise many types of historical studies. Whoever dislikes the incoming paradigm will easily agree with E. G. Hobsbawm's comment that upcoming scholars only can make their mark by demolishing their predecessors' work (Hobsbawm, 1990, p. 105). Other more or less hostile observers will prefer to speak of fashion changes, thereby assimilating paradigm changes to the 'frivolous' occupations of ladies or young men with money to spend. But now that the study of fashion has revealed cultural changes by no means unworthy of serious study, this objection appears in a different perspective (Micklewright, 1990).

Those historians who work in a more or less problem-oriented style, will build on the document-oriented studies already available. The scholar studying Ottoman commerce and urban life, introduced a few pages ago, will attempt to interpret the documents at his/her disposal in the light of broader visions, such as those introduced by Fernand Braudel with his studies on the Mediterranean and the history of merchant capitalism (Braudel, 1966, 1979). Other sources of inspiration include K. N. Chaudhuri and his work on the Indian Ocean as a commercial system, or Philip Curtin's book on the activities of merchant diasporas (Chaudhuri, 1985; Curtin, 1984). All these scholars have been concerned with the Ottoman Empire either marginally or not at all. Braudel was a Europeanist with strong world historical interests, K. N. Chaudhuri focuses on Indian society of the mediaeval and early modern periods, while Curtin's main interest is in African and Latin American studies. One could easily come up with other possible paradigm suppliers, such as the Cambridge Indianist Christopher Bayly (Bayly, 1983, 1989). The latter recently has returned the interest some Ottoman historians have shown for his ideas concerning commercial development in eighteenth and nineteenth-century India (1989, pp. 16–74). These particular historians have been introduced here because I have found their work especially stimulating; if this book had been written by someone else, he/she probably would have substituted different people (for a more extensive discussion, see chapter 7).

But whatever paradigm the historian of Ottoman trade and urban development will decide on, it will come, directly or indirectly, from outside Ottoman history. For as has already been stressed in the introduction, to the present day Ottoman history has not generated its own paradigms, let alone paradigms of use to historians in other fields. Until quite recently, Ottomanist works were not even read by a significant number of researchers outside of the discipline, a situation which was probably not unconnected with the document-oriented (some would say document-fetishist) character of most work being produced. That this state of affairs is beginning to change probably reflects a degree of maturing of Ottoman history as a field. But a great deal remains to be done. Some budding scholars will hopefully feel challenged to produce paradigms which in turn may one day be taken over by historians in other disciplines.

However, the close study of documents is by no means 'out'. It is perfectly possible for scholars well informed of current problématiques to return to the libraries and archives to make new discoveries, and/or to interpret well-known texts in a different light. As a good example one might mention the burgeoning field of women's studies. Archival searches have brought to light quite a few documents relevant to the history of Ottoman women, so that the old objection that this topic cannot be studied due to lack of sources is no longer tenable (for recent examples see Zilfi ed., 1997). Equally, acquaintance with this field has induced Ottoman historians both male and female to question the opinion, dominant until recent times, that the political influence of female members of the Ottoman ruling house was either a cause or else a symptom of 'Ottoman decline' (Peirce, 1993). This in turn has led to a close reading of documents such as account books pertaining to the households of women of the imperial family, which previously had been considered of marginal interest (Artan, 1993, and the same author's forthcoming work on Ottoman royal women).

Or else the new emphasis on women's cultural activities (compare the adage 'Anonymous was a woman' which has recently become popular among feminist literary historians) has inspired Cemal Kafadar to interpret the letters of a seventeenth-century female dervish from the Macedonian town of Üsküp/Skopje (Kafadar, 1992). His sophisticated commentary on this text would have been impossible without previous involvement in the problématique of women's history. Moreover, discussing a primary source after a knowledge of the 'state of the art' has been acquired will also help avoid a common failing of many exclusively 'document-oriented' studies: the reader will not be left wondering why in all the world, of all the documents which have come down to us, the author has selected this particular text for detailed study.

. . . AND NOW YOU ARE ON YOUR OWN: SELECTING A TOPIC

Students usually are asked to do research on a topic which they have been assigned. But once one reaches thesis level, selecting a topic comes to be a fairly important part of overall performance, an activity in which the student can show his/her ingenuity and/or mastery of the field. Quite mundane considerations are often involved in choosing a topic. Accessibility of primary sources will be of major significance for scholars planning to work on areas where political and military conflict has led to the closure, dispersion or destruction of archives. But even in more settled conditions, archive accessibility can be an issue, as apparent from the stimulating and at times wryly amusing polemic against French archive administrations recently put out by Sonia Combe (Combe, 1994). A scholar's language and palaeographical skills will also prove a limiting factor.

But this is not, or at least should not be, the whole story. Even a modest paper involves a lot of work, and it is much more probable that this work will be well performed if the author is convinced of what he/she is doing. It is tempting to select a topic because the documents are close at hand, because an older colleague who has dealt with a similar topic can tender useful advice, or because the necessary linguistic or palaeographical skills have already been acquired. But it is equally important to think carefully about the implications of the topic, and to find something else if the prospective author has serious reservations, no matter how subjective they may sound. It makes no sense for a person with little interest in miniature painting as an art type to study Ottoman miniatures. There is always the danger that such hidden reservations will result in a boring piece of work, and in extreme cases lead to contradictions and involuntary humour in the final text.

APPROACHING YOUR COLLEAGUES

Discussing research findings in public, outside of the seminar room, may sound like a very remote probability to the beginning student. But that is not really true. In the United States, graduate student conferences allow novice researchers a 'trial run' in front of their peers – who may be harder to satisfy than older scholars. Doctoral candidates, and occasionally master students as well, will have fresh findings which are worth presenting in front of a specialist audience. Moreover, it will be a good idea to attend conferences as a listener and possibly discussant before one ventures to present a paper of one's own. For those who wish to try, here are a few hints.

By now there exists a sizeable number of congresses taking place annually, biannually or every three years, which differently from conferences to which one must be invited, are open to anyone in the field. In the United States and Canada, the most obvious place to go is the Middle Eastern Studies Association (MESA) annual convention, which takes place every year in a major city of the US or Canada. There is a special Turkish Studies Association, which as an affiliated organisation, meets at the same time and place. One needs to be a MESA member to present a paper, but a special student rate for membership is available. Once one has become a member, one receives a publication called the *MESA Newsletter*, not to be confused with the *MESA Bulletin* which can count as a regular professional journal. The newsletter gives exact instructions on how to apply. Since conditions and particularly deadlines change slightly from one year to the next, be sure to consult the most up-to-date issue. Sometimes Ottoman history papers can also be read at the American Historical Association, and art historians will frequent the congresses covering their own field. During the last few years, the self-confidence of Ottoman historians seems to have grown, and they increasingly present themselves in front of historians dealing with other fields.

In Europe there also exist some regularly convening congresses which deal with history in general or Middle East history, and where Ottoman historians more or less frequently present themselves. In France the annual congresses of the Association Française d'Études du Monde Arabe et de la Méditerranée (AFÉMAM) meet every year, and though the Arab world takes pride of place, the Ottomanist historical community is also well represented. In Great Britain the British Society for Middle East Studies (BRISMES) acts like a 'little brother' to the far larger MESA; it sponsors regular congresses. In Germany, the Deutscher Historikertag, which meets biannually, also sometimes features panels on Ottoman history; only preorganised panels are accepted, and panels must be submitted more than a year in advance. Unlike those of its French counterpart, the congresses convened by the Deutsche Morgenländische Gesellschaft (German Oriental Society) encompass all of Asia. They also include linguistics and philology, so that Ottoman historians tend to get lost in the crowd. For these reasons budding scholars may prefer the French and British congresses.

There also exists a number of international congresses on Ottoman history which meet at different Turkish and European locations. Special congresses dealing with the Ottoman period of the Arab lands also exist, convened regularly in Tunisia and hosted by the Temimi Foundation (Zaghouan); it is possible to present papers in English or French. For our purposes, the most important periodical congresses are the Congress on Turkish Art, the Congress on Ottoman Social and Economic History and the congress sponsored by the Comité d'Études Ottomanes et Préottomanes (CIÉPO). Though some organisers try to suggest overall topics for the congress they convene, papers presented at the two last-named congresses range widely. These meetings should therefore be regarded more or less as general purpose congresses.

The last-mentioned three congresses quite often meet in Turkey; but in addition, there are congresses on Ottoman history domiciled in Turkey itself which are open to foreign scholars. In Ankara the Turkish Historical Commission (Türk Tarih Kurumu) at irregular intervals organises a large congress. This encompasses not only Ottoman history but also prehistorical and classical archaeology, mediaeval studies and the history of the Turkish Republic, all with special reference to Anatolia. More recent is the series of Ottoman history congresses organised by the Turkish Foundation for Economic and Social History; potential participants will do best to write to the foundation's headquarters in Istanbul (for addresses compare Türkiye Ekonomik ve Toplumsal Tarih Vakfi and T.C. Kültür Bakanlığı, 4. printing, 1996).

Papers presented at all these congresses have often been published by the university or scholarly organisation responsible for the event. But due to the large number of papers presented, organisers often reserve the right to make a selection, and the papers of some congresses remain unpublished in their entirety. Thus one can present a paper at a congress without necessarily being prepared to publish it, and beginners are offered the possibility of a 'dry run'. A willingness to confront criticism is certainly needed; but in my opinion, this is a quality which one needs to cultivate in any case in order to survive in today's world. Invitations to Ottomanist congresses in preparation are usually issued to scholars who have attended previous congresses. A young researcher who wants to get his/her name on the mailing list in most instances should find out where the next congress is scheduled to take place, and write to the local organisers. Frequently, information on impending congresses is most conveniently received from colleagues already established in the field, who may also furnish introductions. Depending on resources available at the congress location, financial aid is often available to students. In any case, it is a good idea to begin attending congresses early; in a small field, much is achieved through personal contacts, and the earlier one builds up a network the better.

SUGGESTED READING

Barkan, Ömer Lütfi (1942). 'Osmanlı İmparatorluğunda bir İskân ve Kolonizasyon Metodu Olarak Vakıflar ve Temlikler', *Vakıflar Dergisi*, II, 279–386 (a classic).

van Bruinessen, Martin M. (1989). *Agha, Scheich und Staat, Politik und Gesellschaft Kurdistans* (Berlin: Edition Parabolis) (thought-provoking; one of the few important studies of eastern Anatolia in Ottoman times).

Clayer, Nathalie (1994). *Mystiques, état & société, les Halvetis dans l'aire balkanique de la fin du XVe siècle à nos jours* (Leiden: E. J. Brill) (a major monograph on the political aspects of dervish orders).

Elvan Çelebi. *Menâkıbu'l-Kudsiyye fî Menâsıbî'l Ünsiyye (Baba İlyas-ı Horasânî ve Sülâlesinin Menkabevî Tarihi)*, ed. Ismail Erünsal and Ahmet Yaşar Ocak (Istanbul: İstanbul Üniversitesi Edebiyat Fakültesi).

[Evliya Çelebi] (1988). *Evliya Çelebi in Diyarbekir, The Relevant Section of the Seyahatname edited with Translation, Commentary and Introduction*, ed. and tr. Martin van Bruinessen and Hendrik Boeschoten (Leiden: E. J. Brill) (among the many partial editions of Evliya texts concerning Ottoman cities, this is possibly the most sophisticated).

[Evliya Çelebi] (1991). *The Intimate Life of an Ottoman Statesman, Melek Ahmed Pasha (1588–1662) as Portrayed in Evliya Çelebi's Book of Travels*, tr. and annotated Robert Dankoff and Rhoads Murphey (Albany: SUNY Press) (pioneering).

Gölpınarlı, Abdülbaki (1953). *Mevlânâ'dan Sonra Mevlevîlik* (Istanbul: Inkilâp).

Inalcık, Halil (1954a). *Hicrî 835 Tarihli Sûret-i Defter-i Sancak-i Arvanid* (Ankara:

Türk Tarih Kurumu) (a classical example of the difficult art of editing *tahrirs*).

Kafadar, Cemal (1992). 'Mütereddit bir Mutasavvıf: Üsküp'lü Asiye Hatun'un Rüya Defteri 1641–43,' *Topkapı Sarayı Müzesi, Yıllık* V, 168–222 (imaginative introduction).

Karamustafa, Ahmet T. (1993). *Vâhîdî's Menâkıb-i Hvoca-i Cihân ve Netîce-i Cân: Critical Edition and Analysis* (Cambridge MA: Harvard).

Köprülü, M. Fuad (1935). *Türk Halk Edebiyatı Ansiklopedisi* . . ., fasc. 1 Aba-Abdal Musa (no more publ.) (Istanbul).

Kütükoğlu, Mübahat (1991). *Osmanlı Tarihinde Usul* (one of the first introductions to our field; information on archival sources).

Kütükoğlu, Mübahat (ed.) (1983). *Osmanlılarda Narh Müessesesi ve 1640 Tarihli Narh Defteri* (Istanbul: Enderun Kitabevi) (superb commentary).

Mélikoff, Irène (1975). 'Le problème kızılbaş', *Turcica*, VI, 49–67.

[Mustafa Âli] (1979, 1982). *Mustafâ ʿÂlî's Counsel for Sultans of 1581*, 2 vols., ed. and tr. by Andreas Tietze (Vienna: Österreichische Akademie der Wissenschaften) (a famous text, made accessible).

Peirce, Leslie P. (1993). *The Imperial Harem, Women and Sovereignty in the Ottoman Empire* (Oxford, New York: Oxford University Press) (novel and fundamental).

Popovic, Alexandre and Gilles Veinstein (eds.) (1996). *Les voies d'Allah, les ordres mystiques dans le monde musulman des origines à aujourd'hui* (Paris: Fayard) (vast overview, wide-ranging in space and time).

3

LOCATING OTTOMAN SOURCES

MANUSCRIPTS AND BOOK COLLECTING

Down into the nineteenth century, when printing became more widespread in the Ottoman realm, most books were manuscripts preserved by collectors, and by copyists who manufactured additional volumes on demand. Many books found their way into endowed libraries. These were numerous especially in Istanbul, either as parts of larger foundations, or, particularly since the seventeenth century, as separate institutions. Most of these manuscript collections have now been brought together in the sixteenth-century buildings of the Süleymaniye. In the provinces, such foundation-sponsored libraries were much less common than in Istanbul (for a union catalogue of Turkish manuscripts, see Collective work, 1979–). But in Konya, there existed and still exists the famed manuscript collection of the Mevlevi dervishes (catalogue published by Gölpınarlı, 1967–72). This library contains such treasures as Elvan Çelebi's fourteenth-century biography of the rebel dervish Baba Ilyas, which we have already encountered (Elvan Çelebi, ed. Erünsal and Ocak, 1984). In the İl Halk Kütüphanesi of the same city, a number of manuscripts go back to another famed thirteenth-century collection, assembled by the mystic Sadreddin-i Konevi. This was the son-in-law and follower of Ibn ʿArabī, one of the great figures of Islamic mysticism. When Sultan Mehmed the Conqueror annexed Konya to the Ottoman Empire in the mid-fifteenth century, he or some of his leading officials apparently were much impressed by these manuscripts. Thus they were recorded in the register of pious foundations prepared immediately after the conquest, and the list was copied several times in the course of the next century (Uzluk, 1958, p. 11).

But *the* major book collectors were not scholars or sheiks, but the

LOCATING OTTOMAN SOURCES

Sultans themselves; Mehmed the Conqueror's activity in this field has been
studied in detail (Raby, 1980). In the sixteenth century, the Ottoman court
sponsored numerous miniatures illustrating dynastic chronicles of the time,
which have come to symbolise the Ottoman arts of the book at their most
brilliant stage. Among later rulers Ahmed III (r. 1703–1730) should be
singled out, for he had a special library constructed in the third courtyard of
the Palace, which can still be visited. But the major treasures of the Palace
library continued to be kept in the bookcases adorning the Revan Köşkü
and Bağdat Köşkü, or else in the Palace treasury itself. The building presently housing the Topkapı Palace library, a sixteenth-century structure, was not
built for its present use, but as a rather unostentatious mosque. It was
converted to its present purpose only after the newly founded Republic of
Turkey had turned the Topkapı Palace into a museum (published catalogue:
Karatay, 1961).

Apart from the Süleymaniye and Topkapı Palace libraries, the
Köprülü Library has attracted scholarly attention (there exists a published
catalogue: Ihsanoğlu *et al*, 1406/1986). Now part of the Atatürk
Kütüphanesi in the Taksim quarter of Istanbul, the Belediye Kütüphanesi is
also worth noting. This is a collection not only of books but also of archival
materials: in the upheavals of the early twentieth century, numerous books
and records were detached from their permanent repositories, and many
were undoubtedly destroyed. But some of them were picked up by private
collectors, among whom the late Izzet Koyunoğlu was probably one of the
best-known. Quite a few of these collectors turned over their treasures to
the public domain, and in Istanbul, the Belediye library was often the
beneficiary. Since the library made no purchases, what it came to possess was
the product of chance, but many materials located here are of high intrinsic
value. For books printed in Turkey, the Beyazit Devlet Kütüphanesi equally
constitutes a major resource (see Ihsanoğlu *et al.*, 1995).[1]

For obvious reasons, private collections deposited in publicly accessible repositories are of importance especially for the nineteenth and
twentieth centuries. In this sector, it is difficult to differentiate between
libraries and archives; since the library aspect is usually very important, we
will introduce these resources here. A foundation known as the Türkiye
Ekonomik ve Sosyal Tarih Vakfı has recently been established (see also

---

[1] Ihsanoğlu *et alii*, 1995 constitutes a one-volume guide to all libraries in Turkey holding manuscripts,
along with the relevant addresses, telephone numbers and short notes on the type of catalogue(s)
available. It includes histories of the more important collections as well as a bibliography of publications
on Turkish libraries. There is also a bibliography of scholarly works, both in Turkish and European
languages, on manuscripts to be found in these collections.

chapter 2). One of the foundation's aims is the collection of publications and private papers germane to late Ottoman social and economic history; however the emphasis is doubtlessly on the Republican period. The foundation is located in Istanbul, with branches in Ankara and Izmir. With respect to women, a similar aim is followed by the Kadın Eserleri Kütüphanesi ('The Library of Women's Works'), also located in Istanbul. In particular, the latter is noted for its collection of the numerous women's journals published at the end of the nineteenth century and during the first decade of the twentieth. Those publications which could not be acquired in the original are at least available in reproduction.

Numerous Ottoman historical manuscripts are also found in European libraries. Interest in Ottoman books developed relatively late; when sixteenth-century collectors such as the Habsburg ambassador Ogier de Busbecq purchased books in the Ottoman Empire, they were concerned with Greek and not with Ottoman manuscripts. In France, the alliance of King François I (r. 1515–1547) with Sultan Süleyman the Magnificent (r. 1520–1566) seems to have stimulated interest in things Ottoman. Thus the Paris royal library, the ancestor of the Bibliothèque Nationale, began to buy Ottoman manuscripts at an early date (Blochet, 1932–33). Both in Paris and in Vienna, the practice of training future consular and embassy personnel to read and write in Ottoman probably stimulated interest in Ottoman chronicles and historical documents. For the 'jeunes de langue', as they were called in France, were prepared for practical duties, such as the conduct of diplomatic correspondence and the translation of treaties. Historical rather than religious texts were regarded as appropriate practice material for this purpose. As a kind of 'graduation thesis' the students were often expected to produce translations of an historical text, which were kept on file in a library, today usually the Bibliothèque Nationale. It goes without saying that the quality of such translations was not always of the first grade (Hitzel ed., 1997).

Since the Germanies outside of the Habsburg lands did not possess a capital before 1871, manuscript collecting was undertaken at a sizeable number of princely courts. After 1871, there was a strenuous effort to enlarge the Berlin collections, and some Ottoman manuscripts were acquired in the late nineteenth and early twentieth centuries. Given this dispersal of holdings, it is helpful that from the 1960s onward, a series of volumes was published describing Ottoman manuscripts in (West) German libraries (Flemming, 1968; Sohrweide, 1974 and 1981; Götz, 1968 and 1979). Of even later date is the collection of Ottoman manuscripts in Prague, mostly purchased during the first third of the twentieth century; it is presently being catalogued. However a catalogue of the Ottoman holdings of the Bratislava University Library has been available for a long time (Blaškovič, Petráček and Vesely, 1961).

Another major European library with large Ottoman holdings is the Gazi-Husrev-Beg Library in Sarajevo. Apart from the original foundation holdings, manuscripts donated by over 120 donors between 1537 and 1980 form part of this collection. Moreover the holdings of many smaller Islamic foundations were concentrated here. By 1980, the library contained approximately 7,500 manuscripts, mostly in Arabic, of which slightly less than one half had been described in two printed catalogues (Zirojevic, 1989). It remains to be seen in what condition these volumes have survived the war which accompanied the dissolution of Yugoslavia.

In summary, our principal guides in tracking down manuscripts containing historical texts are the printed catalogues of major establishments such as the Nationalbibliothek in Vienna (Flügel, 1865–67), the Gazi-Husrev-Beg Library in Sarajevo, the Bibliothèque Nationale in Paris (Blochet, 1932–33), the British Library in London (Rieu, 1881), the Bodleian in Oxford, apart from the Topkapı Palace Library (Karatay, 1961) and the complex of Istanbul foundation libraries now assembled in the Süleymaniye manuscript collection (Collective work, 1943; Ihsanoğlu et al., 1995). These catalogues will contain descriptions of the relevant manuscripts, which in the twentieth century have become increasingly standardised. Physical characteristics such as size, number of lines, type of script, ornamentation and details concerning the binding typically form part of these descriptions. More importantly for our purposes, the authors of catalogues will attempt to identify both the texts and their authors. This is vital for the historian, as there are so few critical editions of Ottoman writings. In addition, the ambitious cataloguer will want to explain by whom and why the texts in question were assembled in a single volume. Often the catalogue description also contains a list of further manuscripts, editions and/or translations of the relevant work. However, the catalogues of certain European collections were compiled about a 100 years ago or even earlier, when there was less information available on authors and manuscripts than is the case today. Later acquisitions may or may not have been recorded in separate published catalogues, so that a letter to the relevant library may be in order.

THE OTTOMAN SECTION OF THE PRIME MINISTER'S ARCHIVE IN ISTANBUL (BAŞBAKANLIK ARŞIVI-OSMANLI ARŞIVI)

The Ottoman central archives, located in the heart of old Istanbul, for most Ottoman historians will constitute *the* major resource. Apart from its incredibly rich holdings, it is also a place where both senior scholars and novices habitually meet. First access is through a published guide (Collective work, 1992, with a supplement of 1995). Whenever new editions of this work become available, they should be preferred, as during the last seven years or so, the process of cataloguing has been much accelerated. New sections are constantly being added. Most of these are relevant to the nineteenth century, but older periods are not neglected. Particularly the section called Başmuhasebe Kalemi constitutes a mine of information to the historian of the eighteenth century.

Individual sections of the Başbakanlık Arşivi open to researchers are covered by special unpublished catalogues; the latter vary widely in comprehensiveness and accuracy of information. Some of the older ones contain nothing but the names of the relevant subsections, the call numbers of the documents contained therein and the years in which these documents were written. But even in many of the more recent catalogues, the documents, both registers (*defter*) and individual documents (*evrak*) are organised by years only, with no index to speed up the work. In certain catalogues however, indices have been included.

A book of its own would be necessary to discuss even the more important sections of this enormously rich archive. The history of archival divisions of course reflects the history of both republican Turkish and Ottoman administration. But that is a vast field which cannot be covered in an introductory text. Thus the few examples given here should merely whet the appetite.

Even in the recent past, the extremely comprehensive section known as Maliyeden Müdevver was the bane of researchers. The only available catalogue consisted of file cards written in pencil in an all but illegible *rik'a* script. A series of bound volumes in Latin typescript has now replaced them. Most scholars studying the sixteenth century will spend much of their time working their way through the Mühimme Defterleri. These comprise copies of the outgoing correspondence of the Sultan's Council *(Divan-ı humayun)*, addressed mainly to provincial governors and judges (kadis), but also to foreign princes. For most of the sixteenth century, the Mühimme catalogues contain summaries of individual documents. But when dealing with later periods, the researcher must be prepared to go through the registers rescript by rescript. Recently several sample registers have been published in facsimile, among them nos. 3, 5 and 12 (Binark *et al.* eds., 1993; 1994; 1996), relating to the years 1558 to 1572, no. 44 (1580–1584, ed. Ünal, 1995) and no. 90, which covers the year 1056/1646–47 (Tulum *et al.* eds., 1993). To protect those often-used registers, most researchers will be given photostats rather than the originals to work with.

From the mid-seventeenth century onward, specialised registers were progressively created, so that the main registers became less and less comprehensive. First the responses to complaints handed in by low-level administrators and ordinary taxpayers were entered into a special series, the so-called Şikâyet Defterleri. From the mid-eighteenth century onwards, separate registers were set up for the more important provinces, known as the Vilayet Ahkâm Defterleri. However the original series continued well into the nineteenth century, and since very few scholars have studied the later registers, they may well contain unknown treasures (for surviving volumes check Collective work, 1992).

Other series which researchers concerned with the early modern period will want to consult are the taxfarming records (Mukataʿa Defterleri). These records can be found not only in the more comprehensive sections such as Maliyeden Müdevver and Kamil Kepeci, but also in specialised ones such as the Bursa Mukataʿası Kalemi, which, as the name suggests, deals with the city of Bursa and the tax farms attached to it. These materials often are not registers, but rather individual documents all related to a single tax farm and bundled together. Considerable ingenuity is needed if the data found in tax-farming documents are meant to serve as the raw material for a study in economic history. However, work by Halil Sahillioğlu (1962–63), Mehmet Genç (1975, 1987), Murat Çızakça (1985), Ariel Salzmann (1995) and Neşe Erim (1991) has demonstrated the enormous potential of these records.

Procedures of document production changed after the great reorganisation of the Ottoman bureaucracy between the 1840s and 1870s known as the Tanzimat. Old series were revamped and new ones were instituted, and the amount of documentation produced increased vastly. Again only a very small sampling of the available series can be introduced here. In certain sectors, continuity with earlier times predominated, at least for a while. For those provinces with Christian and Jewish inhabitants which still remained within the Ottoman Empire, the capitation (cizye) registers were continued between 1838 and 1857. But these later registers were placed in a special section, while older cizye registers are most often found in Maliyeden müdevver. Another series continuing older bureaucratic practice under a different name was the İrade, which in the pre-Tanzimat period had been known as the Hatt-ı humayun. These two terms refer to sultanic commands which down to 1832, the ruler added in his own hand onto a paper on which the Grand Vizier had previously explained the facts of the case. After that date, these summaries were addressed no longer to the ruler himself but to his Chief Scribe, who orally explained the relevant cases to the Sultan and took down the latter's – equally oral – comments. This practice continued down to 1908; after that time, the Sultan as a constitutional ruler merely confirmed the decisions of his Council of Ministers.

The İrade section is organised by at least three different principles, which may oblige the user working on a single topic to check a variety of subdivisions. To begin with, there is a division by time, the cut-off date being 1309/1891–92. Within this temporal division we find a second one according to the ministry or council concerned by a given Sultan's order. This ministry or council probably had prepared the documentation and solicited the ruler's decision in the first place. Secondly, *irades* in the form of files are separated from those which, according to previous practice, were written on individual sheets; incidentally this differentiation between documents on single sheets (*evrak*) and registers (*defter*) is a fundamental organising principle of the entire Prime Minister's Archive, including the older sections. In accordance with a third organising principle, provinces which constituted 'problem areas', such as Egypt, Crete, or the Lebanon Mount were assembled in special sections. All this may sound complicated. But the fairly detailed lists in the published guide, on which the present explanations are based, and supplementary information in the unpublished catalogues should make consultation easier. Moreover, the published guide also contains flow charts which show the way that files took between different government bodies during various periods of the nineteenth century. These charts should be of help when determining which information to expect in which section of the archives. But even so, the advice of an experienced researcher or archive official may often be the surest guide.

We will continue our rapid overview with a series of special interest to the social and economic historian of the nineteenth century, namely the Temettuât Defterleri (Collective work, 1992b, pp. 281ff.). In 1844–45 a tax on profits was instituted, and as a base for this new type of taxation, an overall count of taxpayers was made in certain selected provinces of the eastern Balkans and western as well as central Anatolia. The results were recorded in 17,747 registers, which provide valuable information on both movable property and real estate. Few scholars have as yet made use of this fascinating series. During the Tanzimat years, certain novel authorities were also created, usually on the basis of older bureaus. Among these the ministries of War, Finance, and Foreign Affairs are of special importance, and excepting the Ministry of Foreign Affairs, ministry records are also located in the Başbakanlık archives.

But one of the most important divisions for historians dealing with the later nineteenth century are surely the Yıldız Archives, named after the palace which Sultan Abdülhamid II (r. 1876–1909) built for himself on a hill overlooking Beşiktâş, and from which he conducted governmental business (Collective work, 1992b, pp. 366–73). Because of this practice, the Yıldız section contains records such as the minutes of the Council of Ministers (*Meclis-i Vükela Mazbataları*), which one would not ordinarily expect in a palace archive. An especially rich series (15,679 registers) comprises the Yıldız Petition Registers (*Yıldız Maruzat Defterleri*). Here we find the requests submitted to Sultan Abdülhamid II throughout his long reign, which in 1992, had been catalogued down to the year 1904. Another important section is known as *Yıldız Esas Evrakı*, which contains documentation on affairs with which the ruler occupied himself without necessarily involving a government office. Another set of series specific to this period, also found in the Yıldız collection, emanates from the so-called inspectorate of Rumelia, instituted from 1902 onward upon Austrian and Russian pressure. This material is indispensible for researchers concerning themselves with the wars, uprisings and negotiations which accompanied the last decades of the Ottoman Empire.

THE TOPKAPI PALACE ARCHIVES

After the middle of the nineteenth century the famous Topkapı Sarayı was not used as the main residence of the court. Therefore the archive of this palace is largely concerned with the pre-Tanzimat period. It is again divided up into a section which consists of individual papers, and a second one containing registers. Moreover, the archive is quite separate from the Topkapı Palace Library, located in the same compound, which has been briefly introduced above (Collective work, 1938–40). The Topkapı Sarayı archives concentrate on materials connected with the functioning of the palace, particularly its extensive kitchens, which on certain days needed to feed thousands of people. But there is a lot of overlap with the Prime Minister's Archive. On the one hand, documents concerning the operation of the Palace kitchen are also found in the central archive. On the other hand, quite a few accounts pertaining to pious foundations have found their way into the Topkapı Sarayı archives, even though one would normally expect them in the Maliyeden Müdevver series of the central archives instead.

One of the richest holdings of the Topkapı Palace consists of the Sultan's correspondence with the khanate of Crimea. From 1475 onward, this relic of the once powerful Golden Horde was a vassal principality of the Ottoman Empire. While the khans were appointed by the authorities in

Istanbul, the Sultans were obliged to choose them from among the members of the ruling Giray family. Since documentation concerning the khanate is sparse, the texts in the Topkapı Palace archive are of special value. They have been made accessible by a published guide with an ample index, which also contains reproductions of a few dozen documents (Benningsen et al., 1978).

In addition there exists a catalogue which was meant to cover the holdings of the Topkapı Sarayı Archive in its entirety. Two fascicules were published in 1938 and 1940 respectively; but this work has not proceeded beyond the letter 'H' (Collective work, 1938–40). The publication in question consists of indices of proper names along with the call numbers of the documents in which the relevant personages occur. In addition, there are some sample documents published in facsimile, with descriptions. Two fascicles of a catalogue encompassing sultanic commands are also available (Uzunçarşılı et al., 1985–86). However most of the documents still have to be located through unpublished catalogues. Unfortunately these repertories but rarely indicate whether the document being sought is in a good enough state of preservation to be shown to researchers (by contrast, some of the catalogues of the Başbakanlık Arşivi do provide this information). A fund of patience and good humour is therefore essential.

THE TAPU VE KADASTRO AND VAKIFLAR ARCHIVES

The first-named archive is attached to the General Directorate for the Cadastre, located in downtown Ankara. Primarily the Tapu ve Kadastro archive is meant to serve as a source of information in land disputes, and there is no published catalogue; historians are however admitted. Apart from a sizeable number of foundation deeds (vakıfname, vakfiye), this archive contains a remarkable collection of tax and foundation registers. Apart from the register of central Anatolian foundations prepared for Mehmed the Conqueror, which we have already encountered, this archive contains some priceless foundation registers documenting middle and late sixteenth century Istanbul (one of them published by Barkan and Ayverdi, 1970).

But the main reason for mentioning the Tapu ve Kadastro archive is the fact that it holds the entire series of tax registers prepared under Sultan Murad III (r. 1575–1595). These registers contain lists of settlements, taxpayers and taxes, and form the basis for any study of the socio–economic structure of sixteenth-century Ottoman society (see chapter 4). The documents in the Tapu ve Kadastro archives constitute the last series of registers covering, at least in intention, the entire Ottoman Empire. 1584 seems to have been a target date at least where central Anatolia is concerned; for this is the year very often mentioned in the prefaces. For certain parts of eastern Anatolia, no other registers have been preserved. However such single items are of limited utility, as scholars who have gained experience with Ottoman tax registers stress the need never to consult a individual text on its own. Wherever possible, the entire group of registers pertaining to a given region must be compared and analysed (Lowry, 1992). A researcher planning a study of a given sixteenth-century province thus should make sure to pay a visit to the Tapu ve Kadastro archive.

The archives of the Administration of Pious Foundations equally serve primarily the official body to which they are linked. Yet they also constitute a major resource for researchers dealing with pious foundations. Of particular value are the nineteenth-century certified copies (*hüccet*) of foundation documents, of which this archive possesses a large number. For many of the originals were in the hands of private persons, and given the vicissitudes of the last 100 years, often have not been preserved. Of course these copies may contain misreadings, particularly where older obsolete place names are concerned. But even problematic copies are better than no evidence at all. . .

THE KADI REGISTERS

Apart from the Prime Minister's archives, the thousands of surviving kadi registers (*kadı sicilleri, sicil*) should be regarded as *the* major resource for the Ottoman historian. They are found on Turkish territory, but also in other Ottoman successor states such as Greece, Macedonia, Jordan, Syria and Egypt. Those preserved in Turkey are now, apart from the major exception of the Istanbul registers and a few minor ones, located in the National Library (*Milli Kütüphane*) in Ankara. Istanbul's registers can be consulted in the office of the Chief Islamic Jurisconsult (*Müftülük*) in the Süleymaniye quarter of Istanbul. A published guide is available, the newest version of which allows the prospective user to determine the years covered by each register in addition to the call number (Akgündüz *et al.*, 1988–89). Moreover this guide contains a selection of reproduced documents. Many users claim that they find the scripts used in the kadi registers fairly easy to read; but of course there are variations from one volume to another.

Kadi registers of the larger cities will consist of two parts. One section begins where books written in the Arabic script normally begin, namely at what is, to us, the last page of the volume in question. A second section will then begin at what to the scribes was the last section of the register, and which we regard as the first. Starting from the end of the volume we find transactions notarised in the local court, such as sales, loans, agreements concerning divorces or manumissions of slaves. These transactions were not contentious and the parties involved had them recorded so that proof of the sale, divorce or manumission should be easily available. This purpose explains why we normally find the names of three, four or five witnesses under the relevant text (*şühud ül-hal*), who could be called upon as need arose. In addition, the kadi registers documented cases of litigation, which might concern the division of an inheritance, but also any number of miscellaneous complaints (for a broad selection of published documents from the mid-eighteenth-century Istanbul registers, see Kal'a *et al.*, 1997–).

More serious matters such as rape, robbery and murder are also recorded, but not very frequently. Islamic religious law (*şeriat*) regarded murder without robbery as something which, to a major extent, concerned the family of the victim, and on the other hand, the Ottoman state demanded monetary penalties and particularly a share of the blood money (*öşr-i diyet*). Thus there was some incentive to settle out of court. Many cases which by our categories would be regarded as penal simply contain the 'facts of the case' as established by the witnesses' depositions. Presumably the case was then referred to the Sultan's Council in Istanbul. But after having been seized of such an affair, the Council, according to the evidence of the Mühimme and Şikâyet Registers, in most cases merely issued an order to the relevant kadi to judge the matter according to the *şeriat*. Therefore in most cases, neither one nor the other source will inform us of the judgments issued and the manner of their execution.

The other half of the registers was taken up with orders issued by the Sultan's Council. Some of these were addressed to a large number of kadis and provincial authorities; they were sometimes distributed empire-wide, sometimes merely over a given region. Other sultanic commands were concerned with matters specifically assigned to a particular kadi and/or governor. These included responses to complaints by local inhabitants, such as creditors unable to recover loans.

Occasionally a rescript may occur both in the Registers of Important Affairs and in the local kadi registers. But that is fairly rare, as both the registers of the kadis and the records prepared in Istanbul have not survived in their totality. In addition, we cannot be sure how great was the percentage of documents which for one reason or another, escaped registration at either the central or the local end of the bureaucratic process.

In the largest cities, such as Bursa or Cairo, there were also separate registers for inheritance inventories (*muhallefat, tereke*). By this term we mean a list of the goods left by the deceased, including both movable property and real estate. Debts and money owed to the deceased were also included, as well as provisos concerning the testament of the man or woman in question, especially where the status of slaves to be liberated was involved. In Edirne and Istanbul, there were special registers covering the *askeri*, that is the servitors of the Sultans whose inheritances were liable to confiscation. However, these registers were not the responsibilty of the kadi but of a special official known as the *askeri kassam*.

In cases where no children or absent people were involved, the heirs could divide up the inheritance without recourse to the kadi and consequently without the compilation of an inheritance inventory. This means that only a relatively small share of all inheritance cases was recorded. Merchants were probably overrepresented among the surviving records, as they were likely to possess substantial fortunes and often died while away from home. By the same token, women and the poor were underrepresented. When the inheritance was small, it was to the advantage of all heirs to avoid reducing it further by paying the fees charged by the kadi's court. In addition, the frequency of inheritance disputes shows that manipulations to disinherit minors and women were common. Whenever the inventory does not explicitly say that the estate was sold by public auction, the prices assigned to individual goods in the register also should be regarded with a degree of scepticism. Used goods are notoriously difficult to value, even with the best of intentions.

The kadi's registers must have been kept in the court building of the district centre, and this explains why the registers did not before the late twentieth century find their way into a central deposit. It was the responsibility of the outgoing kadi to hand the registers accumulated in his office over to his successor. Occasionally we hear of kadis who did not do this, due to accidents or because they had something to hide. No Ottoman court buildings older than the mid nineteenth century have survived. But documentary and narrative sources show that by the seventeenth century they existed at least in the larger towns. Presumably an Ottoman court building more or less resembled the residence of a well-to-do family, with habitations surrounding two courtyards. In the first, corresponding to the men's part of a house (*selamlık*), the business of the court must have been transacted, while the family dwelt in the second courtyard. Outgoing kadis presumably moved out to make room for their successors (compare the article 'Sidjill' in *EI*, 2nd edn).

PRIVATE ARCHIVES

These may belong to persons or to non-governmental institutions such as dervish convents (*zaviye*s, *tekke*s). In Turkey, private archives with large numbers of pre-nineteenth-century documents are relatively rare, due largely to the wars and civil wars attendant upon the dissolution of the Ottoman Empire. But things were different in Syria; the city of Damascus holds substantial private archives down to the present day (Deguilhem, 1991 is partly based upon materials in private hands).

Zaviye archives were especially vulnerable when in 1826, Sultan Mahmud II closed down the janissary corps and in its wake, the Bektaşi order of dervishes as well. This was accompanied by the sale of the *zaviye*s' lands and the destruction of much movable property. Many collections of appointment documents (*berat*), which all *zaviye* sheiks needed in order to maintain themselves in office, disappeared during the turmoil (Faroqhi, 1981, pp. 107–28). A century later, in 1925, all dervish convents in the Republic of Turkey were closed down, and some of their movable property ended up in museums. But the dervishes' archives were mostly dispersed, with one major exception, namely the central *tekke* of the Mevlevis in Konya (Gölpınarlı, 1955–56). This collection has been described by the former Mevlevi Abdülbaki Gölpınarlı, who during his long life developed into a major specialist on Ottoman religious history. Moreover the archives of a small but ancient *zaviye*, known as Emirci Sultan and located in the vicinity of Çorum, have survived the upheavals of twentieth-century Anatolian history. They have been studied by Ahmet Yaşar Ocak (Ocak, 1978). Scholars working on the later nineteenth century will probably have somewhat better luck in locating private collections of documents.

MAJOR ARCHIVAL HOLDINGS RELEVANT TO OTTOMAN HISTORY OUTSIDE THE REPUBLIC OF TURKEY: THE EMPIRE'S 'SUCCESSOR STATES'

On the Balkan peninsula, the two major collections of Ottoman documents are found in Sarajevo and Sofia. Ottoman documents in Sarajevo's Gazi Husrev Beg Library deserve special mention (Zirojevic, 1989): 3,909 items are stored here, including the records of the Gazi Husrev Beg foundation itself. The number of foundation documents amounts to 1200, and the library also possesses the registers of the Sarajevo kadis, which begin in the sixteenth century. These registers have escaped destruction in the recent war, while the losses of library and archival materials kept in Sarajevo's Oriental Institute are apparently very heavy. In this same city, the Historical Archive also possesses a rich stock of materials, ranging in time from 1651 to 1900. This collection includes kadi registers from Temeşvar (Timişoara) in modern Roumania, which passed out of Ottoman hands in 1718. Some family archives also have found their way into the same institution, in addition to 1,762 manuscripts; these include some Slavic texts written in the Arabic script. In many instances, the distinction between library and archival materials is quite fluid.

In Sofia, Ottoman holdings are concentrated in the Oriental section of the Cyril and Methodius National Library. Kadi registers of Sofia, Vidin and Ruse (Ottoman Rusçuk) can be found here. These registers begin in the seventeenth century and seem to get much fuller in the eighteenth. Unfortunately the oldest register of Sofia, dating from 1550, disappeared during World War II (Duda, Galabov, 1960). It can still be consulted in a volume of summaries prepared by Galab Galabov and Heribert Duda during the war years, but published only in 1960. In addition, the National Library holds seventeenth-century records concerning the delivery of live sheep for the consumption of Istanbul (Cvetkova, 1976). For the nineteenth century, documents become more numerous; social and economic historians will note a large number of rulings connected with artisans.

Some provincial Bulgarian towns also contain important archives. Memorable are a few parish registers dating from the 1830s and located mainly in the City and District Archives of Plovdiv, but also in the National Historical Museum in Sofia. In one case, such registers are even found in the archive of the parish church for which they were first compiled (Todorova, 1993). These volumes concern Catholic parishes whose priests recorded baptisms, marriages and funerals according to the norms standard in the Roman Catholic church after the council of Trent. As such registers were not widespread in the Orthodox church, these few volumes have become a major source for the historical demography of the Ottoman provinces which a few decades later, were to form the kingdom of Bulgaria.

In the Arab countries, the two major treasurehouses of Ottoman documents are Cairo and Damascus. In Cairo the documentation for the Ottoman period (which we will assume to have ended with the British occupation of 1882) is especially ample. As early as 1930, Jean Deny published an inventory of the Ottoman documents accessible at that time (Deny, 1930). Since then, the history of Ottoman Cairo has all but developed into a separate discipline. Again the kadi registers constitute the historian's principal resource. They are located in the archives of the Mahkama al-shar'iyya, which in 1956 changed its name to Mahkama li'-l-ahwāl al- shakhṣiyya (Tribunal concerning Matters of Personal Status). Unfortunately, very few registers survive for the sixteenth century, and those which we do possess are not concentrated in any particular section of the city (Hanna, 1991, pp. 249–50). While the historian of the sixteenth century thus has to work largely with chronicles and Venetian records, scholars dealing with more recent periods have ample Ottoman archival sources at their disposal. One of the most remarkable is surely the magnificent series of inheritance inventories. This has permitted the construction of continuous series of prices and currency exchange rates, reflecting the major tendencies in Cairo's social and economic history during the seventeenth and eighteenth centuries (Raymond, 1973–74).

In addition, the Egyptian National Archives (Dār al-maḥfūẓat al-ʿumūmiyya) are also of interest to the Ottoman historian. They are located in the Citadel of Cairo. Here we find tax farming registers similar to those familiar from the Istanbul archives, known as the Daftar uṣūl māl djamārik (Registers concerning the Perception of Customs Duties). The National Archives also contain a series of documents emanating from Cairo's law courts, known as the Ḥudjadj sharʿiyya (Religious Law Documents). For the reign of Muḥammad ʿAlī (or Mehmed Ali Pasha if one prefers the Ottoman version of his name, r. 1805–1849) the Egyptian Government Archives provide ample information in the sections Maʾiyya Thāniyya, Turkī and ʿArabī, in addition to Abḥāth, Baḥr Barra, Sūdān, Shām and Diwān Khidiwī (Marsot, 1984, p. 291). Separately from the National Archives, the Ministry of Pious Foundations maintains a collection of numerous foundation deeds going back beyond the Ottoman into the Mamluk period. Some of these foundation deeds, comparable to their Istanbul or Damascus counterparts, deal with the construction of shops, workshops and covered markets. They thus constitute a major resource for the urban historian (Behrens-Abouseif, 1994).

For Damascus, the principal Ottoman archives are in the Markaz al-wathāʾiḳ al-tārīkhiyya (Centre for Historical Documents). This collection contains not only the kadi registers of Damascus itself (1583–1920), but also those of Aleppo (1555–1925) and of Hama (16th–17th centuries). We find some very fine samples of eighteenth-century inheritance inventories relevant to the city of Damascus. Of special interest is also the series known as Awāmir al-sulṭāniyya (Sultanic Orders); differently from what was customary in Anatolian cities, the larger Syrian courts entered the sultanic commands which they received not into the back sections of their regular registers, but into separate record books; for the period from 1780 to 1910, twelve such registers survive. In addition the Damascus archives, both the Markaz al-wathāʾiḳ and the Ḳaṣr al ʿadliyya (Palace of Justice) house numerous documents covering local pious foundations, and the same applies to the

National Archives located in the al-ʿAẓm Palace. In these different archives, the researcher can follow the history of numerous pious foundations from Ottoman times until their abolition in 1949, or in certain instances to the present day. Some foundation deeds are also preserved in the Damascene library of al-Ẓāhiriyya (Deguilhem, 1991; Rafeq, 1976; Abdel Nour, 1982, pp. 1–4).

MAJOR ARCHIVES OUTSIDE OF THE FORMER OTTOMAN TERRITORIES: THE CASE OF FRANCE

The Ottoman documents to be considered here may have arrived in France (or Venice, or the Netherlands) in the normal course of business; this applies to the letters Ottoman Sultans sent to foreign rulers. Or else documents may have been captured in wartime, or purchased by collectors and ultimately turned over to some public repository (for an example concerning the Germanies: Babinger, 1931). In the latter case, the documents in question were often esteemed for their artistic decoration rather than for their contents, and thus wound up not in archives but in museums. In addition, documents composed by Frenchmen or other non-Ottomans may provide vital information on Ottoman subjects who came to France or some other European country as visitors or prisoners of war, remained as long-term residents or even made the foreign country in question their permanent home (Eldem, 1999). Since a great many archives, libraries and museums hold documents falling into one or another of these categories, only a selection can be introduced here.

To the economic historian of the Ottoman Empire, the archives of the Marseilles Chambre de Commerce constitute one of *the* major document collections available, with supplementary information to be gained in the Archives du Port de Toulon (Panzac, 1985, pp. 521–4; Panzac, 1996a, p. 58). At certain times French shippers carrying goods for Ottoman merchants both Muslim and non-Muslim were encouraged to deposit their freight contracts with the relevant consular authorities. Thus two registers from Toulon provide a unique reflection of French and Ottoman Mediterranean commerce in the later eighteenth century. The importance of the much larger Marseilles archives for the history of French commerce in the eastern Mediterranean has been known for over a century (Masson, 1896). Consular correspondence preserved in Marseilles, preserved due to the semi-official role devolving on the Chambre de Commerce, refers to the conditions under which French traders operated. But even more revealing is the Fonds Roux, the archive of an eighteenth- and nineteenth-century Marseilles firm with numerous correspondents in Istanbul, Izmir and other

Ottoman cities. Moreover, the registers of ships entering the port of Marseilles, located in the departmental archives of Bouches-de-Rhone, for the eighteenth century provide valuable information on the presence or absence of plague in the ports shippers had visited. Particularly after the catastrophic epidemic which hit Marseilles and Provence in 1720, these registers were kept with scrupulous care.

Only those places in which French merchants resided on a long-term basis are documented in the Chambre de Commerce records. Apart from Aleppo, these were mainly port towns. Izmir has generated a major amount of documentation, all the more precious as due to wars and earthquakes, little survives *in situ*. Istanbul was a city where Frenchmen sold a great deal, often valuable goods of superior quality. Salonica emerged in the seventeenth and eighteenth centuries as a centre of French trade (Svoronos, 1956). Ottoman Crete was visited by Provençal shippers interested in the country's olive crop (Sabatier, 1976). Among the Syrian ports Sayda was usually the most frequented, except for a period in the late eighteenth century when a local magnate by the name of Cezzar Ahmed Pasha succeeded in rerouting traffic through his port of Acre. As to the Ottoman provinces on the African continent, Alexandria was frequented by French traders doing business with Cairo. From the late sixteenth century and especially from the seventeenth, Tunis also attracted a contingent of Frenchmen, who traded in coral and the abundant olive crop of the Sahel area (Sadok, 1987).

The archives of the Chambre de Commerce have been used extensively by a group of distinguished French historians who in the 1950s, brought out a collective work on the history of the trade of Marseilles (Rambert ed., 1951–57). For our purposes, mainly vols. 3–5 are relevant. Throughout, the authors have documented the quantities of goods traded in the port and the changing priorities of local traders. In that sense this massive and detailed study is a work of economic history, with a quantitative slant. But even so, the French economic historians of the 1950s were not concerned with the Ottoman Empire *per se*. Sayda, Izmir or Salonica were not treated as commercial centres in their own right, but simply as sites on which Marseilles merchants did their buying and selling. By contrast Daniel Panzac has pioneered the use of French archival materials for the study of Ottoman social and economic history: plague, caravan routes and the continuing commercial activity of eighteenth-century Muslim Egyptians form part of his agenda (Panzac, 1985, 1992, 1996).

In Paris and Nantes, the Archives Nationales and the Archives des

Affaires Étrangères (Ministry of Foreign Affairs) provide additional sources of information. French public archives are often classified according to a standard scheme, so that the researcher will encounter certain series in many different archives. Thus the series 'B' is connected with the activities of the various ministries. Apart from the Foreign Ministry, the Ottoman historian may have recourse to the records of the Ministry of the Navy, or else consult the series 'F', concerned with 'Administration générale'. Robert Mantran (1962), Elena Frangakis-Syrett (1992), Boubaker Sadok (1987) and Daniel Panzac (1985) have all provided very full lists of French archival documents in the bibliographies of their respective monographs, and a researcher beginning work in the French national archives will be well advised to take these authors as his/her guides.

To figure out what kind of documentation to expect in French state archives, we need to know something about the functioning of early modern ambassadorial and consular services. Diplomats were appointed by the King, but the merchants themselves were made to defray the expenses of consular officials who, in theory, existed only to take care of commercial interests. In real life, things might turn out quite differently. Thus in the seventeenth century the office of consul was farmed out, and the appointee collected fees from the merchants in order to obtain a profit on his investment. Under these circumstances, massive conflicts of interest between merchants and consul were by no means rare, and this has generated correspondence informative to the present-day historian (Steensgaard, 1968; Goffman, 1990). Even the ambassador, whose duty it was to mediate relations between his sovereign and the Ottoman ruler, often was financed by the merchants doing business in the Sultan's domains. At least in the seventeenth century this situation might lead to chaotic conditions: the most notorious case was that of the ambassador de Cécy who ran up massive debts in Istanbul in the course of furthering French trade. But the merchants were unwilling to reimburse him, and the matter dragged on for decades.

Diplomatic and consular archives particularly of the seventeenth century will thus tell us more about the internal tensions between merchants and diplomatic personnel than about commercial business. This is a great disappointment for the economic historian concerned with the production of silk or cotton thread, the role of commercial intermediaries or the impact of credit. But this documentation admirably suited older historians, such as the late nineteenth-century French scholar Paul Masson. For Masson was concerned exactly with the internal affairs of the French expatriate community, in addition to the relation between the Frenchmen resident on Ottoman territory on the one hand, and their commercial principals and government on the other (1896; 1911). Even today, by no means everything of interest has been said about European expatriates living in seventeenth-century Istanbul or Izmir. Daniel Goffman has discussed the manner in which the English Civil War was fought out on Ottoman soil (Goffman, 1998). Kemal Beydilli has shown that Ottoman archives contain considerable evidence on the repercussions of the French Revolution upon the Istanbul diplomatic community (Beydilli, 1984).

French consular reports of the eighteenth and early nineteenth centuries are of particular interest, as their authors' families were stationed on Ottoman territory over several generations and often able to establish close local contacts. Young men getting ready to step into their fathers' shoes were sent to France for a period of study, an arrangement which also ensured that they did not completely blend into local society. Upon return they would be awarded a vacant consular position. Among the consuls whose writing is especially valuable to the historian we find the Peysonnels, father and son, frequently the guests of one or another member of the Izmir magnate family known as the Karaosmanoğulları (Veinstein, 1975). In the early nineteenth century, Aleppo was the scene of the activities of Consul Rousseau, a relative of the philosopher, whose instructive reports on the eastern trade of this city have been analysed (Wirth, 1986).

OTHER IMPORTANT EUROPEAN ARCHIVES

Information on Dutch trade in the Ottoman Empire can be collected in the Algemeen Rijksarchief in The Hague. Official standing was granted to Dutch merchants in 1612, when Sultan Ahmed I issued a privilege known in Ottoman parlance as an *ahidname*. These privileges (capitulations in European historical terminology) consist of Sultans' rescripts establishing the conditions under which trade could be conducted, along with the status of consular and diplomatic officials (de Groot, 1978, pp. 231–259). Moreover, for certain years, the series 'Resolutions of the States General', which is particularly germane to Ottoman–Dutch relations, is available in print. The Rijksarchiev also contains records of the Dutch embassy in Istanbul (legatie Turkije voor 1785) and of the consulate in Izmir. In addition, the entire Board of Levant Trade archive (archief van de directie van de Levantse Handel) has been deposited here (de Groot, 1978, pp. 340–3). Documents concerning Levant trade and diplomatic relations between the Ottoman Sultan and the Dutch may also turn up in provincial archives. But on the whole, the historian will work with the well catalogued materials in the Den Haag collection. A selection of published documents on Levant trade is also available (Heeringa and Nanninga eds. 1910–17).

Little work has been done by Ottomanist historians on the Dutch records, probably because the Levant was a secondary venue for Dutch traders of the 'Golden Age'. Two monographs based on Dutch sources (Van Lutterveld, 1958; de Groot, 1978) concern the life of the Istanbul embassy, including its artistic personnel. A most valuable contribution to Ottoman commercial history is found in a monograph on Dutch trade of the sixteenth to eighteenth centuries, well known among Europeanists but rarely read by Ottomanists (Israel, 1989). Students of the Ankara mohair trade have long known that mohair yarn was exported in considerable quantities, to the point that local weavers complained of a scarcity of raw material. Apparently the main customers for this fibre were the Dutch, as in the seventeenth century, the town of Leiden wove a sizeable amount of camlets out of mohair. It would be very interesting to find out what happened to Ankara mohair in the eighteenth century, when the demand generated by the Leiden camlet industries fell away dramatically. The figures published by Frangakis-Syrett demonstrate that even in this later period, the export of mohair by way of Izmir was not insignificant (Frangakis-Syrett, 1992, pp. 302ff.).

Both Dutch and English merchants traded in the Levant through chartered companies, so that the sources available in the two countries resemble each other to some extent. Among the material which the Ottoman historian will wish to consult in the London Public Record Office, the Levant Company Archives take pride of place. In the seventeenth and eighteenth centuries, any English merchant who legally wished to trade in the eastern Mediterranean was obliged to become a member ('freeman') of the company. 'Interlopers' were not unknown, but their activities are less well documented. In the Levant Company archives we find registers of various dues paid by English merchants. A section known as the Aleppo Chancellery possesses a sizeable collection of commercial correspondence, including order and invoice books. However, the business of private English traders is richly documented in other collections as well, particularly the Radcliffe Manuscripts. These are located partly in the Guildhall Library of London and partly in the Hertfordshire Record Office in Hertford. The Radcliffes, a commercial family active in Aleppo, have left an exceptional quantity of letters, but other firms are also well documented. Commercial correspondence dealing with the Levant is equally found in the Essex Record Office at Chelmsford (Davis, 1967, pp. xi–xii).

For the nineteenth century, British consular reports often contain considerable evidence on the commercial possibilities of the region in which their authors were stationed. For a published example, concerning the otherwise little known district of Kayseri in 1880, we will take a brief look at the report by the British vice-consul Ferdinand Bennet (*House of Commons Accounts and Papers*, vol. 100, no. 6, 1881, pp. 268–82, publ. Karpat, 1980). Bennet's report, as other well-prepared documents of this type, contains some statistical information, culled both from Ottoman published sources and day-to-day observation of the local market. Thus we find a list of the principal goods traded, along with their prices, a listing of taxes levied, and – due to their importance for the safety of the roads – information on the gendarmerie (*zaptiye*) stationed in the district. While Bennet shared with many of his European *confrères* a tendency to regard anything Ottoman as inferior *per se*, he was conscientious enough to record what he had actually observed, even if it did not fit in with his preconceived mental map (Bennet ed. Karpat, 1980, p. 108).

In Italy, one of the richest resources for the Ottomanist historian is the Archivio di Stato in Venice. The Turkish-language documents (Documenti Turchi) have now been made accessible through a published inventory (Pedani Fabris, 1994a). This new catalogue includes the extensive summaries prepared during the war years by Alessio Bombaci, and constitutes the result of a major reorganisation of the whole section. Until the recent past, various nineteenth- and twentieth-century attempts at organising the Ottoman material, most of them incomplete, had resulted in making this important collection extremely difficult of access. A sizeable number of materials concern the enforcement of the peace treaty of Passarowitz (1718); particularly the correspondence of a Venetian official charged with this matter in Dalmatia is of importance here. A selection of Ottoman documents pertaining to the reign of Süleyman the Magnificent (r. 1520–66) was published, more than thirty years ago, by Tayyip Gökbilgin (Gökbilgin, 1964). This publication includes not only political correspondence, but also more or less personal letters, dealing for instance with the purchase of luxury goods. These shed a vivid light on the relationship between individual members of the Venetian and Ottoman elites.

Venetian ambassadors, and this includes the *baili* posted to Istanbul, after their return needed to present a comprehensive report (*relazione*) before the Venetian Senate, apart from the more informal letters (*dispacci*) which they sent to the relevant authorities while in office. Most of the Venetian ambassadors' comprehensive reports, a favourite source of all nineteenth-century political historians, have been available in print for a hundred years and more. But the *dispacci* concerning Istanbul for the most part remain unpublished, even though they contain valuable information, particularly on the life of the foreign community in Istanbul (Albèri, 1840–45, Barozzi and Berchet, eds., 1871–72; see also Mantran, 1962, pp. 655–659).

For those historians working on Ottoman Christians, the Vatican archives, and particularly those of the Sacra Congregatio de Propaganda Fide, have proven to be a mine of information, even though the number of Catholics under the domination of the Ottoman Sultan was always quite limited. This is due to the strenuous efforts of the Roman Curia, and particularly of its servitors the Jesuits, to persuade the members of eastern Christian churches to acknowledge the supremacy of St Peter's see. Churches willing to comply were allowed to maintain their own languages and rituals; they were known as Uniate. These 'propagandistic' efforts have produced masses of documentation, particularly with respect to those groups most amenable to Roman Catholic missions, such as the Lebanese Maronites, the Aleppine Christians (from the early nineteenth century onward) and a section of the Armenian community (Van Leeuwen, 1994, p. 3; Masters, to be published).

Recently the Inquisition archives in Venice, the Spanish possessions in Italy and of course Spain and Portugal themselves have also turned out to be a valuable if indirect source for Ottoman history. People not on official mission who had dwelt for some time in the Ottoman domains, either in North Africa or in the central provinces, after their return to Spain, Portugal or Spanish-ruled Italy were advised to turn to the Inquisition tribunal of their home province and give an account of their past and present loyalty to the Catholic faith (Bennassar and Bennassar, 1989, pp. 485–486). For captives, the situation was straightforward; even when they admitted to having become Muslims, the court generally assumed that as slaves they had had little choice, and they were let off with a light penance. Highly dangerous however was the position of those men who had been captured with arms in their hands, usually at sea, for in that case a voluntary commitment to Islam was assumed. In such instances, witnesses were sought out, for the accused tried to prove that they were Muslims by birth, and therefore not subject to the Inquisition's jurisdiction. From the depositions of both the accused Muslims or ex-Muslims, and of those who had known these men in their earlier lives, we can gain a fascinating glimpse of personal strategies and motivations, unavailable from any other type of documentation.

Throughout the sixteenth century, the two major competitors for control over the Mediterranean were the Ottoman Empire and Spain. Yet Ottomanist historians have paid very little attention to the documentation available in the Spanish archives, among which the Archivo General de Simancas is probably the most relevant. Among the issues covered, the most prominent is the struggle for power in North Africa, which the Ottomans ultimately won. But this was achieved only after a long sequence of confrontations with many dramatic turning points, including the death of the last king of independent Portugal on a Moroccan battlefield in 1578. These issues are covered by the series E, Guerra Antigua and Cámara de Castilla. But doubtlessly the Spanish archives contain documents relevant to Ottoman history in other sections as well (Hess, 1978, p. 215). Very little is known about the small-scale fighting against Ottoman forces, interrupted by negotiations on the local level, which was conducted by the powerful Spanish viceroys who governed much of Italy during the seventeenth century. Most of the documents will probably deal with the nitty-gritty of false alerts and minor negotiations. But given the fact that Ottomanist historians have so rarely worked in Spanish archives, surprise finds are not excluded either.

Mutatis mutandis, the same thing applies to the Portuguese source materials located in Lisbon, in the State Archives of the Torre do Tombo (Özbaran, 1994, pp. 17–20, see also Özbaran, 1977). The best guide for the researcher wishing to locate Portuguese sources relevant to Ottoman–Portuguese rivalry are the articles of Salih Özbaran, to my knowledge almost the only Ottomanist historian to have concerned himself with the Portuguese archives. The Torre do Tombo materials are divided into two main sections, known as the 'Corpo Cronológico' and the 'Gavetas' ('drawers'). In the 'Corpo Cronológico' section, there are 82,902 documents, organised in 'Maços' ('bundles'). They mainly concern the sixteenth century. A catalogue containing brief summaries of every document, along with an index, is available in the archives. As to the Gavetas, there are twenty-three of them, dealing mainly with the sixteenth century. Among the smaller collections in the Torre do Tombo, which concern Portuguese activities in Asia and therefore Ottoman–Portuguese conflict, Özbaran mentions the Cartas de Ormuz a D. Joao de Castro (letters from Hormuz, the Portuguese port in the Persian Gulf, to the Portuguese Viceroy of India, 1545–48). In addition one should not neglect the so-called Colecçao de S. Lourenço, which consists of letters written to the Portuguese authorities, copied into six volumes. Very little is known about the potential of the Goa archives for the history of Ottoman–Portuguese relations. In addition to their Indian location, the latter can also be consulted on microfilm in Portugal. Since the Goa archive has been used to great advantage by historians concerned with Indian Ocean trade, it is very likely that Ottomanists will also find worthwhile information here.

As the Ottomans and the Austrian Habsburgs shared a long common frontier for centuries, the Austrian state archives in Vienna contain a large number of Turkish documents. Many of them deal with diplomatic matters (for a recent publication see Džaja et al., 1995). For the early period (1480–1574) these documents have all been published in the form of summaries, more or less extensive according to the importance of the text in question (Petritsch, 1991). Moreover those rescripts of Kanuni Sultan Süleyman (r. 1520–1566) located in the Austrian archives have been published in full (Schaendlinger, 1983 and 1986). For archival materials documenting later periods, the researcher will have to consult different archives, namely the Geheime Haus-, Hof- und Staatsarchiv (Secret Archives of the [Habsburg] House, Court and State), in addition to the Kriegsarchiv (War Archive) and the Hofkammerarchiv (Archives of the Aulic Chamber). These archives all form part of the present-day Staatsarchiv. Because of various historical accidents, certain documents may be found not in the section where at first glance one would expect them, but in quite different places. But with the help of the unpublished catalogue and the expertise of the archivists, this should not be a major stumbling block.

Of particular value for the Ottoman historian are the archives of the coastal town of Dubrovnik, until 1808 a miniature vassal state of the Ottoman Empire. Major local archives go back to the fourteenth century. But relations with the Ottomans became significant mainly in the fifteenth, when Dubrovnik was one of the earliest states to regularly receive 'capitulations' (ahidname). The first surviving document in this series, written in what used to be called Serbo-Croatian and in the Cyrillic script, dates from 1430 (Biegman, 1967, Carter, 1972). Dubrovnik, which down into the sixteenth century flourished due to its extensive trade between Catholic Europe and the Ottoman lands, possessed a special Turkish Chancery. Most of the correspondence for which this office was responsible has been preserved. Dubrovnik's archives also hold documents written in Italian, Latin and Serbian-Croatian-Bosnian, which are also often useful to the Ottomanist historian. Records concerning the commercial activities of Dubrovnik citizens in places such as Venice or Sofia also form part of the city's archives. Moreover, this repository as early as the eighteenth century was systematically organised, and in the case of the Ottoman materials, catalogues with summaries of every individual document were prepared. Even though the archives suffered painful losses after the end of Dubrovnik as an independent state – certain documents were carried off to Vienna, Zadar (Zara) and Belgrade, and not all of them survived the move – this is still an exceptionally rich and well-organised collection.

INTRODUCING PALAEOGRAPHY AND
DIPLOMATICS

The formal study of palaeography may be regarded as a kind of paradox. On the one hand, Ottoman archival studies are impossible without a good knowledge of the relevant scripts, and their apprenticeship is a major ingredient in the training of a novice researcher. At the same time, however, nobody has learned palaeography entirely from books. University courses and the private study of published documents are of great value, as they save time when on the spot. However, texts and courses provide no more than a general introduction, and once in the archive, the historian will have to accustom him/herself to the particular documents needed for his/her work. Every type of record and sometimes every individual document has its own special characteristics, so that even the most experienced researchers may fail to read a particular word or phrase. Often it is not so much palaeography, as the knowledge of what is normally said in a given type of document, which provides the solution to the modern reader's difficulty. Therefore the study of the formal structure of documents (diplomatics) is closely linked to that of palaeography. In the end, experience is the crucial factor.

Introducing a few scholars who have studied the formal characteristics of Ottoman documents, we will begin with a brief glance at calligraphy. The aesthetic aspect of writing, characteristic of the more elaborate among Ottoman documents, needs special emphasis. Calligraphy has not been a highly developed art in post-Gutenberg Europe. Therefore, most twentieth-century scholars need to make an intellectual effort to appreciate certain Ottoman documents as works of art – which was what they were originally meant to be. The calligrapher's art begins with his/her writing materials. Thus it comes as no surprise that Süheyl Ünver, one of the best connoisseurs of this art in republican Turkey, should have devoted special attention to paper, watermarks, ink and pens (Ünver, 1960, 1962). Similar matters have equally loomed large in the work of Uğur Derman, who has also written on the aesthetics of script in the narrow sense of the word (for example Derman, 1988).

Numerous are the scholars who have dealt with the structure of Ottoman documents and the modalities of their production. We will begin with a few studies by Ismail Hakkı Uzunçarşılı, Carter Findley and Halil Inalcık. In 1941 Uzunçarşılı published a major article on the *tuğra* of the Ottoman Sultans and the *tuğra*-like signature used by viziers, known as the *pençe* ('claw'). In the same year he also studied the official orders issued by viziers and known as *buyuruldu* ('it has been ordered') (Uzunçarşılı, 1941a and b). But his major contribution probably lies not so much in the study of individual documents, as in his work on the administrative apparatus which produced them (see chapter 8). For the nineteenth century, Uzunçarşılı's work has been continued by Carter Findley with much greater historiographical sophistication (Findley, 1980). In Findley's view, many central government officials down to the Tanzimat, and often even beyond, appear essentially as artisans who specialised in the manufacture of documents. By contrast concern with the content matter of the reports and orders thus issued remained limited to officials in the highest positions (Findley, 1980, p. 85). Findley's work constitutes a study of political and social history, and is certainly not intended as a contribution to Ottoman diplomatics. Yet the researcher concerned with the latter field will learn a great deal from this book.

In Halil Inalcık's *oeuvre*, a concern with diplomatics has often been a by-product of his work on political and economic history. In the early fifties, he published a study of one of the earliest surviving Ottoman tax registers, which also contains essential information on the manner in which this historical source was compiled. Here Inalcık continued a line of research begun in the early 1940s by Ömer Lütfi Barkan, and which after him, engaged the attention of scholars such as Nicoara and Irène Beldiceanu (Barkan, 1940–41; Beldiceanu and Beldiceanu-Steinherr, 1978). A classic from somewhat later years is Inalcık's study of the capitulations (*'Imtiyāzāt'*) in the second edition of the *EI*, which examines these grants of privilege not only in terms of political motivations and economic consequences, but also as documents posing special problems in terms of legal significance. Inalcık also has interested himself in the path taken by individual documents from the moment of composition to the time they were acted upon; of particular interest is his article on the appointment process of an eighteenth-century Istanbul guild warden (Inalcık, 1986).

There exists but a handful of books covering Ottoman palaeography and diplomatics as a whole. For the bibliography, the reader will turn to the work of Valery Stojanov (Stojanov, 1983). One of the pioneers in the study of Ottoman chancery practice was Friedrich Kraelitz (Kraelitz, 1922). But an early 'classic' in the field is owed to the Hungarian scholar Lajos Fekete (Fekete, 1926). This volume treats the characteristics of Ottoman documents from the period between 1526 and 1699, when the sultans controlled most of the former Kingdom of Hungary. When Fekete wrote in the early 1920s, the study of European mediaeval documents was a highly developed discipline, and the author applied categories familiar to him from this field. This was not as inappropriate as it might appear at first glance: Ottoman documents were indeed composed according to traditions elaborated in the Abbasid and Mamluk chanceries, and the scribes working in these institutions in turn seem to have been at least indirectly acquainted with the scribal traditions of late antiquity. Since mediaeval European documents were composed according to models inherited from the same tradition, some similarities go back to a common source. Moreover, the mere purpose of a royal edict may lead to similar forms of expression even if there exist no shared traditions. But Fekete introduced a distinction between documents concerning 'religious matters' and those relevant to 'secular affairs', which makes sense in the context of mediaeval Europe, but much less so in the Ottoman tradition. This categorisation has been criticised by later scholars. But otherwise Fekete's work has been enormously influential. In the books of later authors on the same theme, the intellectual debt to Fekete, particularly where the outline is concerned, is often dramatically obvious.

Fekete's work dominated the field until well after World War II; the useful introduction to palaeography by Mahmud Yazır, published in 1942, does not deal with diplomatics at all (Yazır, 1942). In 1955, Fekete produced another, more specialised work on Ottoman palaeography. In the meantime, he had worked in the Ottoman archives and become acquainted with the intricacies of the script called *siyakat* (Fekete, 1955). This was used by the Ottoman financial administration down into and beyond the eighteenth century. Figures were written not in Arabic numerals but in graphemes derived from the same numbers written out in Arabic words. Because of the abridgements involved, the numerals could no longer be read as words, but had to be memorised as separate entities; understandably, these numerals were not employed in arithmetical operations. Ordinary sentences were written in such a way as to resemble the numerals; they could be read only by people with some prior knowledge of the contents of the document to be deciphered. This script was used to keep the information contained in the relevant documents secret, besides strengthening group consciousness among the limited number of scribes 'in the know'. While other and shorter guides to *siyakat* exist, the documents read and explained by Fekete still form a comprehensive introduction to this thorny subject. Among the shorter ones must name a study by Dündar Günday (Günday, 1974). Its special merit is the inclusion of eighteenth-century *siyakat* material, which Fekete with his Hungarian perspective had rather neglected. As more and more eighteenth-century documents become available in the Istanbul archives, Günday's samples of financial documents from the period will be increasingly appreciated. Finally, there is a pocket-sized volume by Selâheddin Elker, which contains only the *siyakat* figures, without any texts (Elker, 1953). But

Elker's work contains a large number of possible variations; moreover since the tables can easily be removed from the book, it is especially convenient to take along into the archives.

For the English speaker, the most accessible introduction to Ottoman palaeography and diplomatics will probably be the *Handbook of Otto-man-Turkish Diplomatics* by Jan Reychman and Ananiasz Zajaczkowski (Reychman, Zajaczkowski, 1968). This work came out in Polish in 1955, but the editor in charge of the English version, the well-known Ottomanist Tibor Halasi-Kun, has brought the bibliography up to date. In the introduction we find a review of Ottoman published documents, which, however, has been largely superseded by Stojanov's work. The short survey on Ottoman archives equally is out of date, but the more extensive overview of collections of Ottoman documents in Europe is still useful. In the section on palaeography, writing materials and implements are briefly introduced, along with the types of script used in different kinds of documents. As the original edition was directed at Polish readers, information on chancery practice concerns Ottoman–Polish relations, which means that the Crimean Tatars also come in for their share of attention. This is a great advantage, as this kind of information is otherwise hard to come by. But information on Istanbul chanceries is rather meagre; this is scarcely surprising, as the authors must have prepared their book in the extremely difficult conditions of postwar Poland.

In the Roumanian language, Mihail Guboglu has published an introduction to Ottoman palaeography and diplomatics, which judging from the translation of certain sections I was able to obtain from a friendly colleague, is strongly under the influence of Fekete's work (Guboğlu, 1958). However, where Guboglu deals with materials relevant to the three principalities of Moldavia, Wallachia and Transylvania, he has introduced certain documents not covered by Fekete. Moreover he was able to reproduce some documents in colour, which much enhances the visual quality of his work.

In 1979, the Turkish scholar Tayyip Gökbilgin documented his life-long concern with Ottoman archival documents by the publication of a short volume on palaeography and diplomatics, presumably intended for beginners (Gökbilgin, 1979). After briefly discussing his predecessors in the field, the author gives a short account of papers, scripts, seals, and the structure of documents. He shares with Fekete the division of his material into the categories of 'lay' and 'religious'. Special emphasis is placed on the titles used for both Ottoman dignitaries and foreign rulers. An additional division is devoted to documents produced by viziers and other dignitaries, including the khans of the Crimea. By contrast to this fairly developed section, the documents connected in one way or another with 'religious affairs' are given very short shrift; kadi registers, documents establishing pious foundations (*vakfiye*) and legal opinions (*fetva*) are accorded barely a page each.

While not a systematic treatment of our topic, the papers given at a symposium held at Istanbul University and edited by Mübahat Kütükoğlu are of interest here (Kütükoğlu, 1988). A second volume, based on a further symposium devoted to this topic, is in the course of publication. Here we find treatments of particular documents, such as the entry books (*ruzname*, *ruznamce*) kept by the treasury and other offices in order to keep track of goods and money entering and leaving the service in question. Other contributors have concerned themselves with administrative processes reflected in marginal notes to pre-existing texts, or with the document-creating impact of institutions newly established in the nineteenth century.

However, readers wishing to familiarise themselves with the state of the art in Ottoman palaeography and diplomatics now will turn first and foremost to the new volume on the 'language of Ottoman documents' by Mübahat Kütükoğlu (Kütükoğlu, 1994). This volume is notable for the care with which the secondary literature of the last decades has been incorporated. Thus, for instance, the section on paper, which in Fekete's book covered less than two pages, here has been developed into a major chapter. This includes imported papers from both east and west, Ottoman attempts at paper manufacture, watermarks and the types of paper preferred by different official bodies. In the same fashion, the treatment of seals, which Fekete had relegated to a single page, in Mübahat Kütükoğlu's hands has blossomed into an important study. Here we find an introduction to the seals used by sultans, as well as those employed by officeholders in the course of their official functions. Separate sections are devoted to the seals imprinted on foundation documents and those used by private individuals. We even find a discussion of the rules of precedence when a number of people were called upon to add their seals to a single document, and the author also discusses the use of seals containing only a word of authentication (*sahh*).

In similar fashion, the section on sultanic documents has been greatly amplified. Apart from the conventional discussion of their formal structure, the author explains why a sultanic command was emitted in the first place. She also makes clear why documents issued by previous rulers needed confirmation – and how they were often confirmed – whenever a new sultan ascended the throne. There is a section concerning the privileges granted to foreign rulers, often on behalf of 'their' merchants. They were known as *ahidname* in Ottoman and as 'capitulations' in European sources;

Kütükoğlu's analysis is based on original documentation from the archives of the Prime Minister. Of special value is the distinction, introduced by the author, between the older *ahidname* and its nineteenth-century version known as *muahede*. These *muahede*s were the great fetters of Ottoman policymakers in the last century and a half of the Empire's existence, and the changed relationship of the Ottoman Sultan to the outside world was reflected in the minutiae of the relevant documents (see the article 'Imtiyāzāt' in *EI*, 2nd edn by Halil Inalcık).

As *the* major innovation of Kütükoğlu's book, I would regard the attention consistently paid to the nineteenth century; the detailed treatment of the *muahede* constitutes but one example among many. This attention is very timely, since the great work of cataloguing, which has been carried out in the Prime Minister's archives during the last decade or so, has made available enormous quantities of nineteenth-century archival sources. Yet as far as previous work on Ottoman diplomatics was concerned, these recent documents had gone practically unstudied.

Among the texts dating from the earlier part of the nineteenth century, we find adaptations of older formats. Thus the sultans of this period issued commands in their own hand just as their predecessors had done, even if the number of preserved documents is much higher for Mahmud II (r. 1808–89) than for most rulers of the eighteenth century. But after mid-century, usages were instituted which drastically changed the appearance of documents, such as the growing employment of printed forms. In addition, new kinds of officials were introduced, who of course produced records of their deliberations. This applied not only to 'modern' areas such as the developing ministries, but also to sectors which one might have imagined largely immune to change. To name but one example, direct communication between the Sultan and Grand Vizier, for centuries one of the cornerstones of the Ottoman political edifice, was progressively whittled away as a Palace Secretary (*mabeyn baş katibi*) came to be responsible for the entire correspondence of the ruler. Last but not least, new technologies of communication, such as the telegraph, resulted in new archival material. Kütükoglu's work, the first attempt at systematising this vast body of material, ranks as a pioneering effort in the history of Ottoman palaeography and diplomatics.

OTTOMAN DOCUMENTS OUTSIDE OF TURKEY: A BRIEF OVERVIEW OVER SOME SMALLER COLLECTIONS

The empire's 'successor states'

Bosnia (Zirojevic, 1989)

Franciscan conventual archives.
Office of the Pater Provincial in Mostar/Herzegowina: 2,218 Ottoman documents. Official correspondence with the Ottoman authorities between 1844 and 1878. Documents and manuscripts purchased from local Muslim families (seventeenth, eighteenth, nineteenth centuries). Serious damage during the recent war.
Convent of Kresevo and the Franciscan Classical Secondary School of Visoko: archives and manuscript holdings.

Serbia (Zirojevic, 1989)

Belgrade's holdings of Ottoman documents apparently concern the early nineteenth century, after Prince Miloš had been recognised as an Ottoman vassal (Belgrade state archive, 'The Princes' Chancery'). Ministries' archives (foreign, finance), established in the nineteenth century, also contain Ottoman materials.
Orthodox monasteries on Serbian territory frequently maintained correspondences of their own with the Ottoman sultans and high-level dignitaries (Museum of the Serbian Orthodox Church, Belgrade). Maintaining their own archives: Holy Trinity near Plevlja, monastery of Decani.

Macedonia (Zirojevic, 1989)

Skopje (Üsküp in OttomanTurkish parlance)
State archive holds series of Monastir/Bitola kadi registers (early seventeenth century onwards, some registers published). Numerous documents from the late nineteenth and early twentieth centuries.

Albania (Veinstein, 1987)

A kadi register concerning Valona (Ottoman Avlonya, 1567–68), the oldest register of any Albanian town, in the Vatican library. In Albania: kadi registers of Berat (1602–) and Elbasan (1580– , copies only). Other Albanian towns, including Tirana, merely possess kadi registers from the nineteenth century.

Greece (Dimitriadis, 1989)

Macedonian State Archive in Salonica.
Registers containing nineteenth-century inheritance inventories, kadi registers from the countryside around Salonica. Nineteenth-century documents connected with the administration of pious foundations.
Verroia (Gara, 1998).
Kadi registers of the town (in Ottoman: Karaferye, early seventeenth century onwards).
Athos monasteries.
Some monasteries still possess the fourteenth and fifteenth-century rescripts of Ottoman sultans originally issued to them. The Athos does not admit women, and the existence of document publications for many of the larger monasteries is only a minor consolation (for an example: Zachariadou, 1985, xv).
Herakleion.
Extensive series of kadi registers (seventeenth century onwards, see Dimitriadis, 1989, p. 183 for details).

Cyprus (Turkish section) (Altan, McHenry and Jennings, 1977)

In Lefkoşe, a remarkable collection of photomechanical reproductions of Ottoman documents relevant to the island. The local kadi registers constitute the chief treasure of the collection) (late sixteenth century onwards).

Lebanon (Van Leeuwen, 1994, pp. 3–4)

Archives of various Maronite monasteries, some going back to the eighteenth century. Historians have worked in the archives of Dayr al-Kreim (Ghusṭā), Dayr Ḥūb (Tannūrīn) and Dayr Kfifān. Important ecclesiastical archive of the Maronite Patriarchate in Dayr Sayyidat Bkirkī (late seventeenth century onwards, incomplete catalogue). Church affairs apart, documents on the economic and social life of the Maronite community.
Archive of a Maronite notable family, the al-Khāzin (late seventeenth century onward, mainly early nineteenth century). Presently split up among different locations, among others the National Museum of Beirut (Maḥfūẓāt al-mudīriyya al-ʿāmma liʾ-l-āthār, Archives de la Direction générale des Antiquités du Liban), which also contains the correspondence of the Sunni trading family of Bayhum. Privately owned sections in the hands of Dr Farīd al-Khāzin of al-Nakkāsh and Mrs Mona al-Khāzin in Ajaltoun.

Researchers who have worked on these Lebanese collections have had some trouble accessing them, even though most of them enjoyed the support of at least one influential Lebanese personality. This situation was directly and indirectly due to the civil war (1975–1990), which led to the dispersal of collections and also made it impossible to enter certain regions. Ottoman Lebanon is exceptionally rich in private archives, most of them still in the hands of the families that produced them. More than ten go back to the nineteenth century. It is not known whether all these collections have survived the war (Fawaz, 1983, p. 135).

Palestine and Israel (Singer, 1994, Doumani, 1995).

Jerusalem kadi registers in the offices of the Maḥkama al-shar'iyya (1530s–). Many researchers of different backgrounds have expressed their gratitude for the help given to them by the court officials, for whom the arrival of a researcher has meant both extra work and the sharing of already cramped quarters. In addition to the kadi registers of Jerusalem, this repository also contains the registers of Nablus (18th and 19th centuries). Moreover the Tanzimat restructuring of the Ottoman provincial administration gave rise to the so-called Advisory Council, whose copious correspondence also found its way into the Jerusalem archives.

Algiers (Temimi, 1979)

Temimi, 1979 is a good catalogue, essential because the organisation of the documents is due to French archivists equally unfamiliar with Arabic, Ottoman and Ottoman history. Most of this material (late seventeenth century to mid-nineteenth century) also available on microfilm in Paris and Aix-en-Provence. Of the (approximately) 574 registers, about 100 in often scarcely legible Ottoman Turkish. Ample information about the janissaries of Algiers, taxation procedures, trade and the representatives which the Dey of Algiers maintained in various Ottoman ports. Some registers pertaining to the rural hinterland.

Tunisia

Tunis (Mantran, 1961).
State Archives in Dār al-Bek (some seventeenth-century material, but mainly on eighteenth and nineteenth centuries). Published catalogue of the

Turkish documents encompasses over 1,000 items, mostly relating to the business of Tunisian governors with the authorities in Istanbul (Mantran, 1961). In the Arabic section of the archives, registers covering various taxes and customs duties; in addition documentation concerning possessions and expenditures of the state apparatus or *beylik*. After 1885, when a French colonial administration took over, a special archive for land titles (Archives de la Conservation Foncière) was instituted (eighteenth and nineteenth-century documents along with more recent ones). In the 1970s, a collection of documents related to pious foundations was located at the office of the port authority of Tunis.

Outside the Ottoman borders

Italy

Florence
Archivio di Stato, Fondo Archivistico Mediceo No. 4275 in the Archivio di Stato relevant to the rebellion of Canbuladoğlu Ali Paşa (Griswold, 1983, p. 301). Since the second half of the sixteenth century, the Medici Grand Dukes granted a series of privileges to Livorno which soon turned into a hub of Mediterranean trade (Sadok, 1987, pp. 25–27). Some of the material relevant to Livorno's commercial history can be found in Florence.
Livorno (Sadok, 1987, pp. 25–7).
Archivio di Stato, series 'Affari generali e Carteggi di Sanità' important for Tunisian trade (documentation on quarantine). Other sections relevant to the Ottomanist are the series VII, VIII and XI, in addition to the papers known as Affari Guidiziari.

Croatia (Zirojevic, 1989)

Zadar (Zirojevic, 1989)
In the Zadar archive, there is a series known as the Atti del Dragomano Veneto ranging from 1620 to 1796, containing the correspondence between the local Venetian authorities and the Austrian and Ottoman commanders stationed in the area. Incoming letters from a variety of Ottoman provincial governors, kadis and military commanders, not excepting the occasional Bosnian vizier.
Franciscans (Zirojevic, 1989)
Convent of Visovac (on an island in the river Krka): collection of 624 Ottoman documents (1458 – 1724). In the convents of Makarska, Zaostrog, Omis, Sinj and Zivogosce: smaller or larger collections of Ottoman material.

Poland (Abrahamowicz, 1959)
A printed catalogue of Turkish documents (Abrahamowicz, 1959) contains the summaries of over 380 items (1455 – 1672). Only the preface available in a French translation. Remarkable is the extensive collection of letters by Süleyman the Magnificent to the Polish king Zygmunt August. Letters from many Ottoman officials. A commentated edition of all the capitulations granted by Ottoman Sultans to Polish kings, along with English translations, is now in the course of preparation (Kolodziejczyk, forthcoming; for Ottoman embassies, see Unat, 1968).

SUGGESTED READINGS

Barkan, Ömer Lütfi (1966). 'Edirne Askeri Kassamı'na Ait Tereke Defterleri (1545–1659),' *Belgeler*, III, 5–6, 1–479.

Barkan, Ömer Lutfi and Ekrem Hakkı Ayverdi (eds.) (1970). *İstanbul Vakıfları Tahrîr Defteri, 953 (1546) Târîhli* (Istanbul: İstanbul Fetih Cemiyeti) (valuable introduction, special emphasis on research which can be undertaken on the basis of this text).

Behrens-Abouseif, Doris (1994). *Egypt's Adjustment to Ottoman Rule, Institutions, waqf and Architecture in Cairo (16th and 17th Centuries)* (Leiden: E. J. Brill) (on the use of *vakfiye*s by the urban historian).

Bennassar, Bartholomé and Lucile Bennassar (1989). *Les chrétiens d'Allah, l'histoire extraordinaire des renégats* (Paris: Perrin) (innovative use of Inquisition archives, better on North Africa than on Istanbul).

Beydilli, Kemal (1984). 'Ignatius Mouradgea D'Ohsson (Muradcan Tosuniyan)', *İstanbul Üniversitesi Edebiyat Fakültesi Tarih Dergisi*, 34, 247–314 (imaginative use of Ottoman archival sources for the biography of an important intellectual figure)

Beydilli, Kemal (1995). *Türk Bilim ve Matbaacılık Tarihinde Mühendishane, Mühendishâne Matbaası ve Kütüphânesi (1776–1826)* (Istanbul: Eren) (important study of library and publishing history).

Davis, Ralph (1967). *Aleppo and Devonshire Square, English Traders in the Levant in the Eighteenth Century* (London, Melbourne, Toronto: Macmillan) (still one of the best studies on European merchants in the Ottoman Empire).

Gara, Eleni (1998). 'In Search of Communities in Seventeenth-Century Ottoman Sources: The Case of the Kara Ferye District,' *Turcica, xxx*, 135–162.

Goffman, Daniel (1990). *Izmir and the Levantine World, 1550–1650* (Seattle: University of Washington Press) (as a sideline, there is a good treatment of the operations of European diplomatic representatives).

Hitzel, Frédéric (ed.) (1997). *Istanbul et les langues orientales* (Paris: IFEA, L'Harmattan, INALCO) (interesting collection of articles on the study of Turkish in

Europe; special reference to the French 'dragomans' and their training in Istanbul).

Kal'a, Ahmet *et al.* (eds.) (1997–). *İstanbul Külliyatı I İstanbul Ahkâm Defterleri*. . . (Istanbul: Istanbul Büyükşehir Belediyesi) (the volumes of this series bear different titles, thus the first is *İstanbul Esnaf Tarihi*, I; six volumes available in mid-1998, twenty-three volumes projected. The documents, from the middle of the eighteenth century, are given in summary, photographic reproduction and transliteration. A first-rate resource).

Kütükoğlu, Mübahat S. (1994). *Osmanlı Belgelerinin Dili (Diplomatik)* (Istanbul: Kubbealtı Akademisi Kültür ve Sanat Vakfı) (fundamental).

Majer, Hans Georg (ed.) (1984). *Das osmanische 'Registerbuch der Beschwerden' (Şikâyet defteri) vom Jahre 1675* (Vienna: Verlag der Österreichischen Akademie der Wissenschaften) (valuable introduction).

Ocak, Ahmet Yaşar (1978). 'Emirci Sultan ve Zaviyesi', *Tarih Enstitüsü Dergisi*, 9, 129–208 (the record of an extraordinary find).

Todorova, Maria N. (1993). *Balkan Family Structure and the European Pattern, Demographic Developments in Ottoman Bulgaria* (Washington: The American University Press) (this can also be read, and is mentioned here, as a discussion of church records as sources for Ottoman history).

4

RURAL LIFE AS REFLECTED IN ARCHIVAL SOURCES: SELECTED EXAMPLES

As Mübahat Kütükoğlu's book provides such a comprehensive introduction to Ottoman archival materials, our discussion of this topic will be limited to a small selection by way of example (Kütükoğlu, 1994). We will concentrate on documents which the researcher may encounter when preparing a study of Ottoman rural life, confronting the evidence to be gleaned from different types of documents and pointing out areas of continuing uncertainty. This will involve a brief discussion of certain studies on Ottoman rural history which have permitted us to understand the potential and limits of our sources. Such works are relatively few in number due to the lack of primary sources on the Ottoman village. But their importance is greater than their numbers would suggest, as rural society constituted the 'basis' upon which all other sectors of Ottoman state and society depended (Adanir, 1989, 1998).

Peasants paid the taxes which enabled the Ottoman state to function. Their direct contributions consisted of money payments, delivery of crops, and to a decreasing but still important extent, the provision of services (Inalcık, 1973, pp. 107–13; Islamoğlu-Inan, 1994). In addition, peasant-grown grains were delivered to the towns either by merchants or tax farmers, and sold there to feed the townsmen. A large share of the grains consumed by the inhabitants of towns and cities, from the peasants' point of view, were unpaid deliveries, even though the townsmen purchased them on the market. For if tax grains were sold by an official revenue collector, the proceeds benefited the state and not the cultivators. When on the other hand the peasants delivered their grain to a merchant, they were paid, but the money did not stay in their hands for very long. Often they sold mainly to satisfy the tax collector's demand for cash. Moreover, the low level of productivity in agriculture forced a large percentage of the population to labour in this rather unremunerative sector. This situation was by no means unique to the Ottoman Empire, but to a greater or lesser extent, applied to pre-industrial societies in general (Wolf, 1966). As can be expected, the Ottoman administration was well aware of this situation, and therefore tried, not always successfully, to prevent peasants from leaving their villages.

Just as in other pre-industrial societies, village society of the Balkans and Anatolia before 1800 has not left many direct testimonies, since the vast majority of the population was illiterate. Archaeological excavation in the future may provide the answers to some of our questions. But to date, archaeologists dealing with this region have usually been concerned with pre-Ottoman settlements. Some excavation has taken place at Peçin, a ruined town in southwestern Anatolia, which was important in the fifteenth century. This undertaking may yield some information on rural life, even though that was not the archaeologists' primary focus. In Hungary, archaeological investigation of the Ottoman period has included small fortresses (*palankas*) and even the occasional village site. But Hungary, a frontier province where the rural settlement of immigrant Muslims was consciously used in order to promote Ottoman control, cannot be regarded as typical of even southeastern Europe, let alone other parts of the Ottoman realm (Halasi-Kun, 1964).

In the long run, dendrochronological studies may also help the historian investigating Ottoman rural life. This discipline involves the study of tree rings, which turn out broader when the tree in question has access to an adequate water supply, and narrower when this is not the case (Le Roy Ladurie, 1983, vol. I, pp. 30–97). With due allowance for extraneous factors, dendrochronological data thus allow us to make statements about the rain and drought of past centuries; and since so much of Anatolia is steppe, the success or failure of any crop depends crucially on rainfall. Crop failure due to drought may have led to peasant flight, a phenomenon frequently mentioned in archival sources. Even in the second half of the nineteenth century, a major drought could kill off large numbers of men and animals; it would be worth knowing whether similar catastrophes occurred in earlier periods as well, for instance at the time of the uprisings marking the end of Seljuk control. Ottoman peasants complained often of local administrators and rarely of natural catastrophes; but this seems to have been a matter of 'politically correct' petitioning rather than anything else. Perhaps in some cases the weather was at fault, rather than kadis or governors? Moreover, the regular sequences of tree rings, unique to a given time and place, allow us to date wooden beams used in construction, and by implication, the building of which they once formed a part. This may be of help to the historian trying to date village mosques, whose style tended to change little over the

2. *Waterwheel near Çokgöz bridge, on the Kızılırmak (ancient Halys, central Anatolia). This photograph from the late nineteenth century shows the principal source of energy used in milling, but also for the manufacture of gunpowder. That many Anatolian rivers carried sufficient water for milling only during certain months of the year proved a serious constraint on manufacturing.*

centuries and which are therefore not amenable to dating by stylistic criteria.

Dendrochronological researches need to be paid for; and many Ottomanist historians are as yet not very conscious of the possible impact of environmental factors on their chosen field. Thus there has been little demand for the construction of rainfall curves covering different regions of Anatolia from the thirteenth century onward. A few such data have however become available; and in the long run, pollinological analysis of the plant remains preserved in bogs and swamps also may help reconstruct the natural environment in which Ottoman peasants tried to gain a livelihood.

A pioneering effort has been made on a few short pages: Peter Kuniholm, who directs the Dendrochronological Project of Cornell University, has tested a hypothesis previously formulated by William Griswold (Griswold, 1983, pp. 238f). In Griswold's opinion the rural rebellions in late

3. Windmills in Karnabad, modern Bulgaria (1860s to 1870s). Wind-driven mills were less common than the water driven variety. Variations of this type could be found on the Aegean islands, and also on the western coast of Anatolia. Due to their striking visual qualities, windmills have frequently been depicted by European artists from the seventeenth century onwards.

sixteenth- and early seventeenth-century Anatolia, known to Ottomanists as the Celali uprisings, were accompanied by unusually inclement climatic conditions (Kuniholm, 1989). Using a list of grain shortages in various regions of the Ottoman Empire, as recorded in chronicles and official documents, Kuniholm has correlated these scarcities with the dendroch-ronological information generated by his team. Down to 1580, tree ring growth was relatively normal and therefore moisture should have been adequate, even though grain shortages seem to have occurred even at this time. But from 1580 onward, the situation changed for the worse. Now tree ring growth dropped to 79 per cent of normal, and in 1585, only 55 per cent were measured, an all-time low for the entire period stretching from 1564 to 1612. The years around 1585 also were a time of major rebel activity, which seems to have peaked at the beginning of the seventeenth century. From then onward the only year with more than normal tree ring growth (106 per cent) was 1610. Otherwise tree rings grew at a rate amounting at best to ninety percent, but more often only to about three quarters of the normal rate. It is tempting to put all this turmoil down to the 'Little Ice Age', namely the cold winters and wet summers which contributed a good deal to the problems of seventeenth-century European peasants. But that temptation should be resisted: Kuniholm has found evidence of drought, while the 'Little Ice Age' should have brought lower temperatures and more rain, not often the cause of Anatolian harvest failures.

TAX REGISTERS

Given the penury of archaeological studies, and the near-absence of texts directly reflecting the voices of peasants, we have to deal with sources put together by Ottoman officials in order to tax and control peasants and nomads. As the most famous governmental record, we will discuss the Ottoman tax registers of the fifteenth and sixteenth centuries, filed in the Prime Minister's archives under the heading of Tapu-Tahrir. In the second-ary literature, we find the terms '*tapu* register' and '*tahrir* register' used interchangeably. The earliest known example was compiled in 1432 (see chapter 3). It concerns parts of modern Albania and was published by Halil Inalcık (Inalcık, 1954a). Ottoman rulers had such registers prepared when-ever a newly conquered province was placed under direct administration. Vassal principalities, such as Moldavia, Wallachia, Transylvania, those parts of the Crimea controlled by the Tatar Khans, or the most powerful of the Kurdish principalities in the borderlands between the Ottoman Empire and Iran, were normally exempt.

Tax registers were meant to provide a basis for the assignment of revenue sources to cavallerists in the Ottoman army or to provincial admin-istrators. Important revenues also accrued to the ruler himself, his viziers and members of his family (Beldiceanu, 1980; article 'Timar' in *İA* by Ömer Lütfi Barkan). Cavallerists received grants of small or moderate size (*timar, zeamet*), while the larger assignments (*has*) generally went to members of the court and higher administrative personnel. These grants were not hered-itary, and even within a lifetime, a *timar* or *zeamet*-holder might be assigned revenues in different provinces of the empire (Barkan, 1975b). As to the higher-level members of the administration, they were mostly servitors of the Sultan who, while not exactly slaves, held their offices at the ruler's will and pleasure (on provincial governors, see Kunt, 1983). As a result there was considerable turnover at all levels. In order to make the appropriate addi-

4. *A Bulgarian peasant dwelling near Süčündol in present-day Bulgaria*
(1860s–1870s). In the foreground a new bride, who still wears the flower-
decorated headdress of her wedding day. It may not be purely by chance that
Kanitz, with his ardent commitment to Bulgarian independence, mobilises
the favourable associations so easily awakened by the image of the 'flower'.

tions to or subtractions from a given grant, the Ottoman financial administration needed to know what revenues individual villages, semi-nomadic
tribesmen or bridge tolls produced in an average year. In principle, the tax
registers were therefore to be renewed every thirty years, even though both
longer and shorter intervals were common enough.

*Tahrir*s were organised geographically. Comprehensive (*mufassal*)
registers normally were compiled at the rate of one for every sub-province

5. *Turkish village house near Dzumali in present-day Bulgaria (1860s–1870s). Although the house is quite similar to its counterpart on figure 4, the artist shows no animals apart from sheep and goats. By foregrounding the fence, he conveys a picture of diminished animation, even though the number of people depicted in the two etchings is not too different.*

(*sancak*). Very often a whole province (*vilayet*) was covered at the same time, which facilitated the later compilation of summary registers (*icmal*), as well as special lists recording only privately owned lands (*mülk*) and pious foundations (*vakıf*). Within each sub-province, villages were grouped by district (*kaza*) and sub-district (*nahiye*); however in many registers, the distinction between *kaza* and *nahiye* remained rather vague. Towns and large villages were further subdivided into quarters or wards; in settlements with non-Muslim residents, the latter were listed separately, after the Muslims. Within each town quarter, village or tribal unit, taxpayers were listed by given name and father's name. Under the heading of *bive* (widow), women householders were often recorded in the registers of the Balkan provinces. Boys generally went unrecorded until puberty, although some registers, particularly those covering peasant foot soldiers (*yaya, müsellem*) included them as well (Barkan, 1940–41; Elifoğlu, 1984).

These lists of taxpayers constitute our only more or less reliable source for the size of the Ottoman population before the late nineteenth century, when censuses of the total population were first attempted. When the *tahrirs* were introduced to the historians' world in the late 1930s and early 1940s, they were regarded, somewhat optimistically, as very reliable reflections of population size (Barkan, 1940–41). Since that time, a good many monographs based on *tahrir* data have been published, and a degree of disillusionment has accompanied our more sophisticated understanding of the manner in which the *tahrirs* were put together. Among other things, we must take into account the conditions of transport and communications as they existed in the sixteenth century. Certain taxpayers may well have hidden and thus avoided registration. If verification was sometimes attempted by asking the opinion of a local *timar*-holder, that procedure may not have necessarily been very effective either. For the revenue collector may well have benefited if there were more taxpayers in 'his' village than recorded in the register. In certain Palestinian kadi registers, we find documents about peasants who made fun of the registrar and refused to reply to his questions (Singer, 1994, p. 91). One irate taxpayer even suggested that the Sultan should subdue seven infidel kings before he asked his subjects for money . . . (Singer, 1990, p. 114). Cases of this sort have not so far been located in Anatolian sources, but that does not mean that every registrar was given the information he demanded. When no data was available about a given settlement, some registrars made a note of the fact; but that necessitated a degree of self-confidence which not all bureaucrats can have possessed.

To better evaluate the information given in the *tahrirs*, historians have assembled and analysed the rather lacunary sources relating to the manner of their compilation. Thus we know something about the appointment of information-gathering officials and the credentials considered desirable in a man who was to undertake this difficult and responsible job (Beldiceanu and Beldiceanu-Steinherr, 1978). Officials surveying a given district carried copies of earlier registers and noted changes which had intervened since the previous record (*defter-i atik*) had been compiled. At least in the record-keeping office, if not in the field itself, the compilers also compared their notes with the register preceding the *defter-i atik*, the so-called *defter-i köhne* (Inalcık, 1954a). When we follow their example, we will often find individual villages or even larger units whose data have been copied wholesale from an earlier register. While it is of course possible that little had changed between two counts only ten or twelve years apart, unacknowledged verbatim quotations should always arouse the historian's suspicions.

Once we have computed the total number of taxpayers for a village, we need to multiply it with a coefficient in order to arrive at an estimate of total population. Independent evidence of family and household size before the late nineteenth century constitutes the rarest of exceptions, though the registers do tell us whether a man was married or single. Ömer Lütfi Barkan, when he first pointed out the possible use of the *tahrirs* for demographic history, suggested multiplying the number of married men by five, and then adding the total of single ones (Barkan, 1951). This does not of course mean that no more than three children were born to the average family; but due to high infant mortality, at any given point in time the average family would have had no more than three children living. There is no basis for this figure except general experience with better-documented Mediterranean populations, and there must have been areas in which there were more or fewer children per average family. But even so, when we compare maximum and minimum values arrived at by more sophisticated techniques, the 'Barkan estimate' is normally located between the two extremes.

A more reliable means of estimating total population on the basis of the *tahrir* data employs the age pyramids of documented populations, of which we possess a great many for the nineteenth and twentieth centuries, and a sizeable number for earlier periods as well (Erder, 1975). It turns out that in these documented populations, the men beyond puberty, who roughly correspond to the age group covered by the *tahrirs*, constitute between one-third and one quarter of the entire population. This means that if we multiply the number of taxpayers documented in the *tahrir* by 3, we arrive at the minimum, if we multiply with 4, at the maximum value for the population in its entirety. However this procedure will work only if the area under discussion is reasonably large, so that anomalies such as military garrisons – or monasteries in Christian parts of the empire – 'get lost in the crowd'. In a single town, such accumulations of unmarried men may suffice to distort average values.

Other problems are connected with the fact that in most parts of the Ottoman Empire, the *tahrirs* of the sixteenth century record very high levels of population growth. This levelled off or even turned into a decline after 1600. Now the sixteenth century was indeed a period of high population increase throughout the Mediterranean basin, and the end of this growth spurt in the late sixteenth century is quite familiar to historians of southern France or Italy (Le Roy Ladurie, tr. John Day, 1974). But in certain Ottoman provinces, the number of taxpayers grew so dramatically within a very short period of time that this phenomenon cannot be due to mere natural increase. Immigration is of course a possibility, but one cannot just assume that large numbers of people entered this or that area without any corroborating evidence. In some cases, nomads and semi-nomads were

6. A Bulgarian peasant family winnowing (Ogost region, 1860s to 1870s). The women with her child weighs down the sledge, which would have been set with sharp stones on the bottom to help separate the corn from the chaff.

re-registered as villagers by the Ottoman authorities, who regarded settled folk as more desirable because they paid more taxes (Orhonlu, 1963, pp. 27–37). As nomads often had escaped registration, reclassification as peasants must have swelled the numbers of recorded taxpayers. Thus some increases may simply reflect more effective counting procedures.

Further difficulties arise when we try to link the population data gathered from the *tahrirs* with later evidence, very often from the nineteenth century. We know that settlements in the dry steppe of central Anatolia or on the margins of the Syrian desert were given up when population growth ceased in the early seventeenth century (Hütteroth, 1968, pp. 163–208; Hütteroth, Abdulfattah, 1977). But does this mean that there was a contraction of overall population? Often it is difficult to be sure; in Anatolia, the coastal region whose new centre Izmir mushroomed in the seventeenth century, may well have absorbed migrants from central Anatolia (Goffman,

1990). In the same vein the coastal region of Palestine should have attracted migrants who found agriculture on the margins of the desert increasingly unrewarding (Hütteroth, Abdulfattah, 1977). Whatever ingenious methods are devised to deal with these problems, significant margins of error will doubtlessly remain.

At the end of each settlement as recorded in the *tahrir* followed a list of taxes due from its inhabitants. However not all taxes were included. Thus the goods, money payments or labour services forming part of the irregularly levied *avarız* tax were not listed, and the same thing often (but not always) applied to the head tax payable by non-Muslims (*cizye*). Special emphasis was placed on the tithe (*öşür*), demanded from almost all agricultural products. In spite of its name, the tithe generally amounted to more than one tenth of the crop, but the share actually demanded varied widely from province to province. On the basis of these tithe lists, agricultural maps of the entire sixteenth-century Ottoman Empire can be drawn, but such maps have as yet been published for only a few provinces (Hütteroth, 1968; Hütteroth, Abdulfattah, 1977). Through the *tahrirs*, we know something about the different agricultural landscapes of the sixteenth century: the grain monoculture of the Anatolian plateau, the fields of cotton and sesame so characteristic of the Mediterranean coastal plains and even the cultivation of high-quality fruit in the immediate vicinity of Malatya (Islamoğlu, Faroqhi, 1979).

Less instructive are the listings of bridge tolls and market dues paid by the inhabitants of the more important villages as well as by townsmen. For even in the sixteenth century, these dues, which usually formed part of the crown revenues, were not collected directly but farmed out to the highest bidder. This meant that the actual amounts of money collected varied widely, and the sum recorded in the register might have but a tenuous relationship with real receipts. But in spite of this limitation, records of market dues and craftsmen's taxes collected in small settlements are particularly valuable for our purposes. Obviously these entries mean that the inhabitants of such places did not make their living merely from agriculture. Yet until recently there existed a model of the Ottoman countryside which assumed that money was all but unknown and links to the towns non-existent except for the conveyance of tax grains. Therefore evidence for specialised rural production, particularly in the textile sector, and links to often remote markets are of great interest even if we have trouble expressing them in quantitative terms (Faroqhi, 1979).

With the increase of tax-farming at the beginning of the seventeenth century, the expensive and labour-consuming compilation of *tahrir* registers was largely dropped. Only *timars*, in so far as they survived, were

7. Manufacturing attar of roses in the countryside of present-day Bulgaria (1860s–1870s). When Kanitz travelled the area, he made drawings, later converted into etchings by a specialist. Kanitz was an ardent partisan of Bulgarian independence, who respected few Ottomans except for Midhat Paşa. the reforming governor and later architect of the first Ottoman constitution.

still recorded in separate registers, which modern archivists class with the *tahrir*s. These later texts do not, however, contain the demographic data which make the older registers so valuable. Occasionally, registers of tax-payers were compiled for one district or another even in the seventeenth and eighteenth centuries (for example, Tapu ve Kadastro Genel Müdürlüğü, Ankara, Kuyudu Kadime No. 21, on the Haymana district to the west of Ankara). But comprehensive information on large regions was no longer made available.

As a result, the historian trying to arrive at estimates of rural population for the seventeenth and eighteenth centuries is obliged to work with a rather intractable documentation. For the Christian population, there are the head tax (*cizye*) registers, which of course exist for older periods as well, and some of the oldest have even been published (Barkan, 1964). But before the reform of *cizye* collection undertaken in the 1690s many localities paid their head taxes as lump sums, so that the records are not of much use to the historian of Ottoman population. Only the reform of the 1690s established that all males liable to the tax (women, children and handicapped persons were exempted) should be accounted for individually (McGowan, 1981). In those regions of the Balkans where non-Muslims formed the quasi-totality of the population, our information for the eighteenth century is thus reasonably reliable.

But where the Muslim population is concerned, we need to have recourse to the *avarız* registers. This constitutes a problem, because *avarız* taxes were not collected from real households, but from so-called 'tax houses', a mere figment of the bureaucratic imagination (*İA* article 'avarız'; McGowan, 1981, pp. 105–14). Every tax house was liable for the same amount as every other when the *avarız* was collected, although demands varied from year to year. To compensate for the differences in wealth among households, more poor families were joined into a 'tax house' than was true of their wealthier fellow villagers. This means that only if we possess information on the size of 'tax houses' in a particular locality at a particular time, do we know by what coefficient to multiply the number of tax houses in order to arrive at the number of taxpayers. Unfortunately for us, the coefficient in question varies between three or four and fifteen! Moreover, exemption from *avarız* was frequently granted to people who performed services to the Ottoman state. Villagers who repaired roads or guarded dangerous passes were typically exonerated from these often burdensome levies thus making the historian's work more difficult (Orhonlu, 1967, pp. 50–6).

Thus only under special circumstances do these data permit us to establish the total number of taxpayers inhabiting a given region. But with due precautions, they do allow comparisons between different regions of the Ottoman Empire, or between the population levels of a single region at different points in time. Given numerous wars and local uprisings, we can assume that a decrease in the number of *avarız* 'tax houses' meant grave difficulties. Either the population was impoverished to the point that the Ottoman administration granted tax rebates, and/or the taxable population had declined. Increases in the number of 'tax houses' are less easy to interpret. They do not necessarily mean a growth of wealth and/or population. After all, the administration may have assumed that the taxpayers had recovered to the point of being able to pay higher taxes when this was far from being the case. Local circumstances have to be examined in detail before an interpretation is possible. Fortunately the number of surviving *avarız* registers is very large indeed.

Tahrir and even *avarız* registers have interested researchers because they provide protostatistical evidence and thereby allow us to study 'macro' trends in both economy and society. Admittedly the numerical data contained in the *tahrirs* are the despair of present-day statisticians. Yet critical analysis of such material, preferably by scholars with training in demography or some other social science, can be of great help in determining the potential and limits of the *tahrir* as an historical source (for a good example, see Erder, 1975). However during the last few years, it seems that *tahrirs* occupy a less central place on the agenda of Ottomanist historians. This may partly be due to the fact that today we understand the limitations of this source better than we did thirty years ago (Lowry, 1992). But the main reason is that in the historiography of the 1990s, qualitative analysis happens to be in favour. Concomitantly 'hard data' are no longer regarded as the sole desirable result of historical study. Historians and their readers now wish to find out something not merely about economic and demographic structure, but also about the political assumptions and world view held by a given social group (Abou-El-Haj, 1991, pp. 20ff.; Findley, 1989, pp. 35–9). These new preoccupations have induced Indianist historians to examine statistical compilations, particularly from the British colonial period, for the hidden agendas which determined their manufacture (Ludden, 1989, pp. 119–23). By contrast Ottomanists have tended to simply move away to sources in which the subjective intentions of the author are more obvious. An analysis of the mind and world view of the compilers of *tahrir* registers remains a desideratum.

NEW LIGHT ON THE PEASANTRY: ARCHIVAL RECORDS OF THE EIGHTEENTH AND NINETEENTH CENTURIES

As the next step, we will take a brief look at the sources to be used by a researcher who undertakes the study of an eighteenth- or nineteenth-century village. Apart from the kadi registers, if available, it is worth consulting the *ahkâm defterleri* (see chapter 3), particularly if the province in question is relatively small; for then the likelihood of finding information on individual settlements increases significantly. Disputes between *timar* holders and foundation administrators, frequently documented in these registers, may prove rather tedious reading. But they sometimes permit conclusions concerning the limits between villages, and the 'gray zones' separating rural settlements. Complaints about robberies may serve as a source for rural trade, often important but very little known. An occasional murder story may be used as an indicator of power relations within the village, or of currents of migration linking the countryside to the towns. But it is difficult to predict what information may be available in any individual case. Therefore it may be best to concentrate not on a single village, but on a group of settlements, possibly on one of the sub-districts known as a *nahiye* in Ottoman administrative parlance.

In recent years, numerous sections of the Prime Minister's Archive in Istanbul have been catalogued, some of which are at least indirectly relevant to rural life. Thus we now have access to fifty-four registers concerning the sheep tax, a series which begins in 919/1513 and extends until 1251/1835. While in later centuries, this tax, like most others, was farmed out, in the earliest period officials were sent out to count the sheep and collect taxes according to a rate fixed by the local tax regulations (*kanunname*). Further evidence on sheep breeding can be found in the Ganem Mukata'ası Kalemi, which dealt with the sheep Balkan drovers needed to supply for the consumption of Istanbul. While here the series consists of an imposing 369 registers (973/1565 to 1256/1840), again this tax was often farmed out, which does not exactly facilitate the interpretation of the available data (Collective work, 1992).

Within one of the newly opened sections, the Harameyn Muhasebesi, which in principle concerns Mecca and Medina, we encounter documentation on pious foundations (*vakıf*) helpful for our purposes. When evaluating this material, we must keep in mind that pious foundations were more frequent in the rural surroundings of major towns than in the open countryside. *Vakıf* accounts, theoretically prepared year by year but surviving only as fragments, often contain precious evidence not on dues as they were anticipated, but as they were actually collected. Most of the registers in the Harameyn Muhasebesi concern the eighteenth and nineteenth centuries, although earlier material is occasionally included. In addition, it is worth consulting the nineteenth-century registers located in the archives of the Vakıflar Genel Müdürlüğü (see chapter 3). Particularly interesting from our point of view are the records concerning the construction of endowed village mosques. Apparently rural mosques had not very been common in the sixteenth century, but were built in increasing numbers during the nineteenth. In particular, it would be worth finding out whether the initiative generally came from the state or from local people. Ultimately the history of village mosques may fill a major gap in our understanding, for the sources examined to date tell us much more about economic activity and social structure than about peasant world views, which remain a *terra incognita*.

For the period which followed upon the mid-nineteenth-century reorganisation of the Ottoman administrative service, novel types of sources should be consulted by the historian of rural life. One of the most important is known as the Temettuât Defterleri, compiled in 1260–61/1844–45 (see chapter 3 and Collective work, 1992, p. 281). From the 17,747 registers covering western and central Anatolia, the Aegean islands as well as certain sections of the eastern Balkans, a great deal of information on village life may be collected. Household by household, the *temettuât* registers record real property and animals. To name but one example, the mere existence of over 2,000 volumes for the province of Bursa (Hüdavendigâr) alone demonstrates that much of the province's rural wealth must have been documented.

HISTORY WRITING FROM *TAHRIRS*: THE PIONEERS

From the time when the *tahrirs* first became available to historians, they potentially offered a unique 'window' on Ottoman peasant society. Even so however, the actual output of *tahrir*-based peasant studies has been limited. Many of the early contributions are the work of Ömer Lütfi Barkan, a major pioneer in Ottomanist historiography. Among other contributions, he published the first monograph on Ottoman agrarian history, dealing with the question of agricultural labour (Barkan, 1939–40). But most of Barkan's studies focus on the impact of non-peasants on the Ottoman countryside; both the state and local elites set the directions in which village society was expected to move. This approach had some connection with the world view of early Republican intellectuals, who in spite of a notable tendency to glorify village life, had little faith in the peasantry's capacity for self-determined action. But it would be unfair to overlook the biases inherent in the *tahrirs* themselves. These texts often provide valuable information on the persons holding the right to collect dues in a given village (Islamoğlu-Inan, 1994, pp. 56–77). But these documents contain only a modicum of information on individual peasant households.

In quite a few cases, the tax status of a given village depended on agreements between the Ottoman central government and rural power-holders. Barkan has studied the manner in which pre-Ottoman Muslim landholders were integrated into the Ottoman polity, though he may not have felt very comfortable admitting this presence of non-peasants in the countryside (Barkan, 1939). In his view, the ideal situation was that in which the officials serving the state confronted the rural population directly, without intermediaries of any kind. Moreover, Barkan had adopted the notion, which the growing numbers of sixteenth-century registers seemed to confirm, of an early Ottoman rural society evolving towards the ideal model of direct state-peasant relations.

Following this culmination point, however, around 1600 there occurred a precipitous decline of state power accompanied by a dissolution of the socio-political fabric – and in any case, by that time tax-farming had crowded out the *timar*, and *tahrirs* had become irrelevant (Barkan, 1975a and b). This crisis was due to the intervention of merchant capital, partly domestic, in the form of usury, but mainly in the shape of foreign traders responsible for introducing the sixteenth-century price revolution. Barkan's outlook had been determined by the profound economic difficulties of the 1930s and 1940s. In consequence, the hard-to-prove, but highly probable expansion of the monetary economy during the sixteenth century was to him a deeply disturbing phenomenon (Barkan, 1966, pp. 31–3). A supposedly harmonious division of labour between the peasantry and state administrators had been subverted by the power of capital (Barkan, 1975a).

At the very beginning of his involvement with Ottoman rural society, Ömer Lutfi Barkan devoted a large-scale study to a single category of the rural population. In the *tahrirs* these people are known as the *ortakçı kullar*, and many of them lived in the vicinity of Istanbul and Edirne. They seem to have been former slaves, who – presumably to protect the owner's property – could only marry among themselves (Barkan, 1939–40; Beldiceanu-Steinherr, 1976). Moreover they paid higher taxes than other peasants, and apparently had fewer options when it came to disposing of their time and labour. While the *ortakçı kullar* were never more than a tiny minority of the peasant population, Barkan was interested in them on account of what he regarded as their heuristic value. For while he viewed Ottoman society as a phenomenon *sui generis* fundamentally different from European feudal society, he was willing to admit that the Ottoman socio-political system accommodated pockets of older and presumably more primitive social formations. The *ortakçı kullar*, regarded as a variety of serf, appeared as just such a relic, absorbed into the 'regular' peasant population during the sixteenth century.[1]

Throughout the 1950s, the assumption that certain categories of Ottoman peasants for a considerable time showed some of the 'marks' of serfdom or slavery, informed Halil Inalcık's work on rural history (Inalcık, 1959). Novel was the insistence that the Ottoman tax régime could not be

---

[1] One should not however underestimate the conservatism of Ottoman record keepers; in the Edirne region, there are references to *ortakçı kullar* even at the very end of the seventeenth century: compare Başbakanlik Arşivi, Istanbul, D.HSK 25631/60.

properly understood without including the Byzantine component in its makeup (Inalcık, 1958). Inalcık also found evidence in the early *tahrirs* that fifteenth or sixteenth-century peasants paid money dues in place of the physical services demanded from their ancestors. With the increasing use of money, peasants were thus able to liberate themselves from labour services, one of the tell-tale marks of serfdom. Thus differently from Barkan, Inalcık was favourable to the concept of money economy, not only in the towns but in the countryside as well.

In Inalcık's early work, the *tahrirs* appeared as a tool by which the Ottoman central state established domination over newly conquered provinces, including their peasant base (Inalcık, 1954b). His edition of the earliest extant *tahrir* can be regarded as an outcome of this interest in the chronology and methods of Ottoman state building (chapter 3; Inalcık, 1954a). The same author's influential introduction to the 'classical age' of Ottoman history relegated the peasantry to a chapter on provincial administration; this also indicates how strongly Inalcık in the early period of his career concentrated upon state structure (Berktay, 1992, p. 159). Only at a much later stage of his development was Inalcık to emphasise the centrality of the peasant farm and household as the basis of the Ottoman economy and socio-political system (Inalcık, 1994).

In the brief introduction attempted here, not all *tahrir*-based studies can be discussed, far from it, and the selection is somewhat subjective. Bruce McGowan has converted the hypothetical harvests of various southeast European provinces as recorded in the *tahrirs*, upon which Ottoman tithes were based, into 'economic wheat equivalents' (McGowan, 1969). By this interesting experiment, he has attempted to compare levels of prosperity in different provinces of the empire. Moreover, by confronting sixteenth- and twentieth-century data, McGowan's work may allow us to determine whether Ottoman hypothetical harvests permitted the peasants as recorded in the *tahrirs* to live and reproduce themselves. Since a population unable to feed itself will not survive, these calculations will establish whether the recording officials had come up with more or less reliable data. McGowan's work has not been followed up, possibly because most Ottomanist historians have not been convinced that twentieth-century 'subsistence economies' are similar enough to their Ottoman counterparts to permit useful comparisons. But it is quite likely that more sophisticated attempts to place Ottoman agricultural production in a comparative framework will be helpful; hopefully, that kind of work will regain favour in the foreseeable future.

DEALING WITH *TAHRIRS*: A SOURCE FOR PRE-OTTOMAN HISTORY

Modern historians concerned with the *tahrirs* have emphasised the gaps and limitations of the information provided (Lowry, 1992). Yet in spite of all its shortcomings, this material is of special value to the mediaevalist. For the earliest *tahrirs* document, albeit indirectly, the state of rural settlement in central Anatolia when under the domination of the Karamanids. The same applies to the island of Lemnos during the last period of Byzantine rule, and even to Albania when still controlled by local princes (Beldiceanu and Beldiceanu-Steinherr, 1968; Lowry, in Bryer and Lowry, 1986; Inalcık, 1954a). Without the Ottoman *tahrirs*, we would know very little about this pre-Ottoman period in Anatolian and Balkan history. Thus there has developed a branch of Seljuk-Byzantine-Ottoman studies dealing with the transitions from one of these régimes to the next, in which *tahrirs* play a central role. Nicoara Beldiceanu and Irène Beldiceanu-Steinherr have ransacked the early *tahrirs* of Karaman for records of rural power relations under the Karamanid dynasty. Continuing Barkan's work, Irène Beldiceanu-Steinherr has concentrated on the early history of the *ortakçı kullar*, discussing individual villages whose history can be followed back into the mediaeval period (Beldiceanu-Steinherr, 1976). Faruk Sümer has studied the traces of major mediaeval nomadic confederations in Anatolian toponymy, a crucial indicator for the transition from Byzantine to Seljuk and Ottoman Anatolia (Sümer, 1980).

From a geographer's point of view, the same question has been investigated by Xavier de Planhol, who regards the immigration of central Asian nomads into Anatolia as part of a much broader process of what he calls 'beduinisation' of the Near East in the Middle Ages (de Planhol, 1968). Whatever the merits and demerits of this view, de Planhol has stressed the specificity of Anatolia, where rainfall agriculture is possible everywhere, and the settlement of nomads therefore came about within a relatively short time period. By the sixteenth century, the *tahrirs* already recorded a territory settled essentially by peasants, with nomads of major importance mainly in eastern Anatolia.

One of the regions favoured by scholars engaged in 'transition studies' is the Grand Komnenoi principality of Trabzon, conquered by Mehmed II in 1464. This preference is due to the fact that local chroniclers and monasteries have produced documentation on the late Byzantine countryside. On the other hand, the Ottoman conquest was accompanied by extensive deportation (*sürgün*), which has left traces in the *tahrirs*. Anthony Bryer has studied the Byzantine evidence, which includes toponymy, inscriptions and the remains of rural churches (Bryer, in Bryer and Lowry, 1986). Attention has been focused on the rural district of Maçka, where change was less rapid than in Trabzon proper, and where conditions typical of the late Byzantine countryside survived to be reflected in the early Ottoman *tahrirs*. At the same time, the *tahrirs* and kadi registers provide an Ottoman view of conditions obtaining in Maçka during the sixteenth and seventeenth centuries.

The studies of Bryer, Lowry and their collaborators are remarkable for the solid evidence on which they are based (Bryer, 1986; Lowry, 1986b). However, it would be rash in the extreme to assume that their findings applied to all newly conquered Ottoman territories. With its narrow strip of fertile land isolated from the hinterland by high mountain ranges, the northern coast of Anatolia has been a special case throughout recorded history, and should have been in that position during the second half of the fifteenth century as well.

Even so the studies edited by Bryer and Lowry are of major methodological significance; for they show what we can know under the best of circumstances, as well as the limits of our knowledge. Down to the present day, many broad assumptions about the Byzantine–Seljuk–Ottoman transition are based on insufficient evidence. In the absence of even incomplete population counts, nobody knows how many people lived in Anatolia at the end of the eleventh, thirteenth or fifteenth century, how many of them were peasants or nomads, or how many descended from immigrants or could be regarded as 'autochthonous'.[2] But this all but insoluble difficulty has not prevented certain historians from claiming either that territories conquered by the Ottomans were virtually empty, or that a considerable part of the local population was displaced or else converted. In most instances, these claims cannot be substantiated either way, and the work of Bryer and Lowry has shown up the difference between claims based on evidence and assumptions floating in the air.

OUTSIDE THE *TAHRIR*: THE *ÇIFTLIK* DEBATE

In any discussion of Ottoman agricultural history, the *çiftlik* is bound to crop up. In our present account of primary sources, work on *çiftliks* is important because it shows what the historian can do once there are no *tahrirs* available to guide him/her. Unfortunately, the term *çiftlik* is ambiguous, and therefore, we must begin by clarifying its different meanings. A *çift* refers to a pair (yoke) of oxen, and the derivative *çiftlik* can be used to denote

---

[2] That the definition of the term 'autochthonous' varies strongly constitutes yet another problem.

the peasant landholding we have already encountered. However, when referring to such family farms, it is preferable to say 'peasant *çiftlik*', or use the Ottoman term *re'aya çiftliği*. Thus we avoid confusion with what is more often intended when twentieth-century historians speak about *çiftliks*, namely agricultural lands in the hands of non-peasants, cultivated by a combination of slaves, share-croppers and migrant labour. Holders of *çiftliks* might be powerful personages, yet they did not acquire the right of eminent domain which the Sultan reserved for himself. Thus the legal status of such *çiftliks* always remained precarious, as the Ottoman central administration refused to officially endorse the takeover of peasant lands by non-peasants – even if circumstances, particularly in the eighteenth century, might force the Sultan to tolerate such usurpations in practice (McGowan, 1981, pp. 71–72).

A variety of documents has been used for *çiftlik* studies. Ömer Lütfi Barkan's study of the inheritance inventories of the central government's servitors in the region of Edirne has familiarised us with *çiftliks* used as country seats by Ottoman gentlemen (see for example Barkan, 1966, p. 167). In the kadi registers of the district of Bitola/Monastir and other parts of the Balkans, numerous transactions concerning *çiftliks* also have been recorded. This has permitted Halil Inalcık and Bruce McGowan to reconstruct the process by which powerful personages were able either to set up *çiftliks* on vacant land between villages, or else dispossess peasants (Inalcık, 1984; McGowan, 1981, pp. 66–70). Moreover in the eighteenth and early nineteenth centuries, when confiscation of existing *çiftliks* and their reassignment to new possessors were common occurrences, a sizeable documentation was generated. At times these official records include detailed descriptions of such agricultural enterprises (Veinstein, 1986). A few inventories of early nineteenth-century *çiftliks* have been studied in some detail (Faroqhi, 1976, 1991, 1992).

These newly discovered sources have made it clear that certain assumptions concerning *çiftliks* popular in the 1950s or early 1960s are no longer tenable. In the post-war period, Fernand Braudel (Braudel, 1st edn 1949, 2nd edn 1966, vol. II, p. 67) and Traian Stoianovich (Stoianovich, 1953) had both claimed that the *çiftliks* of the seventeenth-century Balkans should be regarded as analogous to the 'second serfdom', which engulfed the peasants of eastern Europe from the sixteenth century onwards. In some cases, the 'second serfdom' was imposed by Polish or Brandenburg lords who in a period of population expansion, wished to take advantage of high grain prices. But in most cases the motivation was less economic than political; in a period when princes consolidated their positions, the conjuncture of the times favoured lordly power on the village level as well (Anderson, 1979, pp. 196–97). In the Russian case (where grain export was not yet an issue) peasant mobility was terminated in order to allow the lower nobility a secure revenue base in exchange for constant military and administrative service to the Tsar (Hellie, 1971). Where Ottoman history was concerned, at one point it seemed tempting to assume that market conditions, that is European demand for cheap grain or cotton, were responsible for the deterioration of the peasant condition brought about by *çiftlik* agriculture (Stoianovich, 1953).

But in the eyes of Europeanist historians, this assumption soon must have appeared rather outmoded. For by the mid-1970s, when Anderson's seminal study first appeared, political developments already were being viewed as the principal factors responsible for the 'second serfdom'. To Ottomanist historians dealing with *çiftliks* however, this turnabout on the 'theoretical' level was at best indirectly significant. More important were empirical considerations, such as the realisation that *çiftliks* held by non-peasants were much less widespread on Ottoman territory than had been originally assumed. McGowan's carefully crafted maps moreover demonstrated that *çiftliks* appeared early and in relatively large numbers in regions such as the Black Sea coasts of modern Bulgaria. However, down to the late eighteenth century these regions specialised in the supply of grain to Istanbul and were not linked to the world market at all (McGowan, 1981, pp. 76–7).

Both Inalcık's and McGowan's work showed that in the Ottoman lands as well, political rather than economic factors often prompted peasant dispossession. Tax farmers and other persons gaining control of agricultural land were often more interested in taking away what could be gotten from the hapless villagers, and assigning this 'surplus' to their numerous retinues. Inserting themselves into the commercial economy, be it domestic or international, must have been alien to these people. By contrast, certain commercially active rural magnates, such as the Karaosmanoğulları of Izmir and Manisa, at least during the eighteenth century sold grain and cotton which they had collected as taxes. Or else they profited from the commercialization of agricultural produce entrusted to them by the farmers of the region, a major commercial force without possessing any *çiftliks* at all (Veinstein, 1975). Relations between *çiftlik* formation and commercialisation have thus turned out to be both more tenuous and more complicated than had originally been assumed.

THE IMPACT OF PEASANT STUDIES

Quite apart from these empirical considerations, from the 1970s onward, Ottoman rural history has received a new impulse through the work of scholars with a background in peasant studies. Among the approaches thus 'imported' into Ottoman rural historiography, we will take a closer look at the peasant economy as seen by the Russian scholar A. V. Chayanov, a victim of the Stalinist purges of the 1930s (Chayanov, English translation, 1966). This economist claimed that the peasant household was not a capitalist undertaking, and peasant families did not strive to maximise their money returns. To the contrary, the amount of labour peasants were willing to invest in their holding depended not on market opportunities, but on the family's stage in the life cycle. Young married couples whose children were not yet able to work might rent additional land, and engage in what Chayanov described as self-exploitation in order to feed their offspring. But with the older children marrying and leaving the holding, the parent couple would scale down the size of its enterprise before finally relinquishing it to the next generation.

Chayanov's theory is built on the assumption that the peasant economy is different *in kind* from its capitalist counterpart, so that the findings valid for capitalist enterprises do not apply here. He has therefore been classed with the 'substantivists', who assume that pre- or non-capitalist societies obey laws totally different from those governing their capitalist-industrial counterparts. While there is as yet no monograph of an Ottoman village explicitly using Chayanov's theories as a framework, his ideas have been important for Ottoman rural historians none the less. For the assumption that social relations rather than market laws govern the behaviour of peasants has had considerable appeal to all those who wish to show capitalism as an historical social formation with definite limits, rather than a universally valid category.

Among other peasant studies with an impact on Ottoman historians, we may mention the work of Emmanuel Le Roy Ladurie on the peasants of Languedoc in the sixteenth and seventeenth centuries (Le Roy Ladurie, tr. John Day, 1974). This work can be classed as 'neo-Malthusian', because the author takes up ideas developed by the eighteenth-century English economist Malthus, and also as 'formalist'. By 'formalists' we denote scholars who assume that certain fundamental economic laws apply, no matter which social formation is being studied. Malthus had developed his theories concerning the linkage of population growth and secular wage decline when the early industrial economy of England was already fully developed. But when building his theory, which implied that people would multiply until they pressed down wages to subsistence level (unless they 'prudentially' limited the number of their offspring), Malthus assumed secular stagnation in agricultural output. He chose to ignore the increase in yields which the 'new husbandry' of the time was making possible.

Le Roy Ladurie has reformulated Malthus' concept to suit the realities of sixteenth-century Languedoc, where indeed technological progress in agriculture was limited. He has defended the view that the sixteenth-century population increase resulted in exactly the consequences Malthus had predicted, namely wage decline and increase in food prices. These in turn led to the stagnation of population during the seventeenth century (Le Roy Ladurie, tr. John Day 1974, pp. 98–113, 239–245). Le Roy Ladurie's views obviously are based on the 'formalist' premise that capitalist categories can usefully be applied to an early modern peasant economy. In the Ottoman context, neo-Malthusian ideas, to a degree, have informed the work of Michael Cook on selected Anatolian districts. Cook has attempted to answer the fundamental question, first posed by Fernand Braudel, whether the sixteenth-century increase in rural population led to a scarcity in land or 'population pressure' as the author calls it (Cook, 1972, pp. 1–9). This question, which has its place in the framework generated by Malthus and his predecessor Ricardo, Cook has answered with a qualified 'yes' (Cook, 1972, p. 29). In concrete terms, he has shown that 'marginal', that is relatively infertile, land was being taken into cultivation. Moreover, in spite of Ottoman rules prohibiting the subdivision of peasant holdings, larger farms were split up to accommodate a growing number of heirs.

By contrast Huricihan Islamoğlu-Inan in her recent work on the peasants of Çorum and Sivas has taken exception to this point of view, basing herself upon the theory constructed by the development economist Esther Boserup (Islamoğlu-Inan, 1994, pp. 19–20). According to these two authors, population growth is to be seen as a factor promoting rather than limiting economic growth. With increasing population, the peasant family has enough labour available to engage in specialised market-oriented activity – in this statement, one may detect the impact of Chayanov's peasants exploiting themselves in order to feed a young family. One may also link this assumption to the theory of the Dutch economic historian Jan de Vries, which attempts to explain how early modern European wageworkers acquired more consumption goods in spite of stable or declining real wages (de Vries, 1993). In the course of the so-called 'industrious revolution', more women and children were put to work spinning, weaving or growing commercial crops. Thus an increasing number of goods became available at affordable prices in the market. More intensive work compensated for lower wages, and many families, particularly in privileged regions such as the Netherlands, were able to acquire an increasing number of objects.

Islamoğlu-Inan equally assumes that sixteenth-century Anatolian peasants cultivated crops requiring more labour as their numbers increased. Thus peasants in the region of Niksar took up the cultivation of rice, in the sixteenth century still a semi-luxury aimed exclusively at the market. Moreover, rural crafts such as cotton-weaving came to be important. Islamoğlu-Inan has also suggested that the beneficiaries of this increased production of marketable goods were not so much the producers themselves as the tax takers of various types. In her view, this situation may explain why even in the eighteenth century, peasant lands were not expropriated (Islamoğlu-Inan, 1987, pp. 122–26). While this particular period was marked by decentralisation and the rise of local magnates, these powerholders could cream off the profits of peasant production without land ownership, and therefore without much managerial effort of their own.

SOCIAL ANTHROPOLOGY AND RURAL HISTORY

Studies of the peasant economy, and its place in the larger socio-political system of which the peasantry forms a part, tend toward a relatively high level of abstraction. Many historians will seek theoretical inspiration less abstract and closer to the concrete data. Sometimes this inspiration can be found in the work of social anthropologists, who have written monographs of village societies the world over, modern Turkey not excluded. As a genre, the village monograph has come in for a good deal of – often justified – criticism. Critics have shown that the effects of society-wide developments, such as the spread of capitalism, are not treated adequately when the researcher focuses on personal interaction taking place at the local level, particularly within the family and kin. But on the other hand, concentration on interpersonal relations will allow us to see aspects of peasant behaviour which cannot be brought into focus when broader developments monopolise our attention. There is something to be said in favour of a pluralism of methods.

One rather attractive approach would be to combine village history, based upon the *tahrir* and other archival sources, with anthropological studies dealing with the same village today. But to date this has very rarely been attempted. One reason lies in the fact that social anthropologists select the village to be studied according to practical criteria. Since the scholar preparing a village monograph must spend considerable time in the locality to be studied, coastal villages, wealthier and enjoying a better climate, are obviously preferred. Moreover, since official permission is needed before such a study can be undertaken, areas considered as 'sensitive' by the authorities are usually excluded. More seriously still, many Anatolian villages existing today have a short history. Some were established in the nineteenth century, when immigrants from the Caucasus and the Balkans had to be accommodated within the shrinking confines of the Ottoman Empire. Others took on their present shape only in the twentieth century, when the population exchange with Greece brought an influx of people who were often established in villages abandoned by the Anatolian Greek population. In addition, we encounter former nomads and semi-nomads, who either settled because the Ottoman government forced them to do so, or because increasing population density made the old way of life increasingly impracticable. At times these recent settlers occupied sites which had been villages in the sixteenth century, but had been abandoned after 1600. Thus even in localities where a present-day village occupies a site known from the sixteenth-century *tahrir*, there is no guarantee of village continuity.[3]

Another major difficulty confronts us when we attempt to link up the findings derived from archival documents with the results of anthropological studies concerning the twentieth century. Present-day anthropologists are quite rightfully concerned with present-day problems, such as the social consequences of mechanised agriculture and the growing integration of villagers into the national or world market (see Stirling, 1993). Viewed from the historian's standpoint, the anthropologist works within a 'short' time horizon, often limited to the 1950s, when tractors first became available on a mass basis, or at the very best, to the early years of the Turkish Republic. From the anthropologist's point of view, there is just as much reason for complaint. Cooperation with a historian may seem valuable in theory but of limited utility in practice. For in most cases rural historians cannot say very much about issues such as the secular permanence or otherwise of rural technologies, the impact of commercialisation or the effects of migration.

However, it may be at least partly possible to bridge this gap by taking a closer look not at the villages, but at the towns. Here rural commodities were ultimately consumed, and here migrants from rural areas attempted to make a living. In the larger cities, particularly in Istanbul, there existed registers of fixed prices (*narh*), containing evidence on rural commodities sold in the urban market (for an example, compare Kütükoğlu,

---

[3] Hütteroth (1968) contains a detailed discussion of these issues with respect to the region of Konya.

1983). We also find large numbers of temporary or permanent migrants, identified as such when they turned to the kadi's court. Documents concerning urban life allow us at least a glimpse of certain (former) villagers, which would be impossible to obtain if we were to tackle the villagers in their original habitat. To find such 'roundabout' ways of locating evidence of interest to the anthropologist takes time and experience, but in the end is well worth the effort. For rural history should be seen as a continuity in time, and not as a 'contemporary period' of seventy-odd years separated from 'historical time' by an all but unbridgeable chasm.

SUGGESTED READINGS

Adanır, Fikret (1998). "The Ottoman Peasantries, c. 1360–c. 1860" in *The Peasantries of Europe from the Fourteenth to the Eighteenth Centuries* ed. Tom Scott, (London, New York: Longman, 269–312 (the latest survey of research into Ottoman rural life, clever and superbly documented).

Beldiceanu, Nicoara and Irène Beldiceanu-Steinherr (1978). 'Règlement ottoman concernant le recensement (première moitié du XVIe siècle)', *Südost-Forschungen*, 37, 1–40 (careful empirical study on the mechanics of *tahrir* compilation).

Bryer, Anthony and Heath Lowry (eds.) (1986). *Continuity and Change in Late Byzantine and Early Ottoman Society*, (Birmingham, Washington: The University of Birmingham, Dumbarton Oaks) (a collection of informative, empirical studies).

Chayanov, A. V. (1966). *The Theory of the Peasant Economy* (Homewood, Ill.) (one of the fundamental texts in twentieth-century peasant studies).

Hütteroth, Wolf Dieter and Kamal Abdulfattah (1977). *Historical Geography of Palestine, Transjordan and Southern Syria in the Late 16th Century* (Erlangen/Germany: Fränkische Geographische Gesellschaft) ('lost villages' in the Syrian desert).

Inalcık, Halil (1994). 'The Ottoman State: Economy and Society, 1300–1600,' in *An Economic and Social History of the Ottoman Empire, 1300–1914* ed. Halil Inalcık with Donald Quataert (Cambridge: Cambridge University Press) (paperback version 1997, Inalcık's work appears as vol. 1; explication of Ottoman peasant economies according to Chayanov's model).

İslamoğlu-İnan, Huri (1994). *State and Peasant in the Ottoman Empire, Agrarian Power Relations and Regional Economic Development in Ottoman Anatolia during the Sixteenth Century* (Leiden: E. J. Brill) (to date, the most elaborate attempt to join *tahrir* studies with social theory).

Le Roy Ladurie, Emmanuel (1974). *The Peasants of Languedoc*, tr. John Day (Urbana, III: University of Illinois Press) (pathbreaking study on Mediterranean peasants in the early modern age).

McGowan, Bruce (1981). *Economic Life in Ottoman Europe, Taxation, Trade and the Struggle for Land, 1600–1800* (Cambridge, Paris: Cambridge University Press and Maison des Sciences de l'Homme) (important collection of essays on population and the *çiftlik* problem).

Orhonlu, Cengiz (1967). *Osmanlı İmparatorluğunda Derbend Teşkilâtı* (Istanbul: İstanbul Üniversitesi Edebiyat Fakültesi) (classical study on privileged peasants).

Singer, Amy (1994). *Palestinian Peasants and Ottoman Officials, Rural Administration around Sixteenth-century Jerusalem* (Cambridge: Cambridge University Press) (on a well-documented rural society)

Veinstein, Gilles (1975). 'Ayân de la région d'Izmir et le commerce du Levant (deuxième moitié du XVIIIe siècle)', *Revue de l'Occident musulman et de la Méditerranée*, XX, 131–146 (how a magnate could exercise rural power and commercial initiative without holding *çiftliks*).

5

EUROPEAN SOURCES ON OTTOMAN HISTORY: THE TRAVELLERS

Due to the work of Edward Said and his associates, the biases inherent in European writing on the Middle East have become obvious to many if not most practitioners in the field (Said, 1978). Given the large number of available Ottoman materials, some researchers might therefore envisage basing Ottoman history entirely on Ottoman sources[1]. When dealing with certain topics, studies built almost entirely on local or else Istanbul-based evidence can in fact be undertaken. As an example, one might mention the tax assignments known as *timar*, a characteristic feature of the administration of the central Ottoman realm in the fifteenth or sixteenth century. Since outsiders had only a superficial knowledge of the system's working, their testimony can largely be disregarded. But in other cases, the information relayed by Venetian, English or French travellers and embassy personnel is so important that we cannot simply neglect it. After all, the Ottoman state of the fourteenth to sixteenth centuries defined itself as a state conquering infidels (Inalcık, 1973, p. 6). This means that close contact to Venetian merchants, Balkan princes, and occasionally even members of western European ruling houses existed from the very early phases of Ottoman history. A critical use of European sources thus constitutes a major challenge to the Ottomanist historian.

In this chapter we will discuss some of the problems raised by this situation, concentrating on narrative sources from the sixteenth to eighteenth centuries. In a second, much shorter section, our focus will be European archival materials, with Ottoman port towns of the eighteenth

---

[1] Unfortunately there are very few Chinese, Indian or Japanese travellers' accounts to counterbalance those written by Europeans.

and nineteenth centuries serving as examples. For a critical evaluation of the works of European travellers, we must begin by establishing the purpose of the visit and the socio-political status of the visitor; obviously these two items are closely connected. Moreover the length of time the person in question stayed in the Ottoman Empire, another crucial variable, is linked to the purpose of the visit. As far as the fifteenth and sixteenth centuries are concerned, most of the necessary biographical data are easily available (Yérasimos, 1991).

Yérasimos' fundamental work begins with an introduction of ninety large pages, a monograph in its own right. Here we find some stimulating discussion of travel writing in the appropriation of the world by Europeans from the later middle ages to the twentieth century. This is followed by an equally thought-provoking section on what the travel-account-reading public expected of this kind of literature. In the course of the early modern period, readers slowly developed a taste for (real or imaginary) adventures of individual travellers. By contrast, more or less systematic overviews over the public administration of the Ottoman state, as well as the customs of the subject population, gradually lost favour. This means that even though relatively few travellers' accounts had any pretension to literary merit, considerations of format must have figured among the preoccupations of their authors.

A comprehensive examination of the Ottoman route system during the period under discussion forms the second part of Yérasimos' monograph. Accounts of campaign routes followed by the Sultan's armies, in addition to the writings of European, Ottoman and a few Arab travellers, constitute the documentary basis for this study. Today, 450 longer and shorter descriptions of fifteenth- and sixteenth-century travels in the Ottoman Empire have become known. Almost 100 of them remain unpublished; Yérasimos has used the publishing history of travelogues as a telling indicator of intellectual trends in early modern Europe. In the reference section, apart from the dates at which the traveller in question visited the Ottoman Empire, we find a list of the relevant author's works, both published and in manuscript, including translations if any. An itinerary is also given, often with commentary in the notes. When the travel writer in question is reasonably well documented, these notes contain a capsule biography as well.

Moreover Yérasimos provides us with the modern names of the towns and cities mentioned in each travelogue, along with the variant versions used at the time. This saves the user a good deal of trouble. Geographical dictionaries and atlases of the fifteenth and sixteenth centuries were (and are) both difficult of access and full of gaps and errors. Therefore authors of this period often distorted the names of foreign persons and places so badly that their identification poses major problems, to say nothing of name changes connected with the disappearance and emergence of states since the sixteenth century. As a result, the present-day reader is in dire need of help when trying to make sense of older itineraries, and life would be much easier were studies comparable to Yérasimos' work available for later periods as well.

Since they are not, we must make do with two reference works dating from the nineteenth century (Vivien de St Martin, 1852; Carl Ritter, 1843–). Both authors flourished in the Victorian period, composing their works in order to highlight the contributions of European travellers to the sciences of physical and historical geography. Vivien de St Martin's work concentrates on Anatolia, and is compact and easy to handle. However, due to its early date of publication, many travellers about whom we need information are not included. The same applies to Ritter's work, which by contrast is multi-volume and covers vast sections of Asia never included in the Ottoman Empire. Finding the volumes relevant to our purposes may therefore take some time. Readers concerned with western Anatolia only may therefore turn to the work of Usha M. Luther, an Indian historical geographer (Luther, 1989). Luther's major interest is in the reconstruction of the route network. This involves a critical examination of travellers' itineraries, so that her book contains useful information about the circumstances surrounding seventeenth- to nineteenth-century travelling. But biographical information and the travellers' publishing histories do not form part of Luther's agenda.

MOTIVATIONS FOR THE WRITING OF TRAVEL ACCOUNTS: THE DIPLOMATS

From the fifteenth century onward, numerous foreign diplomats came to do business at the Ottoman court. Some of them composed their own accounts, or at least conveyed the impression that they did so. The best-known diplomat *cum* author was probably Ogier Ghiselin de Busbecq, a Flemish humanist who negotiated with Süleyman the Magnificent's Grand Vizier Rüstem Pasha. Busbecq produced an extensive description not only of Istanbul itself, but of the route leading there. While this account of Balkan travel through Buda, Belgrade and Sofia became a standard fixture of European travelogues, one of the rare and precious features of Busbecq's book is his description of the way from the Ottoman capital through Ankara to Amasya (translations into European languages abound; for an English version, Busbecq tr. Forster, 1968).

Embassy accounts were of course written with a political purpose in mind. The peace conditions Busbecq was able to secure for his ruler Ferdinand I were none too advantageous, and the envoy presumably wanted to show that he had done everything in his power to impress the Sultan and Grand Vizier. Because the standing of a ruler was bound up with that of his servants, considerations of rank always played a most important role in diplomatic accounts. Moreover, during the sixteenth century many European states established permanent embassies in Istanbul, located at short distances from one another in the 'vineyards of Pera' (today Beyoğlu). Thus it became important to impress not only Ottoman dignitaries, but also the French, English or Dutch neighbours whom one might meet in church or street.

Busbecq's elegant Latin has secured him a place among Renaissance writers, and a wide diffusion of his work down to the present day. As Busbecq was not a great lord, but a minor gentleman who had made a career for himself in the service of Ferdinand I, his literary reputation was an important source of prestige, and a political asset in its own right. Literary ambition, on the other hand, made it imperative to adhere to the rules of humanist writing, the genre which the author had chosen for himself. The conventions governing this type of writing must therefore be regarded as a powerful force shaping Busbecq's account.

Quite frequently, diplomats did not themselves compose accounts for publication. A junior member of the embassy wrote a text for print diffusion, while a sober report was penned by the ambassador merely for perusal by his sovereign (Yérasimos, 1991, p. 18). A frequent choice for this task of immortalising the ambassadors' adventures was the embassy chaplain. Thus Joachim von Sintzendorff, Habsburg ambassador to Istanbul 1578–81, hired a young man by the name of Salomon Schweigger, who had recently completed his theological studies and was in search of employment. Schweigger has written an account of his Balkan travels, including a detailed description of the embassy's stay in Istanbul and a more succinct account of his own pilgrimage to the Holy Land. The author's ecclesiastical concerns are apparent throughout the book. Whatever his private convictions may have been, this stress on religion made sense from a worldly point of view. For after the embassy had returned home, the former chaplain would again be in search of a job. His writing might form the basis of the recommendations needed in order to secure more permanent appointment, usually as a parson (the abridged edition of Schweigger 1986 by Heidi Stein contains an informative commentary; Göyünç, 1962–63).

A special tradition of reporting on embassies existed in Venice. Venetian ambassadors to Istanbul, also known as *baili*, throughout the early modern period resided in the Ottoman capital (Pedani Fabris, 1994). The *baili* were expected to produce interim reports which they sent home by messenger whenever they had the chance. After their term of office was over, they also appeared in front of the Senate for a kind of debriefing session. The highly structured report they read at this occasion is known as a *relazione*. Among other things, *relazioni* needed to contain accounts of the physical appearance and personal characteristics of the Sultan(s) and powerful personages at the Ottoman court. This information was considered worth storing for the use of future negotiators. Descriptions of personalities thus might be written for purely practical reasons. But probably it was also significant that such character accounts had their place in the Roman tradition of history writing, the emperors' portraits by Suetonius forming part of the curriculum taught in many Latin courses of the time. And while humanist models of writing in public business were not adopted in Venice quite as readily as they were in Florence, this style did have an impact even here. Obviously the demand for 'personal' information on members of the Ottoman ruling group could result in the inclusion of gossip picked up at the Sultan's court.

Venetian *relazioni* were not originally intended for publication. But in short order, manuscript copies of individual texts were passed on to non-official readers, and today are often found in libraries rather than in archives (Yérasimos, 1991, p. 18). They were held in high esteem by nineteenth-century historians following the example of Leopold von Ranke. As a result, *relazioni* have long been available in print (Albèri, 1840–45; Barozzi and Berchet, 1871–72; Pedani/Fabris, 1996). But the information these documents provide needs to be treated with as much caution as that contained in any other embassy account, even though the established traditions of the Venetian diplomatic service often ensured reporting of a higher calibre than was customary in other countries of early modern Europe (Queller, 1973; see Valensi, 1987 on the manner in which Venetians conceptualised the Ottoman Empire).

PILGRIMS

Another important group of travel writers were the pilgrims. Pilgrimage accounts survive in enormous numbers, and the genre was well established by the time Selim I conquered Palestine in 1517. Down to the 1570s, Venice possessed the monopoly of conveying pilgrims to the Holy Land.

Even after the Ottoman conquest of Cyprus had brought this monopoly to an end, many pilgrims continued to travel by way of Venice. After all, a tradition of travel management had been established in that city. There even existed a special magistrate supervising the entrepreneurs, who, as a kind of early modern travel agents, conveyed pilgrims to the Holy Land. But this mode of travel explains why most pilgrims had very little contact with Ottoman realities. Moreover, even though the publication of a pilgrimage account for many pious and wealthy travellers seems to have almost formed part of the pilgrimage ritual, many of these accounts contain almost no original observations. Comments which at first glance appear personal, such as the numerous remarks concerning the decadence of Palestine under Mamluk or Ottoman rule, upon closer investigation equally turn out to be highly standardised. By ritualistically adhering to the very words of his predecessors, every author demonstrated his adherence to accepted Christian values (Yérasimos, 1991, pp. 19–20).

Salomon Schweigger has already appeared to us in the double identity of an embassy employee and a pilgrim. Quite frequently, people who had come to the Ottoman Empire for business purposes took time off for a pilgrimage to Jerusalem and the other sites known from Biblical history. We will dwell for a moment upon a fairly late example of the genre, namely the account of Henry Maundrell. As Anglican chaplain to the English Levant Company merchants residing in Aleppo, Maundrell visited Jerusalem on an Easter pilgrimage in 1697 (Maundrell, repr. 1963). He stands out for his power of observation and literary gifts; most other pilgrimage accounts are much more pedestrian. English merchants residing in Aleppo organised such a trip to Jerusalem every year, and differently from most other Europeans, they arrived in Palestine by an overland route. Thus there was more to describe, and Maundrell found additional scope for his erudition and literary talent.

In spite of his ecclesiastical calling however, one may debate whether Maundrell should be regarded as a pilgrim. Certainly his abrasive comments on the Orthodox Easter celebrations, with their disparaging description of the ceremonies surrounding a fire supposedly descended from heaven, may be read as confessional polemics of the conventional kind. In this sense, Maundrell's snide remarks fit well into the pilgrimage account of an Anglican gentleman. But it is also possible to see these less than charitable remarks as an expression of the discomfort felt by a young man of rationalist sympathies, when confronted with something that he regarded as the fraudulent exploitation of other people's credulity (Maundrell, repr., 1963, pp. 127–31).

Maundrell had received the classical education normal for an English gentleman of his time, and his account devotes considerable space to the vestiges of antiquity, both Biblical and Greco-Roman. A variant of this pilgrimage account-*cum*-description of classical sites in the eighteenth century was also sometimes written about Anatolia. In this case, the authors visited the sites of the early Christian churches mentioned in the New Testament, quite a few of which, such as Sardis (Sart) and Ephesus (Efes/ Selçuk), were located in the Izmir region. Here the borders between pilgrimage and travel for scholarly or sentimental reasons are especially fluid. By the nineteenth century, authors such the scholarly traveller Otto von Richter, though they might still call their travel books pilgrimage accounts, in fact allowed literary or scholarly concerns to dominate their work (Von Richter, 1822).

RETURNED CAPTIVES

The accounts of returned prisoners constitute a genre in itself; the most famous personage with first-hand experience of captivity is surely Miguel de Cervantes, who fell into the hands of the Algerians in 1575 and did not return to Spain until 1580 (Cervantes, 1997). The stories he wrote on this theme, even though they cannot be considered realistic accounts, are relevant for our purposes because at the time of his captivity, Algiers already formed part of the Ottoman Empire,[2] even though the sea captains and janissaries who dominated the government of this province retained considerable *de facto* autonomy. In particular, they concluded their own treaties with European powers, and did not necessarily feel bound by the privileges and peace conditions granted by the Sultan in Istanbul.

Apart from those taken at sea, most captivity accounts were written by prisoners of war of central European background. Some were taken in battle, others in the frequent frontier raids which commanders on both sides undertook even in peacetime. Among the earliest extant is the account of Hans Schiltberger, a minor knight of Bavaria, taken prisoner during the Ottoman–Hungarian war of 1394. After having been a slave on Ottoman territory, he fell into Timur's hands, when the latter had defeated and imprisoned Bayezid I at the battle of Ankara (1402). As a result, Schiltberger was carried off all the way to eastern Iran, but managed to return to his Bavarian home in 1427. Schiltberger's account is valuable because he writes about a period for which we have very few sources in any language.

[2] 'El amante liberal' and 'La espanola inglesa' are both in the *Novelas ejemplares*, I, pp. 135–88 and 241–83 (Cervantes, ed. Sieber, 1997)

Moreover he stayed on Ottoman territory long enough to recover from the shock of captivity. He travelled widely, if involuntarily, and picked up information on things which happened in out-of-the-way towns such as Samsun. Moreover he enjoyed a good story, and was not above including tales about things that people of the time considered miraculous (Schiltberger, 1983).

Among seventeenth-century captivity accounts, we will briefly mention the work of two men who, with some claim to credibility, state that they had visited the Holy Cities of Mecca and Medina. This means that both Hans Wild and Joseph Pitts must have converted to Islam during their captivity, as the Holy Cities were and are closed to non-Muslims (Wild, ed. Narciß and Teply, 1964; Pitts, ed. Foster, 1949). However, for many returnees it was not easy to admit having abandoned the faith into which they had been born. Possibly this was due to the fact that in the Protestant home countries of both Wild and Pitts, there was no established tradition concerning the reintegration of former Muslims into their home communities.[3] Or else to have stood steadfastly by one's faith was regarded as a major merit, which the returnee had to forego if he admitted to having changed his religion. Be that as it may, Wild managed to write a whole book about his adventures in captivity without ever discussing his twofold change in religious allegiance (Wild, ed. Narciß and Teply, 1964, p. 29). But the former soldier's account can be read, and possibly was read, as a manual of survival skills by those who might fall into Ottoman captivity (Wild, ed. Narcizß and Teply, 1964, pp. 221–2).

The late seventeenth-century Englishman Joseph Pitts had been a slave in Algiers; his account of his pilgrimage to Mecca, complete with a plan of the sanctuary, shows him to have been an educated man with Nonconformist connections. On his return from the Holy Cities, Pitts encountered a sailor from his home town who informed the captive's family that the lost son was still alive; this lucky chance may have facilitated Pitt's ultimate return to England. Given the fact that he must have converted to Islam during his time of slavery, it is worth noting that Pitts ascribes his recovery from plague as a sign of divine favour: 'for I was just return'd from Mecca when this mercy was dispens'd to me' (Pitts, ed. Foster, 1949, p. 49). We may speculate whether Pitts believed that 'this mercy' was dispensed to him on account of his pilgrimage, or granted in spite of the fact that he had abandoned the religion into which he had been born.

---

[3] In Venice, the Papal lands and the territories ruled by the King of Spain, even the fearsome Inquisition considered the conversions of slaves a minor matter, to be settled by a short penance (Bennassar and Bennassar, 1989).

MERCHANTS

Apart from pilgrims to Jerusalem and Bethlehem, merchants probably formed the majority of European travellers to the Ottoman Empire
before the nineteenth century. But due to their involvement with the
practical business of buying and selling, they have not left as high a propor-
tion of travel accounts as the diplomats. A typical Venetian or English
merchant active in the Ottoman Empire wrote business letters to his
principals in Venice or London, not book-length manuscripts for publication. Yet such business-like reports, particularly if available in quantity, can
be of great interest. The English economic historian Ralph Davis has used
merchants' letters to produce a very informative book on English traders
active in Aleppo (Davis, 1967, compare chapter 3). It contains chapters
about the more prominent family firms whose principals in the seventeenth
and eighteenth centuries held shares in the Levant Company and therefore
possessed the right to send their sons and nephews to Aleppo as 'factors'. A
factor was supposed to observe the market closely, so that his reports might
contain information on local developments such as fashion changes. For
contrary to widespread opinion, the tastes of wealthier Ottoman customers
were not immutable. A good factor would also inform his principals of the
arrival, or failure to arrive, of caravans from Iran. After all, a large share of the
English woollen cloth imported into Aleppo merely passed through the
Ottoman Empire in transit to Bandar 'Abbas and Isfahan. General information on financial crisis at the Ottoman centre also might be included, as the
well-to-do Ottomans who could afford imported cloth might be less inclined to buy in times of monetary instability. Last but not least, as factors
were cooped up together for much of the time in a single khan, even the
most sober business correspondent might be tempted to include some gossip
on his colleagues.

When merchants wrote with an eye to publication, they often
produced small booklets with lists of the different coins, weights and
measurements current in the places they had visited. Such booklets have a
long tradition, one of the oldest and best known being the *Practica della
mercatura* by the fourteenth-century Florentine merchant Pegolotti
(Pegolotti, ed. Evans, 1936). This treatise lists the goods most profitably
purchased in certain places of the eastern Mediterranean; it includes
Anatolia, at that time controlled by a multitude of Turkish princes. As a
result, we know something about the quality of fourteenth-century Adana
cotton in contrast to the same material as produced in Cyprus or Syria. But
detailed information of this kind is not a standard feature; in fact, many
merchants might have considered it a trade secret to be guarded from

competitors. Commercial guidebooks might be used in the training of apprentice merchants. Established merchants also may have read them when planning a business trip into little known territory, or when checking up on the reports sent in by their travelling partners. Most of these opuscula were anything but original; the authors of commercial manuals did not hesitate to copy from their predecessors whatever was still considered as valid information. But through careful interpretation, much can be learned from this material (Kévonian, 1975).

An interesting example, published in Armenian in Amsterdam in 1699, contains information on the trade conducted by Armenian merchants based in the Iranian town of New Djulfa. This commercial network extended as far as Amsterdam, which was reached by way of long-established routes traversing the Ottoman Empire. A newer, less familiar alternative crossed the Caspian Sea; travellers then followed the Wolga, reaching Moscow and ultimately, the Netherlands by way of the Baltic. But as a commercial centre on the older route, Erzurum also was much frequented by Armenian traders, who from there reached Istanbul and Izmir by way of Tokat (Erim, 1991). An enterprising merchant thus needed information on both routes.

Many merchants' accounts were fairly short, and therefore best published in collections. Late sixteenth-century England produced two extensive series of this kind, namely Hakluyt's *Voyages* of 1589 and the editorially less impressive collection known as *Purchas his Pilgrimes*. Both series were presumably compiled to inform English merchants of the opportunities open to them in the expanding world known to European geographers of the time (Beckingham, reprint 1983, No. XX). Of the Hakluyt series, there exist numerous reprints of individual volumes, dating from the nineteenth and twentieth centuries. Present-day readers will prefer them not only on account of their easier availability, but also because many Victorian and Edwardian editors have added extensive introductions. All this publishing activity is due to the efforts of the Hakluyt Society, founded in 1846, which by the end of the 1970s had published 291 volumes of travel accounts, either in the English original or else in translation (Beckingham, reprint 1983, No. IV). In more recent years, C. H. Beckingham has continued critical work on travel accounts, authoring among other things, an article on a sixteenth-century anonymous text, known only due to its publication by Hakluyt. For the first time in European history, the anonymous writer provided reasonably accurate information on the Cairo pilgrimage caravan to Mecca and the traders attached to it (Beckingham, reprint 1983, No. XXI). However this material, in spite of its evident commercial value, was probably compiled not by a merchant but by a former military captive.

A valuable but little known travel account is due to the seventeenth-century Nuremberg merchant Wolfgang Aigen, in Aleppo between 1656 and 1663 (Aigen, ed. Tietze, 1980). At this time, the Thirty Years War (1618–1648) had destroyed the economic potential of southern Germany for a long time to come. So Aigen was not in business on his own account, but acted as a factor to a Venetian merchant, often relying on the protection of the French consul. Possibly Aigen's Venetian principals sent him to Syria because of the Venetian–Ottoman war over Crete (1645–1669); during those tense and difficult years, a Venetian subject might have run into difficulties. But in 1663, the Habsburg emperor and the Sultan being now embroiled with one another, it was Aigen's turn to leave Ottoman territory hurriedly.

Of the one and – probably – only surviving manuscript of Aigen's work, only the chapter on Syria has been published. However, other sections, for instance that covering Dalmatia, may also be of interest to the commercial historian. For Aigen regarded his environment with a merchant's eye. Whenever he visited a place, he carefully listed the local products, often comparing them with similar items available in other places. He liked to dwell upon strange fruit, animals or buildings, while maintaining a sceptical distance from the lore relayed to him by his local Christian acquaintances. The edition by Andreas Tietze retains the spelling and sounds of the original, only the numerous abbreviations of Aigen's manuscript have been written out in full. This may sound daunting; however the text is readily comprehensible to the modern reader, as seventeenth-century German is reasonably close to the language of today.

MISSIONARIES

Missionaries form another numerous group among the writers of travel accounts. According to the Islamic religious law (*şeriat*), apostasy from Islam is punishable by death, and in any case, very few Muslim subjects of the Sultan would ever have wanted to listen to a non-Muslim missionary. So emissaries of the Pope and members of Catholic orders, who visited the Ottoman Empire in substantial numbers from the seventeenth century onward, addressed themselves to the Christian subjects of the Sultan. Protestant missions only became at all widespread in the nineteenth century, and adopted the same policy.

Where the seventeenth century is concerned, Catholic missionary efforts must be seen as part of the movement known as the Counter-

Reformation, and in other contexts as the Catholic Reform. Not merely the Pope and the Spanish kings, but also the French rulers of the Bourbon dynasty were committed to the expansion of the ecclesiastical – but not of the secular – authority of the Pope[4]. This involved encouragement to various Ottoman Christian groups to submit to Papal authority (see p, 67). Those who consented usually retained most of their specific religious ritual, and most importantly, their liturgical languages, that is Greek, Arabic or Armenian as the case might be (Masters, in press).

Franciscan, Dominican and especially Jesuit missionaries were supposed to write reports on what they had seen when travelling in the Ottoman Empire. Particularly in France, these missives were often published, in order to give potential sponsors among the pious laity a sense of what was being achieved. They often figure as 'Lettres édifiantes et curieuses', a title showing the mixture of piety and curiosity about foreign parts that these texts appealed to. Many of the men sent to the Ottoman Empire or the Caucasus knew the language of the people they were expected to address. They thus possessed a distinct advantage over diplomats and merchants, who rarely spoke Ottoman, Arabic or Armenian. Moreover, the missionaries were often interested in the material and social circumstances under which their potential flocks lived. After all the success of their missions, such as it was, depended on an accurate assessment of local power structures. However, the often narrow focus on church affairs explains why seventeenth- and eighteenth-century missionary reports have received relatively little attention from present-day historians.

By far the largest number of missionary publications, however, dates from the nineteenth century, including an important corpus of writings by Anglo-Saxon Protestant missionaries. Quite often married missionaries were accompanied by their wives, who might engage in schoolteaching and social work among women and children. Some of these women wrote about their experiences, forming a separate group among the female visitors to the Ottoman Empire (Melman, 1992, pp. 165–234). Of special interest is the work of Lucy Garnett, who around the turn of the past century, was associated with Robert College, Istanbul, and published extensively about local folklore (Melman, 1992, pp. 106–140). Moreover, some of these female missionaries and missionary wives made an impact on the domestic culture of the people attending mission schools. For the teaching of what these women regarded as 'good housekeeping' formed an important part of

---

[4] Due to the almost continuous warfare between the Ottomans and the Spanish Habsburgs during the sixteenth and early seventeenth centuries, Spanish policies had little impact upon Ottoman Christians.

the curriculum of missionary schools for local girls.[5] Thus the writings of women missionaries also may be read as sources for nineteenth- and early twentieth-century changes in material culture, which were especially noticeable among Ottoman Christians.

TRAVEL WRITING AND SCHOLARSHIP: THE EXAMPLE OF PETRUS GYLLIUS

From the later sixteenth century onward, and more frequently in later times, we encounter people whose main motivation for travel was their desire to write about the places visited. Such books found a public among the English gentry or the French magistrates for whom, by the seventeenth or eighteenth century, the possession of a large library was a matter of social prestige. Following an education in public schools and Oxford or Cambridge in the English case, or the study of law in the French instance, these men were literate enough to read for pleasure. Although they normally knew Latin, they generally preferred non-professional reading in their native languages. A good example of a travel writer addressing himself to this gentlemanly public was the Frenchman Jean Thévenot, who visited Syria and Egypt in the second half of the seventeenth century (Thévenot, ed. Yérasimos, 1980). That he wrote for a leisure-class public may in part explain why the description of public festivities takes up such a considerable share of his book. In the late eighteenth century, a reading public had also come into being that liked its travel books lavishly illustrated, and could afford to pay for engravings. Among others, the last pre-revolutionary French ambassador to Istanbul, the Comte de Choiseul-Gouffier, sponsored and coauthored a series of books directed at this market.

Overlapping with the category of professional writers were scholars interested in the Roman or Greek antiquities of Istanbul, Syria and Anatolia, which had acquired special prestige in the eyes of educated Renaissance gentlemen. Such scholars were sometimes financed by a king or nobleman with the proviso that they should purchase manuscripts for the patron's library or artefacts for his collection. Other scholarly travellers were in the business of plant-collecting; particularly from the seventeenth century onward, many powerful personages prided themselves on the rare and exotic plants cultivated in their gardens (Mukerji, 1993).

As an early example of the travel writer who was also a classical scholar, we will take a closer look at the work of the Frenchman Pierre

---

[5] Mrs. Dina Kiskira (Thessaloniki) is currently working on this issue, basing herself on the archives of Anatolia College, Thessaloniki, Greece. The importance of this topic was pointed out to me by Seçil Akgün.

Gilles, or Petrus Gyllius as he called himself in his Latin publications (1490–1555; visits to Istanbul in 1544–47 and 1550). From Gyllius' pen we possess various studies on natural history, particularly on fish; but for our purposes, his most important works concern Istanbul and the Bosphorus. Basing himself on the authors of late antiquity who had described Constantinople, he attempted to locate, and where possible measure, the remnants of the principal buildings of this period (his book on Istanbul has been translated into English by John Ball, ed. Musto, 1988. For a recent translation into Turkish based on the Latin original, see Gyllius, tr. Özbayoğlu, 1997).

Gyllius approached his sources with a good deal of critical sense. When confronted with major discrepancies between physical remains and literary descriptions, he was willing to accept that the ancient author in question might have been mistaken, a conclusion which, for a man of his training, presupposed considerable intellectual independence. His reasoning with respect to oral accounts was often careful as well. Thus he mentioned contemporary Turkish claims that the Aya Sofya had originally been much larger than the building as it stood in the mid sixteenth century (Gyllius, tr. Ball, ed. Musto, 1988, p. 67). By comparing the existing building with the sixth-century description of Procopius, Gyllius was able to determine that the church-turned-mosque itself was intact, except for the loss of a portico. However, he conceded that the Turkish account he heard might have referred to the houses of priests and noblemen which originally had surrounded the church, but of which nothing remained by the middle of the sixteenth century.

However, Gyllius was completely out of sympathy with the concerns of his Istanbul contemporaries, Greeks and Turks alike. All that counted in his eyes was the heritage of Graeco-Roman antiquity. The buildings of mediaeval Byzantium, including such major monuments as the church of Our Saviour in Chora with its frescoes and mosaics (Kariye Camii, today museum) were not even included in his account. At least part of the reason for his negative evaluation of sixteenth-century Istanbullus was their lack of interest in the monuments of classical antiquity, and/or their suspicion of people who walked around the city measuring and sketching. Gyllius' hostility toward his temporary Istanbul neighbours maybe would not have been expressed quite as drastically if the author had lived long enough to edit his work himself. But he died in Rome not long after his second visit to Istanbul, and the editing was completed by his nephew. Antoine Gilles may well have retained Gyllius' original expressions more faithfully than the author himself might have done. For when expressing himself for publication, Gyllius was in the habit of using a neutral 'scholarly' diction.

Due to his almost monomaniacal fascination with antiquity, Gyllius will sometimes attribute buildings to this particular period for no better reason than that he found them impressive. A good example is his account of the two Istanbul covered markets (*bedestans*), which he was able to view in 'splendid isolation' as a fire had destroyed the surrounding streets whose buildings otherwise obscured them. Gyllius had no doubt that the two structures were basilicas, which is definitely not the case (Gyllius, tr. Ball, 1988, pp. 30–31). But European authors down into the twentieth century had the tendency to mistake Ottoman buildings, including the bridge of Mostar, for Roman ones. Gyllius' error, which incidentally was not noticed by his recent American editor, thus falls into a well-established pattern.

Gyllius' discourse is relevant to modern writing about Istanbul in yet another fashion. Toward the end of his book, he mentioned the intense Ottoman construction going on in his time, claiming that there were 300 mosques in use, and over a hundred public baths, of which 50 were of monumental size. Gyllius was not very happy about all this construction activity, because it involved the destruction of many remains of antiquity. With some regret he noted that many houses of his own time had been built of the ruins and re-used elements of ancient buildings. This was probably true, as only about a century had elapsed since the Ottoman conquest. Yet the author was quite aware that the Ottomans were simply doing what their predecessors had done in their own time. Thus the Roman emperor Severus had destroyed the Hellenistic city; as to the emperor Constantine, he tore down pagan monuments to rebuild Byzantium as Constantinopolis, the capital of a Christian empire. No one who reads Doğan Kuban's recent book about the history of Istanbul can fail to be struck by the continuity: Kuban, a major architectural historian who has spent much of his energy on the conservation of Istanbul's architectural heritage, equally deplores the fact that the present-day city is voraciously gobbling up the traces of its Ottoman predecessor (Kuban, 1996).

Modern readers will often encounter Gyllius' work in the translation by John Ball, an eighteenth-century author, which has recently been reissued. The sixteenth-century editions are accessible only in the rare books sections of major libraries. Musto's edition includes Ball's preface of 1729, written almost 200 years after the original volume. When comparing the preface with the remarks of Gyllius himself, it is apparent that for Ball, straightforward rejection had taken the place of the earlier scholar's ambivalences. Now, the Ottomans are not active and monumental builders destroying what had existed before them, but enemies of monumental architecture *per se*. This negative judgement probably should be linked with the loss of power the Sultans had suffered in the recent war over Hungary. I do not dare to judge whether John Ball knew anything about the eighteenth-century preference of the Ottoman elites for small, light and elegant constructions.

Gyllius and other people drawing and measuring monuments were sometimes taken for spies, and given the tense political conditions of the times, there was no lack of people who in fact were out to gather intelligence. Information, both true and false, travelled back and forth between courts and governments. Ottoman Sultans equally maintained their own spies, who informed them of what happened at contemporary European courts (Skilliter, 1976). Embassies gathered intelligence along with their other functions. We can assume that some of the travel writers were also 'debriefed' on their return to French and Habsburg territories. But much of this activity must have been oral and remains untraceable (for a notorious case of intelligence gathering from the sixteenth century, see Nicolay, ed. Gomez-Géraud and Yérasimos, 1989).

RELATING TO ONE'S PREDECESSORS: THE PROBLEM OF 'ORIGINALITY' IN TRAVEL ACCOUNTS

In the sixteenth or eighteenth century, no differently than today, a person's profession or major activity determined the things he/she considered worth reporting. To mention one well-studied example, in the early eighteenth century Mary Wortley Montague, the young, well-educated and intellectually versatile wife of a British ambassador, accompanied her husband to Edirne and Istanbul (ed. Desai and Jack, 1993). As a woman of the aristocracy, she was able to meet high-born Ottoman ladies, an experience totally impossible to any male visitor. Moreover, she learned Ottoman, something that male diplomats almost never attempted. From her description of the manner in which she was received in Istanbul or Edirne, it is clear that Lady Mary was regarded as something of a curiosity, and she enjoyed this reaction as long as it came from people she considered her social equals (for an example see Montague, ed. Desai and Jack, 1993, pp. 86ff.). Needless to say, Lady Mary's sympathies did not extend to men and women outside this charmed circle. But as she was a good observer of her social environment – and also on account of her elegant style – the letters she wrote to her friends at home are still considered a classic of travel literature.

While Lady Mary was thus an innovator in the genre of Ottoman travel writing, she also must be placed within a literary tradition. This was the art of letter writing, as practised by some aristocratic ladies even in the seventeenth century. After all, Madame de Sévigné (1626–1696) has gained herself a place in French literature by her lively accounts of Versailles and Parisian life. Her younger contemporary Elisabeth Charlotte, princess Palatine and sister-in-law to Louis XIV, became a shrewd chronicler of French court life around 1700. Others even approached more abstract topics; thus Sophie Charlotte, the first Prussian queen, discussed religious and philosophical matters in her correspondence with the philosopher Gottfried Leibniz. When reading the accounts of the Vienna and Dresden courts, which in Lady Mary Montague's collection of letters precede those covering the Ottoman Empire, her debt to the tradition of aristocratic female letter writing is especially apparent (ed. Desai and Jack, 1993, pp. 12–44).

The conventions of feminine letter writing forbade Lady Mary to be too demonstrative about her scholarship – although there are exceptions to this rule, such as her letter to the poet Alexander Pope (ed. Desai and Jack, 1993, pp. 73ff). However, the 'male' tradition of travel-writing allowed, indeed encouraged, the presentation of scholarly credentials. We have already encountered Busbecq, Maundrell and Gyllius, for whom scholarship constituted an aspect of their identity to be deployed, not to say flaunted, before their readers. For our purposes, this commitment to scholarship is often not an advantage, but a distinct drawback. For then as now, scholarly activity involves knowing the writings of one's predecessors, and often 'knowing' meant something like 'copying'. As every undergraduate knows, it is often difficult to find words for novel experiences, and travel in the Balkans or Anatolia was a once-in-a-lifetime experience for most writers. Thus, predecessors' formulations might be taken over simply because they were the first thing that came to mind.

But quite often, the matter was much more complicated, and only a brief outline of the problem is possible here. Down to the Renaissance, no particular value was placed on literary invention. Quite to the contrary, even when authors invented a story, they often claimed to have heard it from 'an authority' or read it in a book. With the classical revival of the fifteenth and sixteenth centuries, the number of possible 'authorities' increased, and it became more important to use a philologically correct text. But for all that, the dependence upon predecessors did not necessarily lessen, as the prestige of ancient authors encouraged close imitation of their style. To mention but one example, quite a few sixteenth-century writers dealing with travel in their own times would feel the need to call contemporary peoples by names taken from Greek or Roman sources. Thus the Turks might be called Scythians, even though there is no link between the two peoples. The equation was justified by a philological concern, namely not to commit any 'barbarisms', that is, to avoid using any words unknown to Graeco-Roman authors. That a distortion of reality was involved in all this is a more serious concern to present-day historians than it was to contemporary readers (for an example among many, see Gyllius, tr. Ball, ed. Musto, 1988, p. 222).

That scholarly and literary originality are values to be protected was certainly not a complete novelty in the eighteenth century. But this notion did become much more widespread after about 1700. A link to the expansion of the literary market is clearly visible, and the idea that a certain work is an 'original' has affinities to the nineteenth- and twentieth-century concept of copyright. In England, where capitalism was more advanced than on the continent, the first legal measures to protect the rights of an author were already taken in the early eighteenth century (Wittmann, 1991, pp. 206–8). Only an original work could be protected by copyright, which allowed the author some control over the products of his/her pen.

But the view that a work of travel should rest upon autopsy wherever possible was already 'in the culture' even before copyright was instituted, namely by the seventeenth century. The books of that indefatigable merchant and traveller that was Jean Baptiste Tavernier contain numerous practical hints on caravan travel in the Ottoman Empire and Iran (ed. Yérasimos, 1981, pp. 159ff). This advice derives its authority from the fact that the author had spent a lifetime plying these very roads. From a slightly later period, it is worth taking another look at Lady Mary Montague. Lady Mary claims to have understood certain phenomena of Ottoman social life better than her (male) predecessors, because, as she went to considerable pains to point out, she had access to aspects of Ottoman life which remained a closed book to male writers (ed. Desai and Jack, 1993, p. 60 and elsewhere).

When originality had come to be regarded as a value *per se*, the claim to depend exclusively on observation easily could become a figure of speech with little justification in fact. Such assertions are comparable to the mediaeval author's claim to have derived his/her account from the appropriate authorities. Both conscious and more or less unconscious borrowing from one's predecessors did not disappear, and even worse, this dependence upon remote predecessors has often been carried over into modern scholarship as well (Said, 1978). Intellectual laziness apart, scholars who conflate the accounts of sources remote from each other in time will justify their procedure by claiming that Middle Eastern history moved at a slow pace. In this context, statements made for instance in the sixteenth century are supposed to be equally valid for the eighteenth as well. This claim is not unjustified *ipso facto*, but must be treated with circumspection. Now that the writings of Fernand Braudel have become part of the intellectual baggage of quite a few non-historians, we have become aware that certain aspects of social life moved very slowly, not only in the Middle East but in early modern and even modern Europe as well (Braudel, 2nd edn, 1966). Thus it no longer makes any sense to construct Middle Eastern 'otherness' on the basis of an allegedly slow movement of history. To sum up, it is not illegitimate to use accounts from different periods to elucidate those of another, but the historian will need to exercise great care when doing so.

THE OTTOMAN TOWN VIEWED BY EUROPEAN TRAVELLERS: AN EXERCISE IN COMPARISON

Now that we have introduced the more widespread types of early modern European travel writers, the time has come to attempt a closer analysis of their work. Gyllius' account of sixteenth-century Istanbul has served as a negative example, that is, we have recognised him as a traveller who avoided looking at the Ottoman capital while spending a considerable amount of time in it. This example has shown how obvious realities can be rendered 'invisible'.

But the positive production of urban images is an even more important process, which we will study through a specific example. This involves a comparison between the description of 'foreign' towns or cities on the part of European travellers on the one hand, and similar accounts by one of their most prolific and observant Ottoman counterparts on the other[6]. Such a confrontation of rival images will bring us face to face with the work of the seventeenth-century traveller Evliya Çelebi (Evliya Çelebi, 1314/1896–97 to 1938; for vol. I see the transcription by Gökyay, 1995 and the facsimile put out by Iz and the Tekins, 1989). A comparison of this sort is particularly rewarding, as for some of the places visited by Evliya, especially Vienna, the topography and monuments are very well known. Evliya's procedure of image-making therefore can be studied at close range. By contrast, Ottoman towns generally possess a smaller amount of surviving documentation, and also have been less well studied. This situation can create a real trap. We may be tempted to take European travellers' claims concerning Ottoman towns at face value, when in fact they are producing images, the relationship of which to 'objective' reality cries out for investigation.

We will begin with an analysis of the urban vision which early

---

[6] On Middle Eastern travellers' views of Europe, one may read Lewis, 1982.

modern European visitors brought along in their travelling kits, and which conditioned their observations in Bursa, Aleppo, Sofia or Trabzon. French, English, Italian or German travellers of that period generally expected a major city to possess buildings several stories high. In part this was probably due to the Roman traditions they had all imbibed; in the imperial period, Rome contained numerous plots of land bordered by streets (*insulae*) covered over with residential construction of six to seven storeys. Frequently, the wealthier inhabitants lived on the first floor, while the upper stories were occupied by the poor; a comparable arrangement also existed in some parts of eighteenth-century Paris. Moreover, in the core of the city, business and residence were closely intertwined, with shops occupying the ground floor and residences the remainder of the building. On a practical level, this arrangement probably had something to do with the fact that until the middle of the nineteenth century, most European cities were still surrounded by walls. Outer suburbs existed, but wholesale building in the unwalled areas was often forbidden for defensive reasons. High densities on a small built-up area were the outcome, and a typical French or English visitor to an Ottoman town would be on the lookout for evidence of similar crowding (compare Braudel, 1979, vol. I, pp. 432ff).

Ottoman towns were however arranged according to different considerations. Most of them possessed a citadel which might contain a number of urban quarters. But at least in Anatolia, the commercial district normally lay outside the citadel. Markets might be located in an undefended lower town, probably because most urban sites were remote from endangered frontiers. But even when a city wall might have seemed advisable for security reasons, Ottoman townsmen – or the central administration for that matter – rarely decided to defend the entire built-up area in this fashion. Ankara constitutes one of the few, exceptional instances in which a new city wall was built in the troubled years around 1600; even a century later, this wall still protected the entire built-up space. By contrast, towns in coastal and therefore exposed regions of western and southern Anatolia were rarely protected by a full city wall. Whenever the situation became too dangerous, such settlements therefore contracted until in the case of emergency, the entire population could find refuge in the citadel (Stoianovich, 1970; Ergenç, 1980; Faroqhi, 1984, pp. 23ff.).

As a result of these building patterns, the pressure on Ottoman townsmen to construct a high-density urban core was, at least in the sixteenth century, probably less urgent than in many parts of Europe. Congestion was further relieved by the fact that so many commercial buildings owned by pious foundations accommodated large numbers of shops without adjacent residences. This meant that many tenants of such

8 *Khan and mosque in Razgrad. Note both waggons and load-bearing animals in the courtyard. This was a modest establishment, and being located in a town, not meant to be defended in an emergency. As a result, it was mainly built not of stone, but of wood.*

shops living elsewhere, an Ottoman town spread out over a larger area than its European counterpart, certainly an advantage given the rudimentary sanitation technology of the times. But visitors such as Hans Dernschwam or Petrus Gyllius seem to have felt that a town built of small, flatroofed houses was somehow less of a town, and this opinion has strongly coloured their perceptions (Dernschwam, ed. Babinger, 1923, p. 189).

On a more general level, the notions and prejudices about Turks and Middle Easterners that European travellers subscribed to have also influenced their judgments about Ottoman towns. In the sixteenth century at least, most visitors were highly impressed by the Sultans' military power. To give but one example among many, Busbecq's account is full of praise concerning such features as the lack of an entrenched aristocracy, the single-minded devotion of all military men to the ruler or the discipline and frugality of the janissaries (Busbecq, tr. Forster, 1968). But it seems that, possibly in order to avoid totally revising their mental map of the world, these European authors were unwilling to admit that Ottomans might be good at anything but warfare. Referring once again to the authors of late antiquity, European writers sometimes compared the Ottomans to the Germans or Huns who battered the Roman Empire during its final centuries. Pious commentators might add that the Ottomans were victorious because of the sins of the Christians in general, and more particularly the selfishness and disunity of Christian princes. Praise for non-military achievements in the Ottoman world on the part of contemporary European travellers is therefore rare, and usually hedged in with numerous 'yes, but's. A whole set of definitions was worked out in order to not have to come to terms with Ottomans as artists, craftsmen or musicians. We have already encountered the tendency to regard Ottoman buildings as Roman. A variant of this theme was the tendency to ascribe all the positive sides of Ottoman rule to the activities of converted Christians, a tendency which has not died out even in the late twentieth century.

Attitudes were not any more positive in the eighteenth and nineteenth centuries, when Ottoman power was no longer feared, and conquest by the sultan's armies no longer a risk. This situation might have made it easier for European travellers to appreciate Ottoman performance in the non-military arts. But a few exceptions apart, this did not happen. To give but one example, for many modern viewers eighteenth-century Ottoman architecture in Istanbul or Cairo appears elegant and imaginative, though the buildings are small in size. But as Ottoman palaces did not resemble the massive structures of Versailles and St Petersburg, they were not counted as monumental architecture, witness the negative comments of John Ball as an example among many. In fact, the Topkapı Sarayı, mostly built in an earlier age, came in for its share of adverse criticism for just this reason (Necipoğlu, 1991, p. xiv).

Accusing the Ottoman government of misrule and ineptitude involved a refusal to recognise as permanent the Sultan's rule over his domains. If the Ottomans were unable to provide what their European critics regarded as good government, then, at least by implication, there were competitors in Europe who claimed that they would do better. In his context, travellers' accounts have been interpreted as a means by which Europeans appropriated, for the time being symbolically, spaces located outside the confines of their world (Yérasimos, 1991, p.20).

In this respect, educated Ottomans and their European counterparts seem to have inhabited a comparable world. For Evliya Çelebi adopted a similar stance when he recounted his visit to Vienna in 1665. Evliya seems to have regarded the inhabitants of the Habsburg capital as desirable potential subjects of the Sultan, for the interesting reason that this city boasted an abundance of skilled artisans, musicians and surgeons (Evliya, ed. Kreutel, Prokosch and Teply, 1987, pp. 142–4, pp. 170ff. and elsewhere). By contrast, the Habsburg ruler was an excessively ugly creature, and of course the people were infidels; however the latter point was probably less important to the worldly-wise Evliya than it would have been to many of his Ottoman contemporaries.

Evliya's account of mid seventeenth-century Vienna describes the mementoes of Süleyman the Magnificent's 1529 siege in great detail. He devotes considerable space to the location of the former Ottoman camp, but also to the derring-do of various personages who had supposedly participated in the siege. This was apparently intended as a kind of prefiguration of the ultimate Ottoman conquest; after all, the second siege of Vienna took place less than two decades after Evliya's visit. His account may thus be read as a kind of propaganda leaflet promoting a future conquest, by accentuating the virtues of the city and its inhabitants. This purpose explains why Evliya sometimes goes so far as to invent flourishing towns, supposedly located on the road between Buda and Vienna. The good care that infidels took of their churches, their diligence in arts and handicrafts, and even the handsome appearance of their youths and maidens were all qualities desirable in future subjects of the Sultan.

Evliya also apparently hoped that readers at home might take some of the qualities of the strange peoples he described as so many examples to emulate. If his description of Vienna is any guide, skill, dedication to one's work and artistic talent constituted values the author wished to recommend to his readers. Again this tendency to use the travel account as a moral tale was not a uniquely Ottoman phenomenon, for Busbecq in the sixteenth century had recommended the virtues of the Ottoman slave aristocracy to his own ruler. Yet there was an important difference between the Ottoman traveller and his European counterparts, which seems to reside in perceptions of relative power and potential. Contrary to some of his contemporaries in the Ottoman ruling group, Evliya did not see the Ottoman Empire as 'on the decline', but quite to the contrary, as vigorously expanding. For the representative of such a system, there was no need to deny the positive virtues of the infidels, including their capacity to build flourishing towns; ultimately, they would be incorporated within the Ottoman world. By contrast, resentment and the feeling of being threatened seem to have played a much stronger role in the world view of European travelogue writers: Apparently the latter saw themselves as hampered in their movements and in permanent danger, while from the wisdom of hindsight, we can see that they themselves were actually doing most of the threatening.   .

Evliya's account of his trip to Vienna contains quite a few tall tales. As a result historians for a long time used to doubt that he had ever been there, until documentary evidence of his presence was found in the Austrian archives. It was understood but recently that even his most fantastic tales were not gratuitous, but rather the outcome of his artistic, moral and political intentions in writing his ten-volume travelogue. The same thing, by the way, applies to his contemporaries the French, Italian or English visitors to the Ottoman Empire, who also invented images with the help of the more or less reliable data they had managed to collect. Only in their case, it has taken present-day scholars a lot longer to spot the myth-making.

EVLIYA ÇELEBI AND JEAN BAPTISTE TAVERNIER

Continuing our comparison, let us look more closely at the 'mental grid' which Evliya used when describing Anatolian towns. This we will compare with what is known about the conceptual categories of a seventeenth-century foreign visitor who saw some of the same places. For such an exercise, the travelogue of Jean Baptiste Tavernier, as indefatigable a traveller as Evliya himself, seems a good starting point. Tavernier was born in Paris in 1605, and died in Moscow in 1689, which makes him the exact contemporary of Evliya Çelebi (about 1605 – after 1683; for Tavernier's biography compare the edition by Yérasimos, 1981, vol. I, pp. 7ff., and also chapter 1). On his three separate visits to India, Tavernier obtained an intimate knowledge of the trade routes passing through the Ottoman Empire. On one level, this author wrote for merchants and other professional travellers, discussing in detail how they might protect their possessions, secure water, or deal with the demands of caravaneers. This aspect of his work is quite comparable to Evliya's account of his pilgrimage to Mecca (Evliya, 1314/1896–7 to 1938, vol. ix, pp. 565–842). After all, the format of 'pilgrims' advice literature' as current in the Ottoman world also demanded that practical aspects be given their due. If the two authors had ever met, which they probably just missed doing, we can imagine them exchanging information on safe and unsafe stretches of road. Moreover both authors, as denizens of the proto-statistical age, seem to have shared a marked penchant for the relaying of 'facts and figures'.

But Tavernier's ambitions went beyond merely writing a well-informed travellers' guide. He has produced a separate treatise on the Ottoman Palace in Istanbul, and his travelogue contains chapters on the manner in which Iran and Mughul India supposedly were governed (see Tavernier, ed. Yérasimos, 1981, vol. II for Iran). These texts are not taken very seriously by historians any more, but they were widely read both in their own time and by later generations. In the writings of the eighteenth-century political theoretician Montesquieu, there are sections directly derived from Tavernier's work (ed. Yérasimos, 1981, vol. I, pp. 33–4).[7] However Montesquieu came up with an interpretation not explicitly spelled out in the writing of his seventeenth-century source: Tavernier had described caravan itineraries, linking the largest cities while often avoiding lesser towns on the way, in which supplementary dues might be demanded. Two generations later, Montesquieu assumed that this omission meant that no cities existed in the Ottoman Empire, except for a few emporia frequented by foreign merchants. Thus the stereotype of the once flourishing lands of the Roman Empire gone to waste because of Ottoman ineptitude, while probably more widespread in the eighteenth than in the seventeenth century, at least in part has been derived from Tavernier's account.

In commenting on Tavernier's work, Stéphane Yérasimos has noted that this trader provides very little information on the people he must have encountered in the course of his travels (Tavernier, ed. Yérasimos, 1981, pp. 30ff.). As Tavernier never managed to learn either Persian or Ottoman, he must have had problems in establishing contact, except where his Armenian business friends were involved. Rural life practically never occurs in his account, the countryside is depicted as a deserted area criss-crossed by roads, leading from one town to another – that is, if the traveller is lucky. Yérasimos links this fashion of viewing with Tavernier's preoccupations as a long-distance trader, for whom the countryside did not produce anything to be bought or sold. But once again, Evliya and Tavernier had something in common, for the Ottoman traveller also had very little to say about rural life. In Evliya's case, this did not stem from a preoccupation with trade. But as an Ottoman gentleman, in his own way he was just as much an urbanite as Tavernier. While Evliya might occasionally comment on the behaviour of Beduins and mercenaries, the fate of peasants remained a matter of utter indifference to him.

But if both Tavernier and Evliya were inveterate townsmen, this

---

[7] Among the other sources used by Montesquieu, there is a satirical novel called *L'espion turc*. This has recently been studied by an Ottomanist historian: Aksan, 1994.

did not mean that they saw these towns in quite the same fashion. Evliya proceeded in a fairly systematic way; it was apparently his aim to visit all Ottoman towns of any importance at least once. Both great cities and less important places were described by the application of one and the same mental questionnaire, in which public and private buildings played a central role. Commerce was important, largely because it gave rise to such monuments as khans and *bedestans*; but religious and military-administrative buildings were given pride of place. By contrast, Tavernier was interested only in long-distance trade, and the conditions which furthered or prevented it. When he described religious and other non-commercial public buildings, it was usually a sideline. Either Tavernier's trade had obliged him to spend some time in the place in question, or the monuments he described were connected with his Armenian business partners. Certainly Evliya's subtext, namely to exalt the glory of the Ottoman Empire through its cities, was totally lacking in Tavernier's case, and one encounters few instances in which he expresses admiration for what he saw.

Yet Evliya's relatively optimistic view of his own time does not mean that he simply retailed illusions, the 'rose-red' counterparts to the 'black' image of decline popular among his European contemporaries. This becomes obvious when comparing his description of the city of Urfa (Ruha) to that of Tavernier. Both travellers saw the town in the 1640s, within a few years of one another. Urfa had been hard hit by the Celali rebellions of the late sixteenth and early seventeenth centuries, when the rebel leader Kalenderoğlu had occupied the town (Akdağ, 1963, p. 211; Evliya Çelebi, 1314/1896–97, vol III, pp. 148–169; Tavernier, ed. Yérasimos, 1981, vol. I, pp. 244–246). Evliya acknowledges this fact by stating that Urfa's commercial buildings were not very impressive, even though a large amount of goods was (once again?) available there. Tavernier reports that a large number of houses still lay in ruins, which is another facet of the same reality. By stretching the point a little, we may conclude that both authors refer to the damage Urfa had suffered in the Celali uprisings, but that Evliya is interested in signs of recovery, while Tavernier remains non-committal on this issue.

EUROPEAN ARCHIVAL SOURCES: DEALING WITH NINETEENTH-CENTURY CITIES

Up to this point, our focus has been on narrative sources from the late sixteenth century to the eighteenth. However most of the European evidence on the Ottoman Empire is not narrative at all, but archival. It has been introduced briefly in chapter 3, and in an introductory text such as the present one cannot undertake the systematic evaluation of these materials. But at least a foretaste is in order, and we will briefly discuss the principal European sources which the student working on eighteenth and nineteenth-century Ottoman port cities will want to use. In so doing, we will introduce a few selected monographs on port cities, mostly of recent vintage. During the last fifteen years or so, a great deal of work has been done mainly on the nineteenth century, and Istanbul, Izmir, Beirut, Alexandria and Salonica (Çelik, 1986; Frangakis-Syrett, 1992; Fawaz, 1983; Ilbert, 1996; Anastassiadou, 1997) have all been well covered. On all these cities, French, English and, in some cases, Austrian documentation is quite abundant. Moreover by dwelling on cities with port facilities, we will continue the discussion of urbanism which has characterised earlier sections of this chapter.

A 'long' eighteenth century, extending down to 1820, forms the focus for the study of Izmir by the Greek-American scholar Elena Frangakis-Syrett (Frangakis–Syrett, 1992). In the first three chapters, the port and city themselves are discussed, while the second part of the book is largely concerned with the trade of French and English merchants, who imported woollen cloth and exported raw silk, cotton or mohair. In the London Public Record Office, the author has studied both Levant Company and consular correspondence. As to the French sources, she relies to a considerable extent on the archives of the Foreign Ministry. Both consular correspondences and the series 'Mémoires et Statistiques' furnish information on the volume of trade; these sources are supplemented by the archives of the French Navy and those of the Chambre de Commerce in Marseilles. This focus on trade statistics explains why the author has concentrated on European sources. For, unfortunately, the eighteenth-century documents on Izmir tax farms available in the Ottoman archives usually contain amalgamations of many different revenue sources, and are therefore difficult to interpret from a trade statistician's point of view.

Leila Fawaz, a Boston historian of Lebanese background, has written a study of nineteenth-century Beirut which equally stresses commerce (Fawaz, 1983). Apart from French and English archives, she has made use of Egyptian, Lebanese and US American official repositories. But where the source base is concerned, her most notable achievement is the extensive use of private archives generated by notable Beiruti families (see chapter 3), in addition to interviews with some of their older members. Throughout, Fawaz' history of this major port on the Syrian littoral is overshadowed by the Lebanese civil war, which was going on at the time the book was being written and published. Nineteenth-century migration from rural areas is thus viewed both as a short-term boon and a long-term bane. Migrants within a few decades turned Beirut from an insignificant town into a hub of commerce. But rapid urbanisation also brought with it an increase in sectarian tension, as Christians took advantage of the new opportunities more easily than Muslims. That new-found wealth was often flaunted in lavish consumption certainly did not help matters. Tensions of this type were less overt among prosperous local merchants, Sunni Muslim, Orthodox or Maronite, as the latter found cooperation across sectarian lines an advantage in the face of strong competition from foreign traders. But among poor immigrants, with little to lose, tensions built up which were to have catastrophic results in the century that followed.

While the urban lower classes thus constitute an important player in the model of urban expansion used by Fawaz, Donald Quataert is one of the few scholars to have actually studied porters and boatmen in their very own habitat, namely the Istanbul quais (Quataert, 1983, pp. 95–120). Quataert's interest is not in the port *per se*, but in the beginnings of an Ottoman working class. His port workers thus take their places next to the coal miners of Zonguldak and the employees of the Anatolian railway. Two major themes are interwoven in Quataert's study. On the one hand, he deals with the long-term survival and ultimate dissolution of waterside guilds in Istanbul, and on the other, with the ethnic and sectarian tensions which strongly impeded the coalescence of wageworkers into a modern-style working class. As to the source basis, Quataert has not only brought together Ottoman and French archival material. He has equally made good use of West German archives, but also of materials located, at the time of writing, in the German Democratic Republic's repositories of Potsdam and Merseburg.

But what may be considered the major monograph on nineteenth-century Istanbul has rather a different focus. Zeynep Çelik, an architectural historian based in New York, has produced a study in which the projects of different luminaries from the Paris École des Beaux Arts for the 'beautification' of the Ottoman capital play a central role. This visual material, partially reproduced in her book, has been supplemented by Ottoman archival sources and newspapers. A sense of tragicomedy or black humour dominates the chapter focusing on the Beaux Arts drafts; for the eminent architects consulted projected pretentious squares and vistas often without any knowledge about the topography of the site. Thus, a project for Beyazit Square and the gardens of the War Ministry, which today houses various faculties of Istanbul University, completely ignores the fact that beyond the Beyazit Mosque, lies the vast historical complex of the Grand Bazaar . . . The search for a style appropriate to nineteenth-century official building in Istanbul,

9. Salonica around 1900. Even though the port was being modernised and nineteenth-century architecture was making an appearance (see buildings in the foreground) the general atmosphere was still quite provincial.

which was meant to be ecclectic and yet 'ottomanising', constitutes another major theme of Çelik's work. How stylistic considerations and the constraints of Istanbul's street-level realities were made to coexist, more or less uneasily, is explained with a wealth of illustrations, which contribute toward making this beautifully produced book a classic of its genre (Çelik, 1986).

During the second half of the nineteenth century, large Ottoman cities, and especially the major port towns, acquired such amenities as access to the railway, a modernised harbour, suburbs inhabited at least partly by the better-off, a tram, and a waterfront street lined with shops and cafés. An educational system more adapted to the needs of the time than the Muslim *mekteps* or Jewish Talmud-Thora schools was also instituted. These urban renewal projects were only to a limited extent financed directly by the

Ottoman state, as the administration was overwhelmed by war-related problems. In most cases, the Ottoman state merely laid out the parameters for renewal projects, while the organisation and financing lay in the hands both of local notables and of the European companies which had obtained the relevant contracts.

This is the context in which we can situate the recent monograph on nineteenth-century Salonica by Meropi Anastassiadou (Anastassiadou, 1997). In the period under discussion, the city was still inhabited by large Turkish and Jewish communities, and the events which were to reshape Salonica as a Greek city were as yet looming on the horizon. For her history of late nineteenth-century Salonica, Anastassiadou has brought together Ottoman, French and Greek sources. In the first category, there are kadi registers and records concerning pious foundations, as well as official year-books (*salnames*). Among sources located in France, she has worked exten-sively in the Foreign Ministry archives, where she has used not only the – by now conventional – consular correspondence, but also the estate inventories of French citizens who died in Salonica (on the problems posed by these sources, see Anastassiadou, 1993). Among Greek sources, she has examined the regulations governing different voluntary associations with Greek mem-bership, in addition to a cadastre referring to real estate owned by Greek Orthodox proprietors.

As to the Jewish part of the Salonica population, in Anastassiadou's study it is represented mainly through the archives of the Alliance Israélite Universelle. This French-based organization financed 'modern-style' schools for Jewish children, and demanded regular reports from the teachers whose salaries it paid (Dumont, 1980). These letters include information about the social situation of the parents, or the resistance of conservative rabbinical circles to the 'lay' educational values which the Alliance schools imparted. Courses suggested by the teachers relate to the vocational options perceived by students and their parents, so that the Alliance archives can also be used as a guide to the aspirations of different late-Ottoman Jewish milieus.

Anastassiadou has dealt with Salonica as a late Ottoman city, and the transformations which followed the annexation by Greece in 1912 remain outside of her purview. Robert Ilbert's work on Alexandria also discusses the nineteenth and early twentieth centuries (Ilbert, 1996). But because from the early nineteenth century onward, this city was governed by Mehmed Ali who had managed to establish himself as an autonomous ruler, Alexandria can be characterised as 'late Ottoman' only to a limited extent. Yet this city shares certain features with Salonica, largely linked to the emergence of a fairly cosmopolitan 'Mediterranean port' society in the nineteenth century; this society was rapidly dismantled when the city passed under the control of a national state, be it Greek or Egyptian. Ilbert's major source are the Alexandria municipal archives, with documents partly in French and partly in Arabic. This material is supplemented by the archives of private institutions located in the city, such as schools, but also by documents from the Egyptian state archives and European consular correspondence. In spite of its recent date of publication, Ilbert's work has the spacious proportions of an old-style French *thèse d'état*, and in certain aspects, may be read as a *roman fleuve*. As a standard for comparison, and particularly for the multitude of sources covered, it should not be ignored by researchers working on Ottoman port towns in the narrower sense of the word.

This rapid survey of recent studies of late Ottoman port cities has shown that Western European archival sources remain important, but now are normally confronted with Ottoman, Egyptian or Greek documentation. Studies built exclusively on European materials are becoming increasingly rare. This is partly due to the fact that certain scholars – Çelik, Quataert and Ilbert may be cited in this context – are strongly aware of the imperialist agendas behind a large share of the European documentation. Supplementing it by a different perspective thus becomes an urgent concern. Moreover the interest in archives located in Beirut, Salonica, Istanbul or Alexandria is also due to the fact that quite a few of the studies referred to have been written by people with strong links to the locality in question. These authors have been able to mobilise their local contacts in order to obtain access to archives, quite apart from the sympathies toward a given city's peculiarities which a lengthy residence may induce.[8]

COPING WITH BIASES

Postcolonial historiography has made us aware of the problems inherent in European accounts, both travelogues and scholarly disquisitions. Self criticism on the part of the historical profession is certainly called for: we have seen that the very concern for scholarly standards has blinded many authors to the realities in front of their very eyes. Quite frequently, the 'modern' inhabitants of Anatolia, Egypt or Syria have paled into insignificance before the contemporaries of the Pharaohs or the representatives of Biblical and classical antiquity. Moreover, this selective blindness was not

---

[8] Among the five major port cities of the eastern Mediterranean, Izmir seems to be the locality with the smallest amount of local documentation. This is in large part due to the fire which destroyed the city in 1922.

In a particularly eloquent fashion, the preface of Ilbert to his work on Alexandria voices the emergence of sympathies with local society in the course of research (Ilbert, 1996).

innocent: Middle Eastern contemporaries were often regarded by European scholars as the uncivilised inhabitants of a land of ancient civilisation, which by implication they did not deserve to own.

Religious and ethnic biases further complicate the picture painted by European travellers. To begin with the religious aspect, for the most part, the authors of travel accounts lacked the information to evaluate correctly the Islamic practices they encountered. Even in the Renaissance period, many texts available to the educated layman did not provide an even moderately accurate picture of Islam as a monotheistic religion. In consequence, the ideas of many travellers on this score were contaminated by notions derived from the paganism of classical antiquity, if they were not confabulations pure and simple (Daniel, 1993, pp. 302ff.).

Moreover since many travellers did not know either Ottoman or Arabic, their contacts were limited to people with whom they could converse in Italian, or later in French. This meant that they derived many of their stories from Ottoman Christians, and not necessarily from the most well-informed within this group. Contacts of passing European travellers with long-established Ottoman Christians were often casual; the Latin domination of certain parts of the eastern Mediterranean in the high and later Middle Ages had left a legacy of ill-will that was not easily overcome, and this resentment may have affected the quality of the information relayed to western visitors.

Another possible source of information for the European visitor were the Hungarians, Italians, Germans and Poles who, particularly in the sixteenth and seventeenth centuries, entered the Ottoman realm as captives or volunteers, and in due course became Muslims. Such people were often employed by the Ottoman authorities to manage contacts with infidels. But in all likelihood, many of these newcomers to the Ottoman world spoke only a limited amount of Ottoman Turkish, and nobody knows to what extent they could read the language of their new homeland. As a result, even with the best of intentions on both sides – which cannot always be assumed – much misinformation must have reached the notes of visitors through this channel.

Some of the caveats relevant to travelogues also apply to European archives. Many archival reports possess a degree of affinity to travel accounts, only they are usually shorter and less elaborate. In order to make good use of this narrative material, it is important to understand what demands the author of the relevant report was trying to satisfy. A good consular report for instance contained information useful to merchants of the relevant nation. In addition to economic data, the attitudes of local government officials and/or tax farmers were often relayed and commented upon. Some invest-ments in the local infrastructure were - to a degree - controlled by Ottoman government agents, who could further or hinder the activities of foreign merchants. As a result, the evaluation of the performance of the post-Tanzimat bureaucracy may take up a lot of space in consular reports. Now that we know from which point of view these evaluations were made, we will be able to place them into perspective better, which in some cases may mean that we simply discard them.

In addition, the archives contain quantitative evidence, which has to be treated by simple statistical techniques before it can be of use to the historian. From the eighteenth century onwards, this numerical evidence is quite abundant. It is tempting to assume that these materials provide some relief from the all-pervasive subjectivity of the travellers' accounts and consular reports. Yet we have already noted that quantitative evidence in European archives, no less than its qualitative counterpart, reflects the particular interests of merchants and consular officials, and must be evaluated accordingly.

Economic historians have taken a long time to make allowance for this situation. To mention but one example, goods neither imported nor exported did not normally enter the sphere of interest of foreign merchants. But Ottoman economic history, particularly where the eighteenth and nineteenth centuries were concerned, started life as a discipline largely based upon European sources. This may help to explain why for a long time, scholars have tended to underestimate the internal trade of the Ottoman Empire, as it was not recorded in French or English archives. Recent research has shown up the extent of this misconception, and now that Ottoman documents are becoming accessible in ever increasing quantities, we are, to some extent, able to avoid this particular bias (for a good example of how this can be done, see Genç, 1987). By the same token, we have become aware of the need to examine archival evidence just as critically as literary materials.

SUGGESTED READINGS

Aigen, Wolffgang (1980). *Sieben Jahre in Aleppo (1656–1663), Ein Abschnitt aus den 'Reiß-Beschreibungen' des Wolffgang Aigen*, ed. Andreas Tietze (Vienna: Verlag der Wissenschaftlichen Gesellschaften Österreichs) (Syrian commerce de-scribed by a professional).

Beckingham, C. F. (1983). *Between Islam and Christendom, Travellers, Facts and*

Legends in the Middle Ages and the Renaissance (London: Variorum Reprints) (both critical and colourful).

Busbecq, Ogier Ghiselin de (1968). *The Turkish Letters of Ogier Ghiselin de Busbecq, Imperial Ambassador at Constantinople 1554 – 1562*, tr. Edward Seymour Forster (Oxford) (Sultan Süleyman's empire as viewed by a humanistically trained diplomat).

[Evliya Çelebi] (1990). *Evliya Çelebi in Bitlis, The Relevant Section of the Seyahatname edited with translation, commentary and introduction*, ed. and tr. Robert Dankoff (Leiden: E. J. Brill) (the traveller's adventures at the court of the khan of Bitlis; includes description of the town).

Gilles, Pierre (1988). *The Antiquities of Constantinople*, tr. John Ball and ed. by Ronald G. Musto (New York: Italica Press) ('period' translation with a modern introduction).

Gyllius, Petrus (1997). *Istanbul'un Tarihi Eserleri*, tr. from the Latin original and introduced by Erendiz Özbayoğlu (Istanbul: Eren) (completes the eighteenth-century translation into English currently on the market).

Maundrell, Henry (reprint, 1963). *A Journey from Aleppo to Jerusalem in 1697*, ed. David Howell (Beirut: Khayat) (well written).

Melman, Billie (1992). *Women's Orients, English Women and the Middle East 1718–1918, Sexuality, Religion and Work* (London, Basingstoke: Macmillan) (critical discussion of women's writing on women).

Montague, Lady Mary Wortley (1993). *Turkish Embassy Letters*, ed. Anita Desai and Malcolm Jack (London: Pickering) (the doyenne of women travellers: sophisticated and thought-provoking).

Pedani Fabris, Maria Pia (1996). *Relazione di ambasciatori veneti al senato*, vol. xiv, *Costantinopoli* (Padua: Bottega d'Erasmo and Aldo Ausilio) (hitherto unknown *relazioni*).

Tavernier, Jean Baptiste (1981). *Les six voyages en Turquie et en Perse*, 2 vols., abridged and annotated by Stéphane Yérasimos (Paris: François Maspéro/La Découverte) (important both for his impact on later European thinking on 'Oriental despotism' and for his great travel experience).

Yérasimos, Stéphane (1991). *Les voyageurs dans l'empire ottoman (XIVe–XVIe siècles), Bibliographie, itinéraires et inventaire des lieux habités* (Ankara: Türk Tarih Kurumu) (the standard work on the subject).

6

ON THE RULES OF WRITING (AND READING) OTTOMAN HISTORICAL WORKS

DELINEATING THE TOPIC

In the present chapter we will deal with literary texts in the broadest sense of the word. By the definition used here, the term 'literary' will denote texts either written for the edification and enjoyment of a limited number of readers, more or less known to the author, or for the eyes of an anonymous public. This means that we are concerned with texts intended for publication. But since in the Ottoman world, the printing press did not come into widespread use before the nineteenth century, the term 'publication' is also in need of clarification. Writers and potential writers met in 'salons' (*meclis*) where they might read their works or informally show their manuscripts to their colleagues (Fleischer, 1986, pp. 22–3), one of the major disadvantages which women needed to overcome being their lack of access to such sessions. Presenting one's work at a literary gathering should be regarded as a form of publication, comparable to the reading of a paper at a scholarly conference in our day. But as a more developed form of publication it was customary to have an elaborate presentation copy prepared. This was handed over to an influential patron, such as the Sultan himself, a vizier, or, at least in the eighteenth century, a princess of the imperial family. The recipient was expected to make the author a gift, usually the only direct remuneration the latter might expect. From the reign of Bayezid II (r. 1481–1512) onwards, registers of gifts made by the Sultan have survived; they mention a number of poets whose works must have been brought to the attention of the ruler (Erünsal, 1977–79).

In an introductory volume it is impossible to survey all the literary genres cultivated by educated Ottomans, which may become important to the historian of our time. We will therefore place the main emphasis on chronicles, and more briefly introduce biographical dictionaries, 'first-person narratives' such as letters and memoirs, in addition to a recent favourite among Ottomanist historians, namely the periodical press. Fiction and poetry have been excluded, partly for reasons of space, and partly because they demand a kind of expertise not available to this author. When dealing with these materials, the historian with no training in comparative literature needs to tread warily. For literary genres with an historical con-tent, such as saints' lives, chronicles, biographies or autobiographies have been extensively studied, not only by mediaevalists or Byzantinists, but also by specialists in comparative literary studies (for an early example, see Jolles, 1958). Unfortunately, this kind of work has interested only very few specialists concerned with Ottoman literature, so that there exists no well-developed scholarly tradition which could be introduced to the beginner. Moreover due in part to the lack of cooperation between Ottomanist historians and specialists in comparative literature, we know rather little about the rules by which even the major genres of Ottoman prose fun-ctioned in different periods. As a result, historians have sometimes sought to extract information from literary genres which the latter cannot provide and were not meant to provide, as students of Ottoman hagiographical texts especially have found out to their cost.

FROM FRONTIER PRINCIPALITY TO EMPIRE: THE FIFTEENTH-CENTURY CHRONICLERS

If the surviving texts are any guide, Ottoman chronicle writing began in the fifteenth century, about 150 years after the establishment of the Ottoman principality (Köprülü, 1959 and 1966 constitute early and import-ant attempts to come to terms with the 'mythological' character of so many early Ottoman sources). Within a group of interrelated texts, the works of Oruç (fl. late fifteenth and early sixteenth centuries), Ibn Kemal (1468?–1534), Mevlana Neşrî (d. before 1520) and Aşıkpaşazade (1400–after 1484) merit special attention (for a good explication of this complicated issue, see Imber, 1990, pp. 1–13). The time lag between the events described and the extant chronicles means that authors had to rely on older written sources, such as the chronicle of Yahşi Fakih, and probably on oral testimony as well. This situation obviously facilitated the refashioning of events into a 'usable past'. Exact dating of events was not necessarily a major preoccupation, and the accounts of early Sultans may well have been intended largely as moral statements, contrasting the virtues of the simple and accessible earlier *beys* with the elaborate court ceremonial of Sultan Bayezid I (1389–1402). Or possibly some of these descriptions were intended as indirect criticisms of Sultan Mehmed II (1451–1483), who governed the Ottoman Empire while the authors of the older surviving chronicles were at work.

Establishing the links between different chroniclers has exercised the ingenuity of philologically minded historians ever since the 1920s. But the debate has been considerably advanced by two fairly recent contributions. Stéphane Yérasimos has examined a group of anonymous chroniclers from the end of the fifteenth century, active under Mehmed the Conqueror's son Bayezid II (1481–1512) (Yérasimos, 1990). These authors relayed a number of stories concerning the Aya Sofya, the former Hagia Sophia recently turned into a mosque. Only some of these stories were derived from mediaeval sources either Arab or Byzantine, while for others no source has been located; probably they were fifteenth-century inventions. With great ingenuity, Yérasimos has attempted to determine why stories about pre-Ottoman Istanbul in general, and the Aya Sofya in particular, became popular among chroniclers at just this time. Several of these anonymous writers depict the history of pre-Ottoman Istanbul as uniquely catastrophic; it was the site of various crimes which the construction of the Aya Sofya, perceived as the one major positive event in this sequence of horrors, was unable to counterbalance.

Perhaps these writings should be linked to a political opposition unable to articulate its major tenets in writing while the conquering Sultan was still alive. But once Bayezid II, known for his disagreements with his formidable father, had acceded to the throne, this opposition did produce a few written statements, circulated anonymously for the sake of caution. In Yérasimos' view, the authors of these texts opposed Mehmed II's 'imperial project', and warned the ruling Sultan against its continuation. Instead of defining himself as a world emperor and heir of infidel rulers, set apart by an elaborate court ceremonial, the Ottoman Sultan was admonished to revive the less formalised court life of his more remote ancestors. Or as an alternative, he might follow the example of the four early Caliphs, the immediate successors of the Prophet Muhammad. This political agenda is not overtly expressed in the surviving texts, and its very existence therefore open to debate. But at the present stage of our understanding, an emerging discussion concerning the future fate of Istanbul can be regarded as a most stimulating hypothesis.

Both Yérasimos and Cemal Kafadar, who in a recent study has produced a sophisticated evaluation of Ottoman fifteenth-century chronicles, share an interest in uncovering statements which do not lie at the surface of the text to be examined, but have only been alluded to by the authors (Kafadar, 1995). There are numerous reasons why such 'traces of statements' may be found in a given text. In an older version of a given chronicle, stories may have been related which no longer seemed acceptable in the light of more recent political developments. However, not all editors were really good at their jobs, so that traces of the original statements sometimes remained even after the text had been refashioned. But this does not necessarily mean that the oldest surviving texts contain the most reliable information. Sometimes, as Kafadar points out, relatively recent texts may relay versions probably found in the earliest tradition, no longer available to us, but which had been edited out of the oldest *surviving* texts (Kafadar, 1995, pp. 105–109).

As an example, Kafadar highlights the possibility that, in the course of a disagreement over policy, Sultan Osman, regarded as the founder of the Ottoman state, may have murdered his uncle Dündar. In the reign of Mehmed the Conqueror, when the earliest available chronicles were mostly composed, the rule that a Sultan acceding to the throne should kill his brothers in order to forestall civil war, had only recently been codified. Since this new rule probably aroused opposition both on political and moral grounds, relaying a story of 'murder in the family' might have been considered objectionable in the 1470s or 1480s. But by the early sixteenth century, when the later among the relevant texts were written, the rule of fratricide had become part of the customs of the Ottoman dynasty, even though this did not mean that all criticism of the practice had ceased. Therefore Mevlana Neşrî (d. before 1520) and Ibn Kemal (d. 1534) had few inhibitions about mentioning the stories of Osman's murder of Dündar, which their immediate predecessors had passed over in silence. Unfortunately it could equally well be argued that the murder of Dündar by Osman, if widely believed, would have facilitated the defence of the new practice of murdering princes not acceding to the throne. This alternative possibility should remind us that, given our lack of information, quite a few of the most stimulating assumptions we may generate are not amenable to proof (Kafadar, 1995, p. 105 shows that the author is well aware of the problem).

When engaging in this kind of historical detective work, it is of course helpful if the texts themselves contain indications concerning the manner in which they were put together. If we can compare variant versions, preferably datable ones, we may find out in which parts of their works the relevant chroniclers, or the authors of later revisions, refashioned their texts according to the demands of the times. Unfortunately in the case of the early Ottoman chronicles, so many intertextual relationships remain unknown that it is difficult 'to catch the authors at their tricks'. Kafadar himself expresses his awareness of this difficulty, by the cautious phrase: 'one is tempted to conclude . . .' (Kafadar, 1995, p. 108).

Not in all instances, however, do we need to engage in the ingenious reconstructions outlined above. Some early Ottoman chroniclers seem to have expressed their views much more directly. This is particularly true of Aşıkpaşazade, descendant of a distinguished dervish family, who at the beginning of his long life, had participated in Ottoman campaigns in the Balkans. When he wrote his chronicle of Ottoman Sultans in the 1480s, he was living in retirement in Istanbul, and at least was not any more held back by career considerations (Imber, 1990, p. 258). This may help us explain why Aşıkpaşazade's criticism is often quite blunt. But even he placed his most trenchant remarks in chapters concerning rulers long since deceased, and usually direct attacks were aimed at the rulers' servitors rather than at the Sultans themselves.

Among the people Aşıkpaşazade especially disapproved of we find Mehmed II's vizier Rum Mehmed Paşa. Our chronicler even claims that Mehmed Paşa, of Greek descent, was trying to take revenge for the conquest of Istanbul by sabotaging the Ottoman settlement of the city (Aşıkpaşazade ed. Giese, 1929, pp. 162–166 and elsewhere). But Aşıkpaşazade also had friends among former Christians who had won political influence at court. Mehmed II's Grand Vizier Mahmud Paşa (Angelović) even becomes one of the heroes of the later part of Aşıkpaşazade's chronicle. Yet our author judiciously avoids commenting on Mahmud Paşa's execution at the hands of his Sultan and former friend. The last reference to Mahmud Paşa concerns the Grand Vizier's deposition, accompanied by the author's mournful exclamation 'God knows [it].' (Aşıkpaşazade, ed. Giese, 1929, p. 174).

Another case of some ambiguity concerns Aşıkpaşazade's treatment of Halil Paşa of the Çandarlı family. In the reign of Murad II (1421–1451, with interruptions) Çandarlızade Halil Paşa had pursued a brilliant career, culminating in the position of Grand Vizier during the conquest of Istanbul. But while Aşıkpaşazade sings the praises of both Murad II and Mehmed II, his account of Halil Paşa's end is quite reticent. During the Istanbul siege of 1453, Halil Paşa allegedly had received bribes from the Byzantines, though our author leaves it open whether the Grand Vizier did in fact help the enemy in exchange for the money he had pocketed. Aşıkpaşazade again avoids discussing Halil Paşa's execution; however he does not simply pass the event over in silence. To the contrary, by stating that 'everybody knows about it', he makes the reader take note that something unusual had indeed occurred (Aşıkpaşazade, ed. Giese, 1929, p. 132, Uzunçarşılı, 1974, pp. 87–91). This discussion of Aşıkpaşazade's attitudes could be pursued; but even the few cases noted here demonstrate that he tried to state his political views without confronting the Sultan directly.

HISTORY WRITING IN THE 'CLASSICAL' AGE: MUSTAFA ÂLI AND HIS WORLD

As a result of bureaucratic expansion and a larger number of trained scribes, the later sixteenth century witnessed a veritable explosion in the number of written sources. It is therefore possible to know a great deal more about Mustafa Âli (1541–1600) and his contemporaries than about chroniclers who flourished one or two generations earlier. Moreover, Âli constitutes a special case, as he had a great deal to say about his own life and career, particularly the frustrations encountered in the latter (Fleischer, 1986). Âli was a prolific writer in different genres including chronicles, campaign accounts, artists' biographies, manuals on etiquette, travel accounts and poetry, even though neither contemporaries nor later generations regarded him as a major poet.

Reflection on the reasons for the setbacks in his career, which to an outside observer would appear distinguished though not top-level, permeates Âli's entire history writing. To understand what he is talking about, and to judge whether his strictures on the Ottoman bureaucracy are fair or not, one needs to have a reasonably detailed understanding of the Ottoman bureaucratic setup of his time. Fleischer's study, though intended as an intellectual biography, therefore discusses in some detail the changes which the Ottoman central and provincial administrations underwent during the second half of the sixteenth century (Fleischer, 1986, pp. 201–34). But the focus of Fleischer's study is the reaction of a highly talented and personally quite idiosyncratic member of this Ottoman establishment to the political system in which he pursued his career.

Âli seems to have assumed that the system which refused to promote a man of his talents had some deep-seated flaws, which he identified particularly with the venality of office which was making inroads at the time. Another source of disillusion, closely connected to the first, was his realisation that Ottoman rules of good government (kanun-ı osmani) were often impossible to enforce, especially in frontier provinces (Fleischer, 1986, p. 270). In Âli's view, the weaknesses of government were closely linked to the weaknesses of the incumbent Sultan. At least in the mind of this writer, the ruler was responsible for much if not everything that happened in Ottoman state and society, due to the absolute power he wielded or at least was

presumed to wield. According to Âli, particularly the diffusion and mainte-
nance of Islamic high culture in Anatolia and Rumelia was the direct
responsibility of the Sultan. For this culture had been implanted quite
recently among a population (both Muslim and non-Muslim) which had no
prior experience in handling it, and in Âli's rather jaundiced view, was only
too ready to revert to its accustomed ways (Fleischer, 1986, p. 254).

Paradoxically, Mustafa Âli, perpetually dissatisfied with his own
career, after his death, came to be regarded as a specialist in the production of
bureaucratic ideology, *maître à penser* to numerous intellectually minded
officials of later generations. Though Âli never reached the most prized
positions which the Ottoman governmental system could offer, particularly
his *Counsels for Sultans of 1581* were widely imitated and his claims concerning 'Ottoman decline' enjoyed a long-lived popularity. Down to the second
half of the twentieth century, many Ottomanist historians have accepted
Âli's observations at face value. Only quite recently have some scholars
attempted to place his claims of 'decline' in their literary and political
context (Âli, ed./tr. Tietze, 1979 and 1982; Fleischer, 1986, pp. 267–272;
Fleischer, 1990; Abou-El-Haj, 1991, pp. 23–34).

For all his obsession with his career Âli was a major figure in the
literary scene of his day. A much more modest personage was Mehmed
Fenari, known as Ta'likîzâde, a contemporary of Âli's who was appointed
the fourth court historian (*şehnameci*). This dignity, established in the 1550s,
lapsed in the seventeenth century and was not revived until, under rather
different auspices, either Mustafa Naima or else Raşid was appointed official
historian around 1700 (Woodhead, 1983; see also 'Naʿīmāʾ in *EI*, 2nd edn,
by the same author). Ta'likîzâde and his colleagues (but not eighteenth-
century official chroniclers) were appointed to write about the deeds of their
rulers in verse, modeling themselves on the poet Firdawsī and his epic
recounting the deeds of the rulers of pre-Islamic Iran. Such works were
normally illustrated with miniatures. Ta'likîzâde's *Şehname-i hümayun* re-
counts Mehmed III's campaign into Hungary in 1593–94, along with the
victory of Haçova. His work belongs to the genre of the *gazavatname*,
focusing on a given campaign and celebrating the victories of the commander. In Ta'likîzâde's case, this was the elderly Grand Vizier Sinan Paşa,
incidentally, Âli's mortal enemy. As befits a man of his advanced age, Sinan
Paşa is praised for his prudence in campaign planning. To set off the Grand
Vizier's virtues, another commander is shown as getting into trouble for
assuming that God would help him against the infidels no matter what he
did (Woodhead, 1983, pp. 30–2). Thus while the *gazavatname* was determined by strong genre conventions of extolling bravery, Ta'likîzâde es-

poused a modified version in which mature reflection had a considerable part to play.

FACTIONAL STRUGGLE AND MILITARY PREPAREDNESS: SOME SAMPLES OF 'ADVICE' LITERATURE

As we have seen, Mustafa Âli made a major contribution to this genre by adapting the old Turco-Islamic version of 'advice to rulers' to late sixteenth-century circumstances (on the origins of the genre see the article 'Naṣīḥat al-mulūk' in *EI*, 2nd edn, by C. E. Bosworth). In mediaeval writings of this kind, it had been customary to give general advice to rulers on the manner in which they should conduct their affairs. However the numerous representatives of this genre in the Ottoman world of the seventeenth and eighteenth centuries geared their advice rather to specific crisis situations. Thus Aziz Efendi, whose official responsibilities had long included the relations with Kurdish *beys* along the Iranian frontier, in late 1632 advocated a conciliatory policy toward these potentates: as staunch Sunnis, they could be valuable allies in the campaign for the reconquest of Bagdad which Murad IV was then preparing (Murphey ed., 1985; Howard, 1988).

Other tracts of political advice refer to the parlous state of the military tax assignments (*timar*), which from the late sixteenth century onward, were increasingly reassigned to servitors of the central administration or else to tax farmers. For as the military utility of the *timar*-holding cavallerists declined, the Ottoman financial administration showed no sustained interest in the continuing solvency of *timar* holders. However in the view of many authors of advice memoranda, the *timar* had been *the* symbol of Ottoman prowess, and its abandonment was viewed as both cause and symptom of 'decline'. In this divergence of practice and ideology Douglas Howard sees a clash between 'reality' and 'ideals'. Not rarely, the much-vaunted principle that taxpaying subjects should not be permitted to enter the military was overridden by the need to reward service in the Ottoman armed forces by granting *timars* (Howard, 1988, p. 68).

By the eighteenth century, the *timar* was no longer a central concern of the writers of advice literature. Now the debate rather concerned such matters as the avoidance of wars for which the Ottoman military was insufficiently prepared, and the extent to which 'infidel' novelties might be used by Ottoman soldiers (Aksan, 1993). In surveying this debate, it seems important to keep in mind a point once made by Rifa'at Abou-El-Haj, namely that the advice given by memoranda writers was informed by their position within (or outside of) the Ottoman bureaucracy (Abou-El-Haj,

1991, pp. 24–8). Officials attempting to outmanoeuvre their rivals might use the arsenal of 'political advice to rulers' as a weapon against their opponents. In consequence, the modern historian should use this material with a critical mind. This statement needs underscoring, for 'corruption' and 'decline' have long been favourite topoi not only of seventeenth-century Ottoman 'advice' literature, but also of both modern Turkish and European-American historiography.

HISTORY WRITING IN THE SEVENTEENTH AND EIGHTEENTH CENTURIES

Unfortunately no studies comparable to Fleischer's work have been undertaken for Âli's younger contemporaries Selaniki and Peçevi. However we do possess a few secondary studies relating to authors of the mid seventeenth century. Kâtip Çelebi (1609–1657) produced a chronicle in Arabic and then expanded this work into a Turkish version known as the *Fezleke*. The Turkish text and its sources have been studied by Bekir Kütükoğlu, who has identified the author's autograph (Kütükoğlu, 1974).[1] Also called Hacı Kalfa in European accounts, Kâtip Çelebi was a man of wide interests, active as a cultural critic, geographer, bibliographer and chronicler. His contribution to 'advice literature' is also much esteemed, due to the author's moderation and aversion to fanaticism of any kind (Kâtip Çelebi, tr. Gökyay, 1968, p. 166; Inalcık, 1973, p. 183).

In the present chapter, we are concerned with the manner in which Ottoman writers both established genre conventions and struggled against the limitations involved therein. In this context, a major aspect of Katib Çelebi's work is his interest in the world outside the Islamic oecoumene (on his biography see Collective work, 1957; for a selection of his works in modern Turkish, see Kâtip Çelebi, ed. Gökyay, 1968). Apparently the author felt that there was no reliable information available to the Ottoman reader on the affairs of Europe, which were of considerable political relevance at the time of the Thirty Years War and the Ottoman–Venetian conflict. He therefore commissioned translations of Greek and Latin sources. By collaboration with a former Christian priest, Kâtip Çelebi was able to produce, among other things, a book which contained basic information on European states and the languages spoken therein, and also to give a brief account of the most important tenets of the Christian faith (Kütükoğlu, 1974, p. 7).

From a perusal of the Turkish *Fezleke* it is obvious that Kâtip

---

[1] Apart from the introductory chapter on the uses of history, this chronicle was published in 1286–87/ 1869–71. However, this edition is apparently so unsatisfactory as to be quite misleading (Kütükoğlu, 1974, p. VIII).

Çelebi, in part due to his work as a bibliographer, possessed a broad knowledge both of previous chronicles and of specialised works such as campaign reports. However, when chosing the works on which he based himself, his personal likes and dislikes apparently were not without impact upon his selection. Thus the chronicle of Ibrahim Peçevi (Peçuylu) constituted one of Kâtip Çelebi's favourites. Even where Peçevi summarises texts which our author had also consulted in the original, Kâtip Çelebi at times preferred the version given by Peçevi (Kütükoğlu, 1974, pp. 27–8). On the other hand, Âli's *Künh ül-ahbar*, though extensively used by Ibrahim Peçevi, was regarded with some scepticism by Kâtip Çelebi, who felt that it contained a mass of things both important and unimportant (Kütükoğlu, 1974, p. 17). In Kâtip Çelebi's view, accessibility and brevity were major virtues in an author of historical texts, which he valued over and above literary merit as it was understood by writers such as Âli (Kütükoğlu, 1974, pp. 19, 29).

It would appear that we have here another example of the ancient and still lively opposition between history writing as a literary genre and history as a branch of scholarship. By espousing the scholarly aspect, Kâtip Çelebi may have meant to refer to the *ulema* tradition of history writing as opposed to its courtly counterpart, which, as we have seen, emphasised the literary aspect. But at least toward the end of his life, Kâtip Çelebi also distanced himself rather pointedly from the rigorist movement of the Kadızadeliler which was gaining adherents at that time, and thereby from at least a section of the *ulema* as well (on this movement, see Zilfi, 1986). Thus his emphasis on 'getting the facts right and the message across' also should probably be linked to his involvement, rather special for a man raised in the scribal tradition, with scientific disciplines such as geography.

Istanbul in the seventeenth century boasted a rich crop of intellectuals with an interest in history, and one of them, namely Hüseyin Hezarfenn ('endowed with a thousand skills') continued Kâtip Çelebi's chronicle after the latter's untimely death. Hezarfenn resembled his contemporary Evliya Çelebi in avoiding official posts, and presumably for that reason, no information on him can be found in the biographical dictionaries of the time (*c.* 1610 – *c.* 1691, see Wurm, 1971). However, he was a member of the circle which gathered around the scholarly Grand Vizier Fazıl Ahmed Köprülü. He was also well known to educated members of the French embassy, who admired him and have recorded some details of his life. Hezarfenn also has left traces in the work of the Italian military man and writer Luigi Fernando Marsigli, who considered himself a personal friend (Stoye, 1994).

Hezarfenn's breadth of vision is documented by his 'Tarih-i

devlet-i Rumiye ve Istanbul', which to date has remained unpublished (Wurm, 1971, p. 91). This history of Istanbul in Byzantine times may have been prompted by official interest in the affairs of the Orthodox during the war for Crete (1645–1669). But Hezarfenn was still at work in 1671, after the war had come to an end. Apparently the author did not know any European languages himself, but made good use of the linguistic skills available among his acquaintances. These included the Empire's official translator Nikusios Panagiotis, and also Ali Ulvi, born as the Polish noble-man Albertus Bobovius. In addition, Hezarfenn also composed a kind of world history, known as the 'Tenkih-i Tevarih-i müluk'. Apart from an introductory chapter on the kings of pre-Islamic Egypt and Iran, this work focused on the Islamic world. But later chapters also contained information not only on Rome and Byzantium, but also on China and the discovery of the Americas. A short sampling of 'advice literature', consisting of an almost verbatim quote from Kâtip Çelebi, was integrated into this 'world chronicle' as a concluding chapter, for Hezarfenn obviously believed in the use of history as a guide to practical affairs (Wurm, 1971, p. 98).

For the later seventeenth century and the eighteenth, there are two secondary studies of major chronicle writers, namely Mustafa Naima (Thomas, 1972) and Ahmed Resmi (Aksan, 1995). Thomas' work, edited by Norman Itzkowitz, appeared after the author's death, and is based upon a doctoral dissertation which Thomas undertook under the direc-tion of the formidable Paul Wittek in the immediate post-war years. In its own time, this was a pioneering study, even though a comparison with the work of Fleischer and Aksan shows that great advances have been made in the meantime. Following Wittek's lead, Thomas stays very close to his sources, that is to Naima's chronicle and to the limited number of further texts documenting the life of this writer. Apart from a biography, Thomas provides a summary of certain crucial passages in Naima's chron-icle, in which the author expresses his ideas on the principles of Ottoman statecraft. Naima all but joins two genres, namely the chronicle and 'ad-vice literature'. Thus he explains that states go through a regular sequence of periods, namely formation, consolidation, confident security, surfeit-*cum*-conservatism, and finally disintegration ('the ages of the state', Thomas, 1972, p. 77). This concept had been given a memorable formu-lation in the work of Ibn Khaldun (1332–1382), and was often used by the writers of 'advice' literature. But discourse on this subject was not a common feature in Ottoman chronicles, and by introducing it, Naima took a stand in the political controversies of the time (Abou-El-Haj, 1991, pp. 24–8).

Naima's brief as officially commissioned historian of the Ottoman Empire involved writing up a period which he had not witnessed in person. By contrast, Ahmed Resmi, an active political figure first and foremost, refers to events which had occurred in his own long lifespan (1700–1783). In a sense, Ahmed Resmi's career is characteristic of the new circumstances in which the Ottoman Empire found itself after the treaty of Karlowitz (1699). For while personages such as Mustafa Âli or Naima had wide experience of Ottoman provincial life, they had not travelled beyond the empire's borders; and Evliya Çelebi, who had undertaken such travel, had done so without major official responsibilities. By contrast, Ahmed Resmi fell into the category of ambassador to foreign courts, charged with reporting in detail upon the situation he found there, and he was to pursue a high-level career after his return. This type of political biography was to become typical of Ottoman statesmen in the first half of the nineteenth century (on Ottoman ambassadors' reports, see Unat, 1968).

Ahmed Resmi's two embassies led him to Vienna in 1758 and to Berlin in 1763. While at the time of writing, his embassy reports may not have achieved circulation beyond a small group of high officials, they did possess a significant afterlife (Aksan, 1995, pp. 34–40). In part, these accounts were integrated into later official chronicles, and as separate texts, they went through several editions in the nineteenth-century Ottoman Empire. Ahmed Resmi expressed an interest in economic and cultural phenomena he encountered on his travels. The wry humour with which he recounted the parsimoniousness of the Prussian king Frederick II, and the curiosity of the still rather provincial Berliners for anything exotic, explain why, down to the present day, his account occasionally turns up in publications directed at a non-specialist public.

Even more original were Ahmed Resmi's comments on war and peace, expressed in the accustomed format of advice literature and integrated into an account of the Russo-Ottoman war of 1768–1774 (Aksan, 1995, pp. 198–199). This genre presumably suited the author because by definition it allowed scope for criticism. But Ahmed Resmi went far beyond what had been customary down to his time. He does not hesitate to assume that the same political rules are valid for Muslim and non-Muslim states, warning particularly against an overextension of forces. When a ruler attempts to conquer more lands than his resources and 'natural forces' allow, he will exhaust his subjects with nothing to show for it in the end. As a prime example of this kind of political miscalculation, the author points to Süleyman the Magnificent's expansionist policies in the Yemen and the western Mediterranean, which ultimately produced no lasting results. As Süleyman the Lawgiver was regarded as *the* model Ottoman Sultans were supposed to imitate, Ahmed Resmi's statement constituted a bold departure from the conventions of advice literature. His advocacy of peace as a major asset and his insistence upon the need to stay within 'natural boundaries' implied the assumption that the fortunes of war were determined by this-worldly strategies and resources. In Ahmed Resmi's view, one could not rely on a quasi-automatic expansion of the Islamic realm (Aksan, 1995, pp. 195–205).[2]

NINETEENTH-CENTURY INNOVATIONS

For a nineteenth-century link in the chain of chroniclers *plus* authors of advice literature, we will now turn to the writings of Ahmed Cevdet (1823–1895). Cevdet can be compared to Mustafa Âli due to his training as an *alim* before he transferred into the central administration (Chambers, 1973; Neumann, 1994). But he was much more successful than Âli had ever been, leaving the *ilmiye* after having risen to the position of *kadıasker*. During the reign of Sultan Abdülhamid II (1876–1909) Ahmed Cevdet was at one time Grand Vizier, and played the role of accuser against Midhat Paşa. First a reforming governor of Rumeli and Bagdad, and during his own tenure as Grand Vizier, father of the first Ottoman constitution, Midhat Paşa was banished to Taif, and ultimately murdered. This end to the story has presumably contributed toward the image of Cevdet Paşa as an out-and-out conservative (Meriç, 2nd printing 1979). Yet outside of his official functions, Cevdet Paşa's ideas were much more variegated. Thus, when the Paşa realised that the most talented of his children was a daughter, he had her carefully educated. With his blessing, Fatma Aliye (1862–1936) grew up to be a member of the first generation of modern-style female intellectuals in the Ottoman Empire (for recent studies of her work, see Findley, 1995a and b).

As a public official, Cevdet's major achievement is the codification of the Hanefi version of the *şeriat*. This text was intended to serve as the empire's civil code, but the project was interrupted after some years, and only completed by the family code of 1917 shortly before the collapse of the empire. As a literary figure, Cevdet Paşa is especially noted for his history of

---

[2] As he was both an Ottoman Armenian and, for a while, the Swedish ambassador to the Sultan, it is hard to classify Ignatius Mouradgea d'Ohsson / Muradcan Tosunyan (1740–1807), fluent in Ottoman but writing in French. His well-known *Tableau général de l'Empire othoman*, based upon Ibrāhīm al-Halabī's compendium of Hanefi law and various commentators, is of interest mainly because of the last section, in which the author discusses the Ottoman administration of the later eighteenth century. On d'Ohsson's relations with the representatives of revolutionary France, there is a fascinating article by Kemal Beydilli, fundamental for all subsequent d'Ohsson studies (Beydilli, 1984). Findley (1998) discusses the documentation on this enigmatic figure in French and Swedish archives.

the Ottoman Empire, which encompasses the period from 1774 to 1826. It was commissioned by the textbook task force *cum* academy of sciences known as the Encümen-i Daniş (Neumann, 1994, pp. 17ff.; this book contains information on the publishing history of Cevdet Paşa's works).

Throughout his work, Ahmed Cevdet was concerned with making the wars and diplomatic crises of the period discussed intelligible to his readers. He therefore devoted a major section of the fifth volume of his history to the political history of Europe, with special emphasis on the French Revolution. This interest in the changed international context in which the Ottoman Empire now needed to operate has been regarded not only as a methodological innovation, but also as an indicator of Cevdet Paşa's political agenda. After having lived through the mid-century restructuring of the Ottoman state, known as the Tanzimat, its legitimation through historiography apparently formed a major part of Ahmed Cevdet's intentions (Neumann, 1994, pp. 278–83).

By discussing political constellations and military campaigns in context, Ahmed Cevdet also came to introduce a number of formal innovations into the chronicle genre. Thus at least in certain sections, he abandoned the convention of discussing events year by year, with lists of official appointments and obituaries at the end of each section, a format characteristic of the Ottoman tradition of history writing (Neumann, 1994, p. 33). Instead, appendices containing primary sources were attached to certain volumes; older authors, if they had wished to include such material, had normally integrated it into the text of the narration. Moreover, Ahmed Cevdet, though thoroughly familiar with the elevated Ottoman language in which such chronicles had generally been composed ever since the sixteenth century, himself wrote in a language fairly close to the educated speech of his day. He was very conscious of the fact, and justified this break with tradition by the need to be accessible to a broader spectrum of readers (Neumann, 1994, p. 26).

THE OTTOMAN CHRONICLE: A BRIEF SUMMARY

This bird's eye view of chronicle-writing at, or close to, the Ottoman centre has shown that in the course of four centuries, the genre changed profoundly. Certain chronicles can be read as accounts of 'heroic conquests' (*gazavatname*). But many sixteenth- to eighteenth-century authors, while not spurning the *gazavatname* format altogether, placed more emphasis on events happening in the Ottoman capital, such as the appointment of dignitaries, major fires or rebellions. Language use also varied. Fifteenth-century chronicles were often written in a relatively straightforward Turkish. But from the sixteenth century onward, the use of literary Ottoman became more widespread. In particular, certain eighteenth-century chroniclers are known for their elaborate style and Arabo-Persian vocabulary, which made their texts inaccessible to all but the most highly educated. But even authors who favoured this literary style – and there were gradations even in the seventeenth or eighteenth century – did not necessarily use it from beginning to end in their books. Elevated style might thus serve to emphasise certain sections of a chronicle. In the nineteenth century, as we have seen, the use of elaborate style came to be questioned, first by authors who aimed at a wider public and later, in the last decades of the empire, by nationalists wishing to get rid of non-Turkish words. Unfortunately, the number of chronicle studies taking account of literary style is as yet quite limited, so that it is difficult to make definite statements on the evolution of chronicles from the stylistic point of view (for an exception, see H. Lamers in Van Bruinessen and Boeschoten eds., 1988, pp. 62–70).

On the other hand, certain conventions remained constant throughout the centuries. Authors proceeded year by year and used the reigns of individual Sultans as the basic grid for the organisation of their narrative material. We have noted how Ahmed Cevdet wrestled with this convention when he wished to discuss long-term developments. Another constant was the use of the chronicle as a vehicle of political comment and criticism directed at the author's own time. We have seen that the story of the early Sultans as relayed by fifteenth-century chroniclers was largely governed by such considerations, while nineteenth-century authors such as Ahmed Cevdet and his conservative successor Ahmed Lütfi used their respective histories to debate the merits of the Tanzimat (Neumann, 1994, p. 46).

CHRONICLES IN THE PROVINCES

Ottoman authors who tried to make their way in Istanbul usually had little incentive to discuss provincial concerns. But a number of chronicles, recounting events in a single city or province, do survive. One of the oldest is the seventeenth-century account of life in Serres (today Serrai in Greek Thrace) by a priest named Papa Synadinos. This text relays local events such as famines and epidemics, the arrival of bishops and assorted disputes within the Orthodox community. The author did not hesitate to include information appropriate to a family memorial; thus we hear about his marriage or the births and deaths of his children. Moreover, Synadinos compiled short biographies of Serres Orthodox notables, organised according to the years of their deaths as was also common in chronicles written by Muslims. However, he was less restrained in his comments than the writers of the more formal texts composed in Istanbul, freely relaying not only the virtues, but also the vices and weaknesses of the persons concerned. We learn a great deal about the more or less crooked deals involving the finances of the Serres Orthodox community, nor are deficiencies in the training of local priests passed over in silence (Odorico *et al.* eds., 1996. pp. 71–9, compare also Strauß, to be published).

Even though Papa Synadinos wrote in Greek, his work in certain respects can thus be viewed as part of Ottoman culture in the broader sense of the word. In this short introduction, it is unfortunately impossible to discuss more than a small sample of such provincial writings, especially abundant in eighteenth-century Syria.[3] Mīkhā'īl Burayk, strongly ecclesiastical in orientation, often mentioned his links to Mount Athos, and may have been inspired by Balkan historiography (Masters, 1994). Burayk was an ardent adherent of the Orthodox church and strongly resentful of the activities of Roman Catholic missionaries gathering adherents among the Christians of eighteenth-century Syria. By contrast Yūsuf 'Abbūd, who wrote in Aleppo during the early nineteenth century, was a merchant and an adherent of the movement of Catholic reform, but whose perspective reached beyond ecclesiastical events. Among Syrian Muslims, Aḥmad al-Budayrī is supposed to have been a barber and member of a sufi brotherhood in Damascus. Unfortunately, his work, covering events in his home town, has survived only in an edition by a mid nineteenth century scholar. Ḥasan Aghā al-'Abid was a military man whose responsibilities included the safety of the hajj route. His chronicle is more concerned with political events than is true of the other three accounts. Its value lies in the fact that Ḥasan Aghā relays the view of a man with ample experience of rural Syria, especially the desert routes (Masters, 1994).

All four chronicles, but especially the first three, have been mined by twentieth-century historians for 'facts', but have also been analysed for the cultural attitudes inherent in them. Thus the narrative of 'Abbūd has been extensively used in a major monograph on eighteenth-century Aleppo (Marcus, 1989). All four texts contain a great deal of evidence on the attitudes of Ottoman provincials toward the powers that be, both governors and judiciary. Here there was considerable common ground between Muslims and Christians. But perspectives were similar even beyond the realm of the 'political' in the narrow sense of the term. Thus the misogyny of the Orthodox priest Burayk, always ready to blame the women of his own

---

[3] I thank Arifa Ramovič for pointing out the existence of a local chronicle concerning eighteenth-century Sarajevo, written in Ottoman but to date published only in a Serbo-Croatian translation (Bašeskiya, ed. Mujezinović, 1968).

community for whatever misfortunes might befall the Orthodox, has been viewed as an example of the patriarchal values shared by Muslims and Christians (Masters, 1994).

THE UNIQUENESS OF EVLIYA ÇELEBI

Defying the conventions of genre as accepted by seventeenth-century writers, Evliya Çelebi not only provides the modern historian with mountains of information, but poses special problems of interpretation. The ten volumes of his life's work cover his travels, which mainly took place within the Ottoman frontiers (for the basic biography, see Baysun in *İA*; for later additions, van Bruinessen and Boeschoten, 1988, pp. 3–5). However, in an embassy to Vienna (1665; Kreutel, Prokosch and Teply tr. and annotators, 1987) and visits to western Iran, the Caucasus and East Africa (Prokosch tr. and annotated, 1994) he did move beyond these limits. Within the empire, Evliya apparently possessed the ambition to leave no route untravelled; as a result, he was occasionally tempted to describe places he did not know from personal experience. Evliya crisscrossed Anatolia, the Balkans, Syria, Egypt and the Hijaz, but neither western North Africa nor Mesopotamia seem to have attracted his attention. A focus of interest were the empire's major cities. Thus a whole volume was dedicated to Istanbul, and another to Cairo, while Aleppo, Damascus, Mecca, Medina, Diyarbekir, Bursa or Edirne also were described *in extenso* (see also chapter 6).

Evliya's use of his sources is known through a few monographs focusing on this question (Eren, 1960; Haarmann, 1976) and more cursory treatment by the numerous historians who have analysed sections of his work. Although Evliya had had some training in religious scholarship, a concern with the accurate reporting of statements as found in reputable sources, so typical of the *ulema* ethos, did not determine his writing at all. When discussing Istanbul, for instance, Evliya was quite ready to attribute statements read in one source to another, or to refer to books which he had manifestly never seen (Eren, 1960, p. 127). In cases where his references to inscriptions have been checked against the extant originals, it has been shown that he not infrequently assigned his text to the wrong building. Evliya also used the geographical literature which had begun to flourish in the Ottoman Empire during the sixteenth century, particularly the work of Mehmed Aşık. However, where trustworthy sources gave out, Evliya was not above including stories of his own invention, particularly when narrating the little known 'history' of provincial towns. Thus it seems that Evliya's writing was intended as a travelogue forming part of imaginative literature, and the geographical and historical information for which modern scholars have usually mined Evliya's work is incidental to his purposes (Haarmann, 1976, p. 169).

Evliya Çelebi may have hoped that sorting out the factual from the imaginary would amuse his readers (Haarmann, 1976, p. 168). But before the middle of the nineteenth century, only very few people seem to have read his writings. This lack of interest may be due to the difficulty of placing Evliya's work in any literary genre known at the time. Ottoman literature before the late eighteenth century knew only a few travel accounts, and the narratives of professional story-tellers (*meddah*), which visibly inspired much of Evliya's work, did not form part of written culture. In addition, the traveller's decision to write in an educated but conversational language may also have lowered his prestige, at least before writers began to change their minds on this issue during the second half of the nineteenth century. Evliya's work also included a much broader spectrum of human types than a more conventional Ottoman literary man would have considered appropriate. The craftsmen, merchants, nomads on the hajj route and rebellious soldiers populating his narrative were distinctly beyond the pale of polite society. Last but not least, Evliya's decision to make travelling his chief aim in life, without legitimising this activity by major religious and political motives, must have struck his readers as incomprehensible. Quite conceivably he was regarded as a man who refused the obligation of serving the Sultan, which birth and training had placed upon him, and instead wasted his time on trivialities.

BIOGRAPHICAL COMPENDIA

Throughout the Islamic Middle East, biographical dictionaries encompassing juridical and religious scholars often constituted voluminous works, compiled in order to ascertain the claims of a given scholar to have studied with another. This was meant to ensure an unbroken line in the transmission of Islamic scholarship. Beyond the world of religious scholars, biographical dictionaries were also sometimes compiled, poets constituting a popular subject. This was originally motivated by the view that a close study of Arabic usage, as documented in the works of pre-Islamic and early Islamic poets, was necessary for a proper understanding of the Koran. But even though the study of poets writing in Persian and Ottoman had no religious significance, biographical dictionaries dealing with their lives were also often compiled (Stewart Robinson, 1965)

In such works, biographies were normally grouped according to death dates – in the absence of official registration, the latter were much more widely known than the subjects' dates of birth. In terms of content, these biographies were fairly standard and therefore lend themselves to statistical treatment. It was normal to give some information about the teachers with whom the subject had studied, the offices held, the works authored (if any), a few anecdotes if the compiler was able to get hold of them, in addition to the circumstances surrounding the death of the subject. If the latter had sons who reached prominence in their turn, this was also often noted.

By the sixteenth century this whole tradition had found a secure place in Ottoman history writing. The first representative of the whole genre to be completed in the Ottoman lands was Sehi Bey's dictionary of poets (1538, ed. Kut, 1978) which, as usual in this type of work, also contained samples of verses. During this same period, the scholar Taşköprüzade was working on his voluminous _Shakāık al-nuʿmāniyye_ (compl. 1557–58; German trans. O. Rescher, 1927). Taşköprüzade wrote in Arabic, but his work, which was highly esteemed and much in demand, was soon translated into Ottoman. His continuators preferred to write in this language from the start. Taşköprüzade provided a compendium of scholars and sheiks, in many cases attempting to assess the contribution of a given author to scholarship (Taşköprüzade, trans. O. Rescher, 1927).

In seventeenth-century chronicles, it was not uncommon to end the account of a given Sultan's reign with the biographies of the prominent men who had died during this period. Authors thus combined two genres, namely the chronicle and the biographical compendium. Many buyers must have been happy to acquire two sources of information rolled into one; but the combination may also have been favoured as a means of saving the reader from boredom. For collections of biographies made monotonous reading, and not all users may have been willing to consider variation in linguistic expression a solution to the problem. Nevertheless, the search for variant expressions remained a major preoccupation for anyone who wished to write a successful biographical dictionary; and it has been pointed out that long lists of phrases all meaning 'he died' can be compiled by anyone perusing these compendia (Majer, 1978, p. 51).

Another popular variant were biographical dictionaries dealing with the scholars who had died in a particular _hicri_ century; this tradition had been well established in Mamluk Egypt, and continued in Ottoman times. Thus Nadjm al-dīn al-Ghazzī put together a massive work, containing 6,000 biographies, which covered the tenth _hicri_ century, roughly corresponding to the fifteenth century CE. His work was continued by Muḥammad al-Amīn from the Muḥibbī family, whose members mostly held positions as judges in Syria. Muḥibbī's work comprises 1,290 biographies from the eleventh/seventeenth *hicri* century, while the twelfth/eighteenth century was covered by the work of Muhammad K̲h̲alīl al-Murādī (for further information see the articles on al-Muhibbi and al-Murādī in *EI*, 2nd ed., by C. Brockelmann and H. A. R. Gibb respectively, also Barbir, 1979–80). Al-Muhibbī and al-Murādī were both active in Damascus, and scholars with some connection to that city have therefore been accorded prominent places in their dictionaries. But in principle the net was cast fairly wide. Drafts of biographies obviously intended for inclusion into al-Muhibbī's work have been preserved, concerning people active in the Hijaz and Yemen (see the article al-Muhibbi in *EI*, 2nd edn.).

Among the authors of biographical dictionaries active during the late Ottoman and early Republican periods, Ibnülemin Mahmud Kemal (Inal) takes pride of place (for his biography, compare the relevant article in the *EI*, 2nd edition, by Fahir Iz). Inal produced a biographical dictionary of calligraphers, containing specimens of their work. He also edited poetry with extensive biographical introductions, and in further dictionaries covered both the poets and the Grand Viziers of the later centuries of the Ottoman Empire (for the last named, see Inal, 2nd edn, 1955). Apart from his broad literary culture, Inal's strength lay in his extensive knowledge of archival sources, which he had studied while serving on commissions classifying Ottoman documents, but also in the even-handed approach toward his subjects. A dictionary of Ottoman authors was compiled by Bursalı Mehmed (Mehemmed) Tâhir and published in three volumes, along with a biography of the author (Bursalı Mehemmed Tâhir, 1333–34/ 1914–16 to 1343/1924–25). By contrast, Mehmed Süreyya attempted a dictionary of Ottoman personages from different walks of life, with special emphasis on members of the bureaucracy. Mehmed Süreyya included many people about whom little information is available, and often used the subjects' gravestones as his sources. Since many of these stones have since disappeared, the information relayed by this author is of special value (Mehmed Süreyya, 1308/1890–91 to 1315/1897).

WRITING FOR A RESTRICTED CIRCLE: THE FIRST-PERSON NARRATIVE

For a long time it was assumed that only in very exceptional instances did Ottoman authors write in the first person. Memoirs and autobiographies supposedly came into their own only in the twentieth century. This claim has turned out to be an over-simplification, and while first-person texts are not numerous before the mid nineteenth century, more have been located than had previously been thought possible (Kafadar,

1989). There seem to exist both ideological and technical reasons for the long neglect of texts narrated in the first person. On the ideological plane, European scholars until quite recently have tended to think that first-person narrative is linked to 'individualism'. 'Individualism' and 'enlightenment', however, are regarded as specifically European values, which cannot be found in and should not be attributed to non-European cultures.[4] Moreover, these assumptions often have been endorsed by Turkish writers, many of whom until recently also regarded values such as religion, nationalism or left-wing opinions much more highly than the expression of personal experiences.

But the technical difficulties involved in the search for first-person narratives should not be underestimated either. Texts relaying personal experiences have rarely been copied, and therefore in most cases are available only in a single manuscript. Even worse, such a manuscript may not be extant as a separate volume, but form part of a set of miscellanea bound together (*mecmua*). Such manuscripts, often of extremely diverse content, are notoriously hard to catalogue, and some cataloguers will only record a selection of the works contained in the manuscripts they describe. Certain *mecmua*s may therefore well contain unsuspected treasures, and it is quite possible that totally unknown texts written in the first person will emerge in the future.

Among diary, memoir and letter-writers active down to the Tanzimat, we encounter people from different walks of life, ranging from a *şeyhülislam* to a junior military officer. From the sixteenth century, the most remarkable text of this type is doubtlessly the autobiography of the Chief Architect Mimar Sinan, which, in old age, he dictated to his friend Sâî Mustafa Çelebi (for a publication of the Topkapı Sarayı manuscript and references to earlier publications compare Saatçı, 1990; see also Meriç, 1965). Apart from reporting his diverse professional experiences before becoming the Chief Architect, Sinan's account is memorable for its frank discussion of the author's disputes with powerful personages. For as a janissary officer Sinan fell out with his patron the Grand Vizier over the question whether a bridge he had just built should be fortified or not. The disagreement resulted in Sinan's leaving the janissary corps and becoming a professional architect. More serious was his conflict with Sultan Süleyman, who in the course of his long reign, gave Sinan many of his major commissions. If the old architect's memory was not too treacherous, he seems to have emerged from this conflict as the winner. Sinan's autobiography

---

[4] While these assumptions today carry less conviction among specialists, they are still very prevalent in publications catering for a wider audience.

10. The Süleymaniye, one of Sinan's major works, as it appeared in the early twentieth century. Sinan was permitted to build his own – small and unassuming – mausoleum adjacent to this structure.

demonstrates that in the sixteenth century a major Ottoman architect did not regard himself as an anomymous craftsman, happy to bow to his superiors' judgment. At least in Sinan's case, high-level competence seems to have earned an artist the kind of stature which allowed him to defend his artistic and other choices against viziers and Sultans. That Sinan was able to retain his position even as a very old man, when he had several gifted students waiting to succeed him, indicates that his assessment of the situation may not have been too far wrong.

An even more highly placed memorialist was the late seventeenth-century Şeyhülislam Feyzullah Efendi. In the year 1702, shortly before his death in the uprising known as the 'Edirne event', the head of the Ottoman *ulema* hierarchy recounted both his own career and that of close family members (Türek, Derin, 1969). The two texts written by Feyzullah tell us a good deal about marriage arrangements, family pride and the ways by which the careers of sons and protégés could be advanced by a high Ottoman official. While these strategies were certainly no invention of Feyzullah Efendi's, there is a personal aspect to his story; for when he became the butt of murderous attack in 1703, his nepotism was one of the main points held against him. Feyzullah Efendi thus must have practised family advancement in a way that aroused hostility, possibly because his strategies were spectacularly successful, at least for a time. Incidentally Feyzullah Efendi does not indicate in any way that he was aware of the dangers threatening himself and his family.

Due to the work of Cemal Kafadar, we have already been able to introduce two further seventeenth-century figures who wrote about themselves (Kafadar, 1989, 1992). One of them is the dervish Seyyid Hasan Efendi, whose account constitutes a unique source for everyday life among the propertied classes of seventeenth-century Istanbul. The other text was authored by the only woman of the pre-Tanzimat period whose first-person prose has been published to date, namely Afife Hatun, the female Halveti dervish of Üsküp. From a slightly later period dates the account of Osman Ağa, a junior officer. Captured in 1688, during the Habsburg–Ottoman war of 1683–1699, he did not return to the Ottoman lands until the end of the fighting (Ottoman text, publ. Kreutel, 1980; for a very readable German translation, see Osman Ağa, tr. Kreutel and Spies, 1962).

After the middle of the nineteenth century, personal accounts get somewhat more frequent. We will take a brief look at three examples that have been well studied, namely the memoirs of Leyla (after the adoption of surnames: Saz), the autobiography of Aşçıbaşı Ibrahim Dede and the memoirs of the reforming Grand Vizier Midhat Paşa, which we know only in the shape given to them by the latter's son. Leïla Hanoum (1850–1936), as she is known to the readers of the French version of her book produced by her son Yusuf Razi (Leïla Hanoum, tr. Youssouf Razi, 1991; the Turkish version, bearing the title 'Harem ve saray adat-i kadimesi' was first published as a serial in the daily paper *Vakit* in 1921), was unusually gifted in both poetry and music (Sagaster, 1989, pp. 18–23). Her memoirs were written twice, the extant version having been reconstructed by herself after a fire had destroyed an earlier manuscript before it could be published. But even this first version probably had been written decades after the events it describes, and Leyla Saz was herself acutely conscious of the problems involved. Her principal aim was not to write an autobiography, but to instruct her readers about an institution, namely the Sultan's Harem, on which there was little reliable information. The author thus provides detailed descriptions of furniture and decor. But since a young child presumably did not pay much attention to such matters, Leyla Saz must have collected this information at a later date. She does in fact recount having questioned people who had been in the Imperial Harem at the same time as she was. In the published (second) version of her story, which she had put together from memory when she was in her later sixties, she laments the fact that around 1920, there were no more people living who could have provided details she had forgotten (ed. Youssouf Razi, 1991, pp. xli, 3).

A much longer testimony, reflecting the lives of less highly placed members of the Ottoman bureaucracy, can be found in the memoirs of the civilian army employee Ibrahim b Mehmed Ali (1828–around 1910). Outside office hours, this writer pursued a sufi life in various Mevlevi and Nakşbendi lodges, and is known by the title of Asçıbaşı Dede. His memoirs have been intensively studied (Bremer, 1959; Findley 1983 and 1989), but, possibly due to their great length, only partially published (ed. Koçu, 1960; Bremer, 1959 contains a summary in German). Ibrahim Dede has given a detailed account of his career, including the networks which he developed through marriage, personal service to highly placed officials, and activity in dervish orders. The author did not belong to an elite family and was not highly educated, neither in the established Ottoman style nor in the French-inspired mode that was gaining in career usefulness during the second half of the nineteenth century (Findley, 1989, p. 180). But judicious use of the contacts available permitted him a respectable career, for he had reached the rank of examining clerk (mümeyyiz) in the headquarters of the Second Army, before retiring in 1906, when approaching his eightieth birthday.

The last example to be briefly introduced here is the 'Müdafaaname' ('Book of Defence') by Midhat Paşa. This text is known to us through an edition by Midhat Paşa's son Ali Haydar Midhat (for bibliographical information, see Davison, 1995, p.65). The latter, while in European exile, published a biography of his father in order to vindicate Midhat Paşa's policies, basing himself not only on the 'Müdafaaname', but also on other documents which had been in his father's possession. Both Midhat Paşa's own work and that of his son had political aims, namely to defend the former Grand Vizier against the accusations of the tribunal which had ended the career of the man to whom the Ottoman Empire owed its first constitution. In that sense the Midhat Paşa memoirs as edited by his son constitute one of the first examples of a new mode of writing, namely memoirs written by political figures as a form of self-advertisement and self-defence. As this genre was to flourish in the Ottoman Empire after 1908, as it did in Europe and America, the work of the two Midhats must be viewed as pioneering (Davison, 1995, pp.76–78).

NEWSPAPERS AND THE PERIODICAL PRESS

During the last few years, a considerable amount of work has been done on the periodical press published in the Ottoman centre, as well as in the Balkan and Arab provinces during the second half of the nineteenth century. Locating periodicals has proven an arduous task, sometimes almost as difficult as the original work of publication must have been. Administrative intervention on the part of central and local authorities, and the lack of interest on the part of an as yet very limited reading public frequently forced the publishers of periodicals and papers to abandon the ambitious projects they had originally conceived. Most periodicals were short-lived, and editors who succeeded in publishing a few hundred issues felt a real sense of achievement. The appearance of the one thousandth issue of the magazine *Servet-i fünun* was regarded as a veritable triumph (Kreiser, 1995).

Needless to say, periodicals were regarded as ephemeral and did not arouse the interest of late-nineteenth century book collectors. When a few amateurs became involved in the twentieth century, much material had already disappeared. Moreover the modern historian of periodical literature is hampered by the fact that libraries stocking all publications appearing within the territory of the entire state, or even a given province, did not exist in the Ottoman Empire. As a result, much searching in a multitude of libraries may be required before a full set of a given journal can be assembled, and occasionally we may read of a journal of which no surviving copies could be located. However where the Ottoman provinces comprising modern Turkey are concerned, the task has been facilitated by a number of bibliographical repertories (Özege, 1979; Akbayar, 1985; for an overview over current research, see Prätor, 1998).

The first Ottoman paper, an official gazette known as the *Takvim-i vekayi*, was published in Istanbul from November 1831 onwards. A French version, edited by Alexandre Blacque, began to appear the same year (Koloğlu, 1992a, p.8). As readers of the Ottoman version, there existed a growing number of officials, who could thereby be informed of the intentions of the government. By contrast, the French version was intended for the consumption not only of embassy personnel stationed in Istanbul, but also as a source of information for European newspapers, whose editors would thus be familiarised with the Ottoman point of view. Beginning publication in 1840, the first privately owned paper was the *Ceride-i havadis*, owned by an Englishman named William Churchill; it was heavily subsidised by the Ottoman government (Inuğur, 1992).

But the press did not really become a major feature of Ottoman life until the last quarter of the century, and down to 1908, and again from 1909 onward, it was hampered by censorship rules not only strict but also often unforeseeable in their application. But that was by no means the only difficulty. Given the condition of the roads, it was frequently impossible to bring the papers to out-of-town subscribers within reasonable delays. Moreover, periodicals were available in many coffeehouses, so that the number of individual purchasers was cut down even further. Only in important provincial cities, such as Salonica, Izmir or Beirut, did the relative isolation of readers from the publishing life of the capital permit the development of a lively local press.

Yet in spite of these difficulties, publishing expanded during the last quarter of the nineteenth century. While in Europe, publishing houses long had preceded the emergence of newspapers, in the Ottoman context, it was only the growing demand for newspapers which made the publishing business viable (Koloğlu, 1992 b). During the last decades of the nineteenth century, we also encounter the beginnings of specialised journals, dealing with literature or even philosophy. In some instances, a journal first intended for general circulation gradually might develop a special focus. Thus the composer Sadeddin (Arel) during the years preceding World War I edited the bi-weekly *Şehbal*, modelled on French publications such as *L'illustration*, but increasingly emphasising music. Before the journal ceased publication at the advent of World War I, it had pioneered the new genre of music criticism, organising competitions to find Ottoman words for such novelties as public concerts (Prätor, 1997).

Among the specialist journals, those intended for women have recently attracted some attention. This is due to the activities of scholars with a feminist bent, fascinated by the discovery that a section at least of upper- and middle-class Ottoman women did not passively await the reforms of the early republican period (Çakır, 1994). Quite to the contrary, some of these women took the initiative and campaigned for the improvement of educational and professional opportunities, even though they were usually careful to 'dress up' their demands in suitably altruistic language. The advancement of the younger generation and later, the greater good of the nation constituted favourite legitimising arguments. This kind of rhetoric was all the more persistent as many publications directed at women were written largely by men, the only periodical with an all-women staff being *Kadınlar Dünyası* (Çakır, 1994).

Even under these restrictive circumstances, a few women, sometimes quite young, were able to try their hand at journalism and embark on a professional career in this field. As a notable example one might cite Halide Edip (later: Adivar), who went on to become a novelist, and in her later years, a professor of English literature (Enginün, 1994, pp. 44–45). In late Ottoman Salonica, Sabiha Sertel began to write for the press while still a high-school student. Such work might aid emancipation even on the most personal level. As Sabiha Hanım had decided to marry only a man with whom she had something in common intellectually, but possessed no opportunity to meet eligible young men in the flesh, she selected a fellow journalist whose writings she particularly esteemed (Sertel, 1993, pp. 60–90). In the 1930s and 1940s this husband-and-wife team then took its place among the most distinguished journalists of the early republican period.

Given the impact of censorship, searching the periodical press for the personal opinions of journalists will be more successful outside of the overtly political sections of a given paper. But even here an interpretational effort is often necessary, made difficult by the relative lack of biographical data on people not part of the highest official circles. As one particularly intriguing example, one may cite the case of Beşir Fuad. At the end of the nineteenth century this ex-officer and literary critic, an ardent adherent of the novelist Emile Zola, felt that literature could not be practised without a knowledge of the natural sciences, and wrote essays on this topic. Given the author's convictions, Beşir Fuad's journalistic work on 'popular science' should not be viewed as a simple attempt to diffuse useful knowledge. Presumably these articles were intended as a statement albeit indirect, concerning naturalism in literature. For this topic was highly controversial in the late nineteenth century, not only in the Ottoman Empire but in France as well (Beşir Fuad, ed. Hilav and Özturan, n.d.; Okay, n.d.). There may have been other journalists with hidden agendas which we have not yet succeeded in understanding (for a summary see Faroqhi, 1995, pp. 274–99).

Letters to the editor also at first glance seem to provide an occasion for personal comment, and a recent volume has therefore been devoted to this topic (Herzog et al. eds, 1995). However those contributors who concern themselves with the Ottoman Empire make it clear that personal comment was not a major priority for the editors who selected the material to be published. This fact becomes apparent from a thoughtful study on a journal named al-Muḳtaṭaf, published first in Syria and later in Egypt, which aimed at explaining modern technical inventions and their possible applications in the work of craftsmen, farmers and housewives (Glaß, 1995). More often the 'Letters to the editor' were used as a pedagogical device, to amplify the information already provided in previous articles. This does not imply that the editors necessarily invented the relevant letters; quite possibly they simply made judicious selections from the material at hand. Other studies have shown that in provincial contexts, the correspondence column might be used as a means of relaying local complaints to the centre. Letters which could not be used for this purpose were positively unwelcome to the editors (Strauß, 1995; Prätor, 1995).

WRITING HISTORY AS A FORM OF WRITING

In the present chapter, we have proceeded in a rather empirical fashion, and have not introduced the theoretical discussion concerning history as a branch of literature, which is linked especially to the name of Hayden White (White, 1978; compare also Williams, 1989). But even the down-to-earth, not to say pedestrian, treatment of history-writing as a genre which has been attempted here, is sufficient to show up one of the basic problems of our discipline. Just as Ottoman chroniclers or writers of bio-graphical dictionaries were bound by the conventions of genre, which they could expand and develop but not throw off, our own historical writing is also subject to such conventions. In schools and colleges, to say nothing of graduate school, students spend a good deal of time writing papers, so as to assimilate the conventions of today's expository writing so thoroughly that they become a second nature. We may not any more notice the rules that, for instance, enjoin us to say certain things in the introduction of a book or article. Without further reflection, we will place certain matter in the footnotes rather than in the text. But even so these conventions exist, and limit what we can express just as certainly as the rule that obliged an Ottoman chronicler to organise his material by years and by reigns of Sultans.

We have seen that such conventions did not preclude innovation, and Mustafa Âli, Hüseyin Hezarfenn or Ahmed Cevdet developed new rules concerning language, the use of sources or the arrangement of chap-ters. In fact, so as to avoid creating the impression that genre conventions bound writers hand and foot, this chapter has highlighted the implicit or explicit expression of personal opinion.

But it is still true that often enough, genre conventions limit the capacity of present-day historians fully to understand their sources. After all, these sources have been composed according to rules of genre different from those familiar to the modern reader, who therefore is liable to misinterpret. For this reason, it may be claimed that historical research does not get us any closer to 'the truth'. Viewed in this perspective, writing history is at best a branch of creative writing, and at worst a mere legitimising discourse. Some historians have given up the struggle right from the beginning. Much historical work done in the Nazi period, to cite an extreme case for the sake of clarity, was in fact conceived purely as a legitimising discourse. Many historians of the time explicitly denied being bound by the rules of 'objectivity'. While we would normally see an emphasis on the limitations of all historical work as a preliminary to more, and more sophisticated, criticism, this realisation can also result in an unbounded and therefore uncritical subjectivity.

However most historians do believe that their work is meant to be a hopefully increasingly appropriate interpretation of processes taking place in the outside world. After all, it is the point of books such as the present one to introduce the user to a critical reading of sources, and such an effort would be meaningless if we were not trying to reconstruct developments taking place in a world outside of our consciousness. In consequence, we need to reflect constantly not only on the limits of what could be expressed by a chronicle writer or an author of memoirs in seventeenth or nineteenth-century Istanbul, but also upon our own limitations. This constant dialogue between the researcher and his/her sources would appear to be the very core of our profession. Needless to say, we have no way of knowing how future generations will judge the results of our efforts.

SUGGESTED READING

Aksan, Virginia (1993). 'Ottoman Political Writing, 1768–1808' *International Journal of Middle East Studies*, 25, 53–69 (informative on a period otherwise little studied).

Behar, Cem (1990). *Ali Ufkî ve Mezmurlar* (Istanbul: Pan Yayıncılık) (engaging monograph, by a musicologist, on a seventeenth-century Polish-Ottoman intellectual).

Davison, Roderic H. (1995). 'The Beginning of Published Biographies of Ottoman Statesmen: the Case of Midhat Pasha', in *Türkische Wirtschafts- und Sozialgeschichte von 1071 bis 1920*, ed. Hans Georg Majer and Raoul Motika (Wiesbaden: Harrassowitz), pp. 59–80 (a scholarly 'detective story').

[Evliya Çelebi] (2nd edn., 1987). *Im Reiche des Goldenen Apfels, des türkischen Weltenbummlers Evliya Çelebi denkwürdige Reise in das Giaurenland und in die Stadt und Festung Wien anno 1665*, tr. and annotated Richard F. Kreutel, Erich Prokosch and Karl Teply (Vienna: Verlag Styria) (for fans of Evliya and of Vienna; fascinating annotations).

Findley, Carter Vaughn (1989). *Ottoman Civil Officialdom, A Social History* (Princeton: Princeton University Press) (combines statistics and a qualitative study of an important volume of memoirs; 'required reading')

Howard, Douglas (1988). 'Ottoman Historiography and the Literature of "Decline" in the Sixteenth and Seventeenth Centuries', *Journal of Asian History*, 22,1, 52–76 (useful reading).

Kafadar, Cemal (1989). 'Self and Others: The Diary of a Dervish in Seventeenth-Century Istanbul and First-Person Narratives in Ottoman Literature', *Studia Islamica*, LXIX, 121–50 (put 'first-person narratives' on the agenda of Ottomanist historians).

Köprülü, Fuat (1966b). *Türk Edebiyatı'nda İlk Mutasavvıflar*, 2nd edn. (Ankara: Diyanet İşleri Başkanlığı Yayınları) (one of the books that founded Ottoman history as a discipline).

Kütükoğlu, Bekir (1974). *Kâtip Çelebi 'Fezleke' sinin Kaynakları* (İstanbul: İstanbul Üniversitesi Edebiyat Fakültesi) (by one of the foremost connoisseurs of Ottoman chronicles).

Leıla Hanoum (1991). *Le Harem impérial et les sultanes au XIXe siècle*, tr. and ed. Youssouf Razi, preface by Sophie Basch (Brussels: Editions Complexe) (evocative, but to be read with circumspection).

Neumann, Christoph (1994). *Das indirekte Argument, Ein Plädoyer für die Tanzimat vermittels der Historie, Die geschichtliche Bedeutung von Ahmed Cevdet Paşas Ta'rih* (Münster, Hamburg: Lit Verlag) (intellectual biography; Turkish translation in preparation).

Odorico, Paolo, with S. Asdrachas, T. Karanastassis, K. Kostis and S. Petmézas (1996). *Conseils et mémoires de Synadinos prêtre de Serrès en Macédoine (XVIIe siècle)* (Paris: Association 'Pierre Belon') (beautifully explicates the work of a small town chronicler).

Saatçı, Suphi (ed.) (1990). 'Tezkiret-ül Bünyan'ın Topkapı Sarayı Revan Kitaplığındaki Yazma Nüshası', *Topkapı Sarayı Yıllığı*, 4, 55–102 (perhaps *the* most interesting memoirs of Ottoman literature).

Wurm, Heidrun (1971). *Der osmanische Historiker Hüseyin b. Ǵaᶜfer, genannt Hezār-fenn, und die Istanbuler Gesellschaft in der zweiten Hälfte des 17. Jahrhunderts* (Freiburg i.B.: Klaus Schwarz) (though written in German, this interesting work deserves to be more widely known).

Yérasimos, Stéphane (1990). *La fondation de Constantinople et de Sainte-Sophie dans les traditions turques* (Istanbul, Paris: Institut français d'études anatoliennes and Librairie d'Amérique et d'Orient) (imaginative interpretation).

7

PERCEPTIONS OF EMPIRE: VIEWING THE OTTOMAN EMPIRE THROUGH GENERAL HISTORIES

DELIMITING THE CORPUS OF TEXTS

This chapter is certainly not meant to be a comprehensive and systematic discussion of the manner in which the Ottoman Empire has been perceived in the course of time. Such a topic could easily fill a volume all by itself. More modestly, we will limit ourselves to books written during a relatively short timespan, roughly speaking, the last forty-five years. More-over, the plot does not really thicken until after 1970. At this time Ottoman studies seem to have matured as a discipline, and at least a few Ottomanists began to think they might have something to contribute to the understand-ing of world history[1].

Since we are here concerned with the *history* of Ottoman history-writing, the relevant works have been discussed for the most part in the order of their appearance. However, to avoid losing sight of thematic connections among our texts, a grouping by major topics intersects with the chronological order. In the majority of cases, the first edition has been taken as the basis for classification. But when a later edition has been much amended, in fairness to the author this later text has usually been preferred. Due to the roughly chronological arrangement, we can conveniently high-light the dependence of a given author on his/her predecessors.

In order to delimit a corpus of texts indicating the development of our field, we will concentrate on general works, both single and multi-volume. The period of Ottoman history discussed in the publications to be selected for analysis should be at least a century long. Sections of more

---

[1] But this may well be an optical illusion, an outcome of the fact that my own active participation in the field began at about this time.

encompassing works, for instance on Middle Eastern history as a whole, have been included if the space devoted to Ottoman history consists of at least 120 pages. All the works considered contain some overall evaluation of Ottoman rule and have been written in either Turkish or English[2]. Many of the works under discussion strongly emphasise Balkan history, but histories of individual Balkan countries have not normally been taken into consideration. However, in a few instances, especially where the early history of the Ottoman Empire is involved, books focusing on the territory of modern Turkey have been included in the discussion.

This proceeding has resulted in a choice of thirty-odd books, a limitation unavoidable for pedagogical reasons. But it must be admitted that something is lost by this very selective approach to the field: for many of the finest works on Ottoman history are not general overviews at all, but articles and monographs on more limited topics. In fact, only recently have Ottomanist historians shown much interest in the writing of comprehensive histories of the Ottoman realm. In the 1960s and 1970s, many people believed that such undertakings were premature and should await the time when major research problems as well as limited periods of Ottoman history had been properly explored. In all likelihood, the present-day vogue of general histories also has something to do with cutbacks in library funding. With monographs increasingly difficult to market, scholars are encouraged to write books appealing to a wider public. That general texts cannot be any better than the monographs on which they are based is an unpalatable truth easily forgotten in the process.

When defining our corpus, we have to cope with the fact that the limits between monographs and empire-wide or at least major-region histories are often not clearly perceptible. And what about accounts of the Ottoman world to be found in handbooks of European or general Middle Eastern history? These texts must usually be quite brief, and have therefore been excluded from the present chapter. Yet often they provide the window offering non-Ottomanists a view of what is being done by Ottomanist historians, and have been more influential than their size would lead us to assume.

In applying the rules outlined above, some inconsistencies do occur, and it will always be possible to argue that a given author should have

---

[2] Due to the tyrannical requirements of brevity, French and German publications will be signalled in the reading list along with short comments, rather than discussed in the body of the text. It is most regrettable that I do not read Russian and am therefore unable to evaluate the works published in that language.

been included and another left out. Obviously, subjective factors do play a part, and I do not claim to have found the optimal solution.[3]

FROM THE END OF WORLD WAR II TO 1970

We will begin our bird's eye view of overall Ottoman histories with the works of Ismail Hakkı Uzunçarşılı. Among his major undertakings figures a four-volume history of the Ottoman Empire, which for the nineteenth century was complemented, in three volumes, by Enver Ziya Karal. Since volumes III and IV of Uzunçarşılı's work consist of two parts each, published under separate covers, the number of volumes written by Uzunçarşılı, as they actually appear on the shelf, is six instead of four (2nd printing, 1977–1983). The narrative is organised by reigns of sultans. Campaigns are given pride of place; at appropriate points, the chronological sequence is interrupted to make room for the discussion of the empire's foreign relations, with the material organised state by state. These chapters, which can be found especially in the second section of the third and fourth volumes, discuss agreements with foreign rulers. These sections also contain biographical data on Ottoman officials. The model of Ottoman chronicle design remains visible in the background of Uzunçarşılı's work.

In addition, this author has produced a series of books on five major branches of the Ottoman administration, namely the janissaries and other military corps on the central government's payroll (Uzunçarşılı, 2 vols., 1943; 1944), the Palace (Uzunçarşılı, 1945), the central government itself and the navy (Uzunçarşılı, 1948; the section on the navy now to be supplemented by Bostan, 1992; on finances, see Tabakoğlu, 1985; Cezar, 1986; Darling, 1996). Almost twenty years later, Uzunçarşılı completed the series with a study of the religious *cum* legal scholars who staffed the Ottoman courts and institutions of higher learning (Uzunçarşılı, 1965). Moreover, the whole series is introduced by a volume giving the reader a bird's eye view of Ottoman state organisation (Uzunçarşılı, 1941c).

Uzunçarşılı was an active professor-politician, whose formidable strength lay in his extensive knowledge of archival materials. Equally impressive was his commitment; his last publication of an Ottoman document was mailed to the journal *Belgeler* on the very day of his death (Uzunçarşılı, 1981–86). The principal weakness of his studies of Ottoman administration

---

[3] As the Ottoman sections in the Middle Eastern histories of Lapidus and Hourani only consist of about 50–60 pages each, they have not been included here (Lapidus, 1988; Hourani, 1991). The same thing applies to Geoffrey Lewis' work on the republic of Turkey, where the section on Ottoman history is also but 50 pages long (G. Lewis, 3rd ed. 1965). Stoianovich's recent study has been excluded because of its heavy emphasis on post-1918 developments (Stoianovich, 1994) . In addition, some works may have been inadvertently overlooked.

was probably the assumption that the Ottoman governmental apparatus remained more or less static from the late fifteenth to the early nineteenth century. This basic misconception is all the more remarkable as Uzunçarşılı himself diligently catalogued the eighteenth-century reorganisations of the central bureaucracy. As a result of this static approach, his books have to be read, so to say, against the grain. Factual statements must be placed in their temporal context, which often is quite different from that in which the author has placed them. For this reason Uzunçarşılı's books, while useful to the specialist, should be consulted in moderation by beginners.

On the European side, arguably the most influential work of this period was the two-volume study of H. A. R. Gibb and Harold Bowen on eighteenth-century Ottoman society (Gibb and Bowen, 1950; 1957). The first volume is really a good deal older than the date of publication would suggest, as it was largely written before World War II. On the other hand, the second volume came out in 1957, at a time when Turkish scholars, and even a few foreigners such as Bernard Lewis, had become acquainted at first hand with the riches of the Ottoman archives (Lewis, 1954). This means that the first volume depended much more upon European sources than the second one. In the preface to the second volume, Gibb and Bowen have themselves expressed the predicament in which they found themselves. The authors realised that once the new archival studies got underway, many points of detail, but possibly also major generalisations, would need to be modified or even totally discarded. This is of course true for all books which attempt a broad survey of a given field.

One of the major challenges to the view of seventeenth- and eighteenth-century Ottoman history as proposed by Gibb and Bowen came from Norman Itzkowitz's 1962 article on career lines in the Ottoman bureaucracy. Gibb and Bowen had adopted the interpretation originally proposed by A. Lybyer in his work on Sultan Süleyman the Magnificent. In Lybyer's view, the Ottoman state administration was made up of a so-called 'ruling' and a so-called 'religious' institution, the latter identified with the *ulema* (Lybyer, 1913). Itzkowitz demonstrated that passages from one of these 'career lines' to another were much more frequent than the image of two radically separate institutions would suggest, thus undermining the validity of Gibb and Bowen's synthesis. It is perhaps worth noting that this issue has never troubled Turkish historians of the Ottoman realm, who have generally been closer to the primary sources and less concerned with theoretical constructs. Both Uzunçarşılı and, on a much more sophisticated level, Halil Inalcık, discuss empirically identifiable services such as the Palace, the navy, the soldiers paid by the Porte (*kapıkulları*) or the *ulema*

(Uzunçarşılı, 1948; İnalcık, 1973). Neither of these authors concerns himself with the 'institution' these state officials may have belonged to, if ever such a thing existed. By contrast, the understanding that Ottoman officialdom was organised in two separate divisions has tentatively been taken up again by Carter Findley in his discussion, broadly inspired by Max Weber, of the Ottoman bureaucracy after the reorganisation of the Tanzimat years (Findley, 1980, pp. 44–68).

At the same time, it is only fair to point out that Gibb and Bowen also have made some very pertinent observations. Thus quite a few of today's Ottomanist historians would probably agree with their argument that the Ottoman Empire did not 'decline' because intercontinental trade was diverted by sixteenth-century European merchants from overland to maritime routes, even though this view remained popular long after the publication of their work (Gibb, Bowen, vol. I, pp. 7, 300ff.). Equally, their judgement that the ruin of local handicrafts and the loss of gold to pay for European manufactured goods were basically nineteenth-century phenomena must have sounded novel at the time, but has many adherents today.

As specialists on Islamic history, Gibb and Bowen were particularly concerned with the Arab provinces, to whose history they dedicated a special chapter. The Ottoman Balkans concerned them to a much lesser extent. But considerable work on Balkan history was carried out by other scholars during the 1950s. Especially the massive work of Leften Stavrianos (Stavrianos, 1958), almost 1,000 pages long (850 pages not counting appendices), merits a closer look (Stavrianos, 1958). Chapters are organised chronologically, but at the same time, individual national states are allotted separate chapters under the umbrella of the relevant section title. If a reader wishes to follow, for instance, merely the history of Greece, he/she will find relevant chapters within the sections named 'The Age of Nationalism', 'The Age of Imperialism and Capitalism' and 'The Age of War and Crisis' (referring to the twentieth century).

A pronounced interest in political economy constitutes one of Stavrianos' major virtues. Thus the nineteenth century, from the Congress of Vienna (1815) down to World War I is treated not as a mere sequence of wars and treaties, but discussed in connection with the concepts of 'nationalism', 'imperialism' and 'capitalism'. Both internal and external reasons for the non-development of Balkan economies after independence are analysed in detail. Even though the chapter on Greek national aspirations (pp. 467–82) is written with obvious sympathy for the Greek cause, the author is scrupulously fair to the national projects of Bulgarians, Serbs, Albanians and Roumanians, often enough in open conflict with Greek demands. This restraint is especially obvious in Stavrianos' treatment of the Macedonian imbroglio. Unfortunately, Stavrianos knew much less about the Ottoman Turks than about the Christian peoples of the Balkans. In consequence 'the Turks' are described merely as a 'declining' imperial power. That Turks and Muslims made up the majority of the population in certain sections of the Balkans is thus lost from view. Moreover, while the miseries suffered by Greeks and Macedonians are not absent from the narrative, those afflicting the Turkish population are all too frequently glossed over. All this would have been less meaningful in an ephemeral publication. But having provided a model for his successors due to his many strong points, Stavrianos' major weakness also has found quite a few imitators.

This is perhaps the right place to introduce the work of Roderic Davison, whose major study on the Tanzimat appeared in 1963 (Davison, 2nd printing with new introduction, 1973). While this book, as a mono- graph, does not qualify for inclusion into the present chapter, the author has supplemented it by a later volume of articles grouped into a more or less coherent narrative and covering the period from 1774 to 1923 (Davison, 1990). Davison was one of the first American scholars to learn Ottoman and work in the Istanbul archives. In addition, he possessed a thorough knowl- edge of Ottoman published literature, apart from being conversant with the French and English archival sources which form the traditional 'meat and drink' of the nineteenth-century specialist. This versatility, while not un- usual today, is worth stressing, for most studies of the 'Eastern Question' (a polite term for the division of Ottoman territories) up to that point had been prepared on the basis of European sources exclusively. By contrast Davison regarded Ottoman constitutional history from the viewpoint of the Kemalist republic, and expressed considerable sympathy for the embattled Ottoman ruling class: *Cet animal est très méchant: quand on l'attaque, il se défend* ('this animal is very vicious: if you attack it, it will defend itself', see Davison, 1990, p. 75).

Even though quite short and over thirty years old, William McNeill's study of Ottoman, Polish and Russian relations on "Europe's steppe frontier" (McNeill, 1964) offers the present-day reader both instruc- tion and pleasure. McNeill's perspective is informed by his work on epi- demics of plague and cholera, but also by theories concerning the relations between centres and peripheries of world empires, and, more particularly, geopolitics. As I see it, his book is unusual because it avoids the assumption, not rare in other works of this sort, that geopolitical considerations do not leave the relevant states any choices, and therefore legitimise whatever aggressive policies the rulers in question may decide to engage in.

McNeill is not an Ottomanist, but his account of Ottoman expansion and stagnation in terms of centre–periphery relations makes fascinating reading. In the author's perspective, the expanding Ottoman Empire consisted of a moderately taxed core, and border provinces bearing the cost of expansion through the destruction caused by warfare. With respect to the Ottoman Empire McNeill's view now must be modified, since we have learned that the defence and administration of border areas was often financed by provinces closer to the centre. Thus the load was lighter than Mc Neill had assumed (Barkan, 1953–1954, p. 273; Finkel, 1988, vol. I, p. 308). However, the author's account does retain some validity, because a province such as Hungary suffered great losses in population during the times in which it constituted a disputed and often doubly taxed Ottoman border province. According to McNeill, the differences between centre and periphery tended to even out at a later stage. Now the central provinces were more heavily taxed, while the stabilisation of the frontier allowed the inhabitants of border provinces some breathing space. But of course in the Hungarian instance, this period of recuperation was cut short by the war of 1683 to 1699. McNeill's remarks on the political impact of aristocracies and centralised monarchies on empire-building are also worth pondering.

Bernard Lewis' study of the emergence of modern Turkey will be touched upon rather briefly, for as the title indicates, it focuses on the post-Ottoman period (Lewis, 1961, 2nd edn 1968). But Lewis, who has done research in many different periods of Middle Eastern history, delves deeply into the post-Tanzimat Ottoman Empire, and in certain chapters, into even earlier periods as well. The first section contains an account of historical change from the eighteenth through the twentieth centuries, while the second focuses on key issues confronting a nation state in the process of organising itself. Lewis' work is notable for the effort to understand conservative Ottoman thinking in its own terms (for an example, see p. 107). A long introduction, practically a separate essay, analyses the 'decline' of the Ottoman Empire, which is linked to increasing isolation from world trade routes. Many researchers today would probably disagree with at least some of the points made in this introduction. Thus the focus upon secular 'decline' and the assumption, inherent in the modernisation paradigm, that nation-states necessarily represent human progress seem problematic today. But at the time when Lewis put down his theses in an extraordinarily elegant and polished language, they summarised what many historians thought about the matter.

Roughly from the same period dates the introductory survey of Ottoman and Turkish history by Roderic Davison (Davison with Dodd, 3rd edn, 1998). This is a teaching aid intended for survey courses of twentieth-century history, but about one half of the volume is dedicated to the Ottoman empire. Davison's perspective is comparable to that of Lewis (and numerous other scholars), as Ottoman developments are discussed as a necessary preliminary to the history of modern Turkey. Where the pre-Tanzimat period is concerned, Davison, as a specialist on the nineteenth century, cannot but echo the results and perspectives put forward by his contemporaries, particularly that *tarte à la crème* of 1960s scholars, namely 'Ottoman decline'. But for the nineteenth century, and also for the crisis-ridden last years of the Empire's existence, Davison has produced a very readable account, whose enduring popularity is demonstrated by the numerous editions and reprints which this book has enjoyed. In the most recent version, an attempt has been made to modernise the bibliography, but this does not really change the book's character as a 'period piece'.[4]

THE 1970s AND 1980s

From the very beginnning of our period (1970) dates the publication of *The Cambridge History of Islam* in two massive volumes, edited by Peter Holt, Ann K. S. Lambton and Bernard Lewis. In the first volume, the Ottoman Empire has been allotted a prominent role, with three contributions on political history by Halil Inalcık, and further articles by Uriel Heyd and Peter Holt. By contrast, in the section concerning Islamic society and civilisation, Ottomanists are not much represented, with literature the only aspect of Ottoman culture allowed a separate article (Iz, 1970). To some extent, this reflects the state of research in the 1960s, when the study of Ottoman art was still struggling for recognition as a separate discipline, and specialists on the Arab world and Iran dominated the study of Middle Eastern culture.

In 1976, Inalcık's article from *The Cambridge History*, along with contributions by Vernon J. Parry, Akdes Nimet Kurat and J. S. Bromley to the *New Cambridge Modern History* were issued as a separate volume. This included a new introduction by Michael A. Cook, who provided an elegantly formulated short text on what one might call the 'Ottoman legitimacy deficit'. This text explains how Central Asian royal traditions, the *yasa* (laws) of Cengiz Han and Islamic concepts concerning the caliphate all legitimised only certain aspects of the Ottoman sultanate. Thus authors exalting Ottoman rule were obliged to circumvent the trouble spots as best they could. However Cook's and Inalcık's contributions apart, the texts in

[4] Clement Dodd's reworking concentrates on the history of republican Turkey, so that the most recent edition includes developments of the 1990s.

this volume are for the most part purely narrative, without the analytical component which the beginning pages of the volume would lead one to expect (Parry, Cook *et al.* (eds.), 1976).

In 1973–74, there appeared one of the major syntheses of overall Middle Eastern history published to date, namely the three-volume *Venture of Islam* by the Chicago scholar Marshall Hodgson. However, Hodgson died before completing the third volume, dealing with 'The Gunpowder Empires and Modern Times', that is the Ottoman, Safavi and Mughul empires. His friends and colleagues were able to locate enough drafts to put together the third volume. But it must always be kept in mind that Hodgson did not live to impart a final shape to his text.

Many Ottomanists have responded favourably to Hodgson's idea that the Ottoman, Safavi and Mughul empires, which all governed large territories for relatively long periods of time, had a common technological basis in an expert use of firearms (see for example Inalcık, 1975). Scholars of the pre-Hodgson generation had never given much thought to structural parallels between, for instance, Ottoman and Mughul techniques of rule. Gunpowder use apart, if today a consideration of possible structural parallels between the Ottoman, Safavi and Mughul empires has entered the agenda at least of a few historians, this is largely due to the impact of Hodgson's work.

In 1976, there appeared the first comprehensive account of the Ottoman world to be attempted in several decades, namely the two-volume *History of the Ottoman Empire and the Republic of Turkey* by Stanford Shaw; the second volume was coauthored with Ezel Kural Shaw. While the first volume treated the Ottoman Empire prior to the Tanzimat, the second discussed the final decades of the Empire's existence and the history of the Republic down to 1975. Before publishing this volume, Shaw had made a name for himself as an expert on Ottoman Egypt. He had explored the workings of the provincial administrative structure, virtually a *terra incognita* at the time, and published a sixteenth-century budget of Ottoman Egypt (Shaw, 1962, 1968). But apart from these studies concerning a very important, but also very special, Ottoman province, Shaw was essentially interested in the period of 'reforms' inspired by European examples, which the Ottoman governing class attempted from the eighteenth century onward. This may explain why the first edition of the first volume, which covered earlier periods of Ottoman history, contained more than its fair share of errors. But also where overall views of Ottoman history were concerned, the first volume suffered from the fact that the author had little first-hand experience with the history of the Ottoman 'core area' before 1800. These blind spots have earned Shaw harsh criticism, especially from experts on the

Byzantine-Seljuk and early Ottoman periods (for example Ménage, 1978).

As to the second volume, the Shaws could base themselves on documentary research of their own, with a positive effect upon the quality of their work. Here aggressive criticism, particularly on the part of certain members of the American-Armenian community, has been directed principally at the political stance taken by the authors. In certain cases, these protests unfortunately have far overstepped the boundaries of academic disagreement, involving intimidation and physical attack. On the whole, the Shaws identify themselves with the positions of the Ottoman officials upon whose writings they base their work. Now the prime concern of Ottoman governments, but also of their Young Ottoman and Young Turk opponents, was 'to save the state'. In the foreign policy context, this was for the most part a defensive operation, and therefore an *ex post facto* espousal of Ottoman policy does not give rise to too many problems. But when it comes to internal affairs, particularly during the war years 1912–1923, these attempts at 'saving the state' at times led to brutal repression against rebellious or even just potentially rebellious minorities. In the perspective of the Shaws, these measures also form part of 'legitimate defence'. This constitutes a political statement, with which one may agree or else sharply disagree. But even so, the authors' thorough knowledge of Ottoman documentation has ensured that in the twenty years since its appearance, the second volume of *The History of the Ottoman Empire and Modern Turkey* has been consulted by almost everyone attempting to familiarise him/herself with the nineteenth-century history of the Ottoman Empire. I have learned a great deal from it.

Forming part of a series on eastern and southeastern European history put out by the University of Washington, Peter Sugar's treatment of Balkan history down to 1805 was published in 1977. This work is remarkable for its emphasis on social and economic developments, and for the author's interest in the findings of Ottomanist historians. While the relevant political developments have been sketched in quite a cursory fashion, Sugar devotes long chapters to the operation of the Ottoman land system and to the – for Balkan historians – vexed questions of Turkish immigration into the Balkans and Islamisation. Basing himself particularly on the works of Ömer Lütfi Barkan and Halil Inalcık, Sugar gives an account of the settlement of Anatolian nomads (*yürük*) in areas often left virtually empty by fighting and epidemics, such as Thrace. Concerning conversion to Islam, Sugar accepts that it was usually more or less voluntary, apart from the boys drafted for service in the Ottoman army, the much disputed *devşirme*.

But apart from this special case, even in the sixteenth century, when Ottoman control of the Balkans was for the most part well established and conversion processes underway, the poll tax paid by the Christian population still constituted one of the major sources of government revenue. Thus there was little inducement for administrators to reduce revenues by enforcing mass conversion. For the most part, the latter took place on the 'non-official' level. In the wake of Hasluck, Köprülü, Barkan and Vryonis, Sugar highlights the activity of colonising dervishes, who were willing to accommodate the folk beliefs of populations long estranged from the 'high-cultural' version of Orthodoxy, and thus won over the hearts and minds of local people to Islam (Hasluck, 1929; Köprülü, 1966b; Barkan, 1942; Vryonis, 1971).

In all this, Sugar for the most part follows what has become the majority opinion of the Ottomanist community. His personal views are more apparent in his evaluation of the effects of Ottoman administration. While most Ottomanists have emphasised the Sultans' capacity to develop an intricately organised governmental system that survived several centuries, Sugar sees this matter in a rather different light. In the author's perspective, 'overadministration' to the contrary may have constituted the Ottoman régime's major weakness. A set of stringent rules and regulations, minutely enforced, tended to make life rather dull and monotonous for the Sultan's subjects, especially for non-Muslims. This monotony may have contributed substantially to the disaffection even of the most unambitious and undemanding of Balkan Christian peasants (pp. 34, 110).

There is little doubt that this view of the motivations of sixteenth- or seventeenth-century Balkan villagers, about which we have almost no direct evidence, is highly speculative. A twentieth-century citizen's frustration with constant bureaucratic interference doubtlessly plays a major role in the genesis of Sugar's interpretation. Elements of the 'American dream' are not absent either. Whether this construct has a basis in seventeenth-century reality, is another matter entirely.

Also in 1977, the American Balkanists Charles and Barbara Jelavich published a history of the Balkan states in the 'long' nineteenth century (1804–1920). It appeared in the same series as Sugar's work, and therefore shares the overall format: approximate length, the preference for a bibliographical essay instead of a conventional bibliography and limited footnoting. But while Sugar's work is oriented toward Ottoman life, the Jelaviches' volume shares Stavrianos' focus upon Balkan nationalism, making little attempt to discuss the Ottoman point of view. However, the authors do give a balanced account of the violence which accompanied the dissolution of the Ottoman Empire in the Balkans. Thus we hear not only of the Ottoman massacre on Chios (1822), immortalised by Eugène Delacroix' painting, but also of the murder of Turkish merchants in Jassy (1821) or of the Muslim population of Tripolitsa (1821, pp. 42–4). But we do not find much discussion of the changing Ottoman social structure of the nineteenth century.

By contrast, the Jelaviches do emphasise the link between the conflictual domestic politics of the various Balkan states and indigenous social tensions. In some cases they have identified outright class struggle, although class tensions were not always easily recognisable in the prevailing factional strife. Only in Roumania, with its powerful boyar class and disinherited peasantry, were class tensions acted out completely in the open. Thus, an inside view of the emerging Balkan nation states characterises the Jelaviches' work, contrasting with an outsider's perspective where Ottoman society is involved. This latter aspect is unfortunate, as the reader may come away with the impression, probably not intended by the authors, that Ottoman politics could be neatly separated from the Balkan context, and were somehow less amenable to rational analysis those of the new national states.

It would appear that at least one of the authors concerned became aware of this problem. For when in 1983, Barbara Jelavich issued a two-volume study of Balkan history on her own, she emphasised the comparative aspect. Where the eighteenth century was concerned, B. Jelavich highlighted those problems shared by the Habsburg and Ottoman empires. A first chapter, entitled 'Balkan Christians under Ottoman rule', discussed religious tensions between a Muslim ruling establishment and a subject population largely non-Muslim, at least in most parts of the Balkans. The second chapter was called 'Balkan nationalities under Habsburg rule'. This title, both a parallel to and a variation on the first, seems to me a fortunate choice. For in the eighteenth century, the Habsburgs did not yet possess any Muslim subjects. But religious and political tension between an aggressively Catholic government and a subject population which after 1699, comprised both Hungarian Protestants and Orthodox Serbs, was present just the same. Moreover, during the eighteenth century, religious conflicts were beginning to shade over into national ones. The third chapter proceeds to a formal comparison between the two empires in the eighteenth century. By emphasising religious dissidents' and peasants' points of view, B. Jelavich shows that the advantages were by no means all on the Habsburg side.

One of the most remarkable attempts by a Turkish historian to address the problem of Balkan independence movements was undertaken by Ilber Ortaylı (Ortaylı, 1983). *İmparatorluğun en uzun yüzyılı* ('the Empire's longest century') begins with a discussion of the conflicts surrounding

Mahmud II's accession to the throne. A second chapter deals with early Balkan nationalism, under the evocative title the 'modern period of Ottoman nations'. Ortaylı then addresses the dominance of the Grand Vizier's office (Bab-ı Ali, or Sublime Porte) and its centralist policies during the early stage of the state restructuring known as the Tanzimat. A section called the 'impasse of the reformers' contains an analysis of the tension between a society which changed but slowly, both in the economic and the demographic sense of the term, and a bureaucracy aiming at fairly rapid reforms. A final chapter is dedicated to the intellectual world of the new-style Ottoman officials.

Ortaylı's study is based on a 'classical' concept of modernisation. But its strength lies not so much in the construction of models as in the breadth of the author's perspective and information. Reading Russian and familiar with research on Russian history, a rare achievement among Ottomanist historians of any nationality, Ortaylı refuses to demonise the Czarist empire. By stressing the local roots of Balkan nationalism he asserts that these were not a simple Russian or other ploy, but possessed a legitimacy of their own. The same matter-of-fact approach is apparent in his dicussion of economic mentality. Ortaylı links phenomena such as the long survival of Ottoman guilds not to immemorial habits of thought, as was common enough among older historians, but more straightforwardly, to conjunctural factors (Ortaylı, 1983, pp. 152–3).

OTTOMAN–TURKISH SETTLEMENT AND CONQUEST AS HISTORIOGRAPHICAL PROBLEMS

In the works introduced up to this point, the eighteenth and nineteenth centuries constitute the focus of discussion. However, during this same period, the earliest years of the Ottoman Empire also attracted some historians interested in synthesis. In 1971, the Byzantinist Speros Vryonis published a massive work on the decline of the Byzantine and Orthodox presence in Asia Minor and the Islamisation and turkification of the peninsula (Vryonis, 1971). Vryonis takes the story through the fifteenth century, and makes a point of including the Ottomans. Thus his work, differently from that of his older contemporary Claude Cahen, is relevant to Ottoman history (Cahen, 1968, 2nd, considerably revised edn 1988). In a sense, Vryonis' work can be viewed as a response to the studies of Köprülü, Barkan and Inalcık (works cited above, and Inalcık, 1954a and b). While the latter have recounted the islamisation and Turkish settlement of Anatolia and part of the Balkans as a success story, Vryonis discusses the process from the losers' point of view.

For the Ottomanist, the section of Vryonis' work dealing with the reactions of late Byzantine writers to the loss of Anatolia is of special interest. Also relevant is the last chapter, dealing with the Byzantine residues in Ottoman Anatolia, some of which survived down to the Greco-Turkish exchange of populations in 1923. Vryonis used Turkish secondary literature in the preparation of his work, and thus was one of the first scholars to acknowledge that the Byzantino-Ottoman transition period needed to be studied from the Byzantine, Seljuk and Ottoman angles. This was a fertile departure, which in the next generation was to result in a well-cultivated field known as Byzantino-Ottoman transition studies. When set against this innovation, it is probably less relevant that something resembling 'Byzantine nationalism' is discernible on many pages of Vryonis' book.

Two years later, there appeared another study which has continued to shape our perceptions of the early Ottoman period, namely Halil Inalcık's account of the empire's 'classical age' (1300–1600). By a seminal article on 'Ottoman methods of conquest', in addition to a series of studies on fifteenth-century trade and Ottoman control of the Black Sea, Inalcık had established himself as the foremost specialist on early Ottoman history as viewed in a global context (Inalcık, 1954a and b, 1960a and b). State making and trade also form the principal concerns of the 1973 volume. Here a brief treatment of political history is joined to a second, much more innovative section on the operation of Ottoman government. Institutions and their personnel, such as the dynasty, the Palace, or the *timar* holders occupy centre-stage. But more abstract ideas are also allotted considerable attention, particularly the differentiation between state servitors and tax-paying subjects, often known as the Ottoman class system.

A third section highlights international trade, including the attempts by Mehmed the Conqueror to turn Bursa into a spice entrepôt. Competition between the Ottoman Empire and the Portuguese in the Indian Ocean is linked to this concern with trade. By emphasising the success of Muslim merchants during the early centuries of the empire, Inalcık implicitly rejects the old view that in the Ottoman Empire, the division of labour was more or less immutable, being based on religious and ethnic criteria. Views of this kind had frequently been found in works dealing with the nineteenth century (for an example see Issawi, 1966, p. 114). By contrast, Inalcık demonstrates that the division of labour was historically determined and could therefore change. This point has an important place in the argumentation of those historians who wish to show that Ottoman history has its own economic dynamic, and is not based on some supposedly immutable priciples of religiously based social organisation.

On the borderlines between monograph and comprehensive account of fourteenth- and fifteenth-century Anatolian history, we find Rudi Lindner's reconstruction of the role of nomads in the early years of the Empire (Lindner, 1983). Basing himself on the studies of recent tribal societies untertaken by social anthropologists, Lindner attempts 'to bring back in' the nomad component of early Ottoman history. In so doing, he challenges the views of previous historians, who had recounted the story from the vantage point of sedentary rulers and their court chroniclers. This approach also casts doubt on the assumption that frontier warriors arriving from all over Anatolia, rather than the early Ottoman Sultans' fellow tribesmen, had played the crucial role in propelling a backwoods Bithynian principality onto the historical stage. In challenging the frontier warriors, Lindner has not remained alone. However, his 'Ottoman tribe', which supposedly formed and unravelled without leaving unambiguous traces in the historical record, has not gained much of a following in the fifteen-odd years which have elapsed since the publication of *Nomads and Ottomans* (Lindner, 1983, pp. 36–7).

SOCIAL AND ECONOMIC HISTORY: THE FIRST ATTEMPTS AT SYNTHESIS

If one disregards Mustafa Akdağ's rather premature attempt, the first books to summarise the available body of knowledge on socio-economic history were authored by Niyazi Berkes (Akdağ, 1959, 1971; Berkes, 1969, 1970). These volumes appeared in a series with the title *Yüz soruda* 'In a hundred questions', loosely inspired by the French series *Que sais-je?* The structure of the series made it necessary to divide the material into 100 short chapters per volume; footnotes or suggestions for further reading were impossible. Presumably the series editors aimed at high school students, teachers and undergraduates as their prospective audience.

In the first volume, Berkes discussed modes of production and defined the Ottoman economy as a war economy, where riches were accumulated mainly as a form of booty. In his view, periods in Ottoman history were best established by using a set of categories originally invented by Ibn Khaldun. Berkes distinguished between the formation, consolidation, crisis and decline of the Ottoman state, the ultimate collapse being followed by the attempt to build a totally new kind of polity. Berkes also suggested that one reason for the decline of the Ottoman Empire was the inability of its ruling class to make a clear choice between war and the more conventional types of capital formation (Berkes, 1969, pp. 11–15). A second section was devoted to the relations between state and society, in which the author stressed the relative distance of the state from all social forces, a concept which was to play a significant role in discussions down to the present day (for recent examples, see Haldon, 1992 and 1993). Further chapters were devoted to the Ottoman ruling group, problems connected with taxation and socio-political tensions within the system. These latter conflicts conditioned the manner in which European trade and imperialism came to reshape the Ottoman economy.

The European impact upon the eastern Mediterranean scene constitutes the topic of the second volume. This begins by confronting 'European feudalism' and 'Eastern despotism'. In concrete terms, this section deals with the Ottoman conquest of Egypt (1517) and the sixteenth-century conflict with the naval powers of early modern Europe. Further sections cover the impact of mercantilism, the importation of bullion, the monetary crisis of the sixteenth and seventeenth centuries, and the changes in the established class structure resulting from all these developments. A final section treats the early stages of direct Ottoman confrontation with European imperialism, which the author places in the years around 1800.

Berkes' books were veritable pioneers at the time they were written, but of course they could only relay what was known in the 1960s. Thus we do not find very much information on the concrete activities of Ottoman peasants, sailors, caravan merchants and owners of capital. On the whole the Ottoman Empire is viewed in its confrontation with Europe, which constitutes an important aspect of Ottoman history, but by no means the total story. As a result of his limited perspective, Berkes' books have not aged well, and this explains why before 1988, the series editors commissioned a new volume on 'Ottoman economic history, 1500–1914'. The author was Şevket Pamuk, who had worked on cotton and the European world economy and was later to focus on monetary history (Pamuk, 1987, 1994). As a significant change in format, the book now contained a reading list with titles in Turkish and English. While themes such as 'state and society' continued to be central issues, Pamuk highlighted the course of time more strongly than Berkes had done. Even the chapter headings each contained a reference to the century treated in the relevant text.

The introduction of Pamuk's work deals with the period down to the fifteenth century; the emergence of the Ottoman state is discussed in connection with the basic problem of 'situating' Ottoman history in the context of world history. To Pamuk, this undertaking necessitates a discussion of 'modes of production' as a concept of Marxian political economy. The feudal mode of production, a category derived from mediaeval European socio-political relations, is contrasted with the Asiatic Mode of Production (AMP), a concept Marx had developed on the basis of a rather flawed image of pre-colonial Indian society (for an introduction to the whole issue, see Anderson, 1979, pp. 462–549, Berktay, 1985). But in the 1980s, modes of production were no longer viewed as monolithic entities. Pamuk thus emphasises that modes of production are abstract models, and any concrete society will show a combination of different modes. This articulation of various modes of production does not however, in Pamuk's view, produce a combination unique to Ottoman history; for by inventing a new, specifically Ottoman mode of production, one returns full circle to the 'uniqueness of Ottoman history', a notion dear to nationalist historiography. However, the author does suggest that it maybe worth experimenting with an 'intermediate' mode, with characteristics of both the 'feudal' and 'Asiatic' modes.

A rather different form of presenting Ottoman economic history has been attempted by Charles Issawi, who in 1980, published a selection of readings covering the economic history of the late Ottoman Empire (1800–1914). The format is similar to that of the author's older works on the economic history of the Fertile Crescent and Iran. Given the availibility of the previous volumes, the author has not included materials relating to the Arab provinces in his book of 1980, and the Balkans have also been excluded. Thus the use of the word 'Turkey' in the title is appropriate, for the only places covered, apart from present-day Turkey, are Macedonia and some of the Aegean islands. Many though not all of the 126 readings translated by Issawi and his collaborators have been taken from primary sources previously unpublished, the Foreign Office series in London's Public Record Office constituting a major treasure trove. Other selections come from the reports concerning commercial matters in the archives of the French Ministry of Foreign Affairs. Excerpts from publications in languages less accessible to English-speaking readers, particularly Russian and Turkish, have also been provided. Issawi's own contribution consists of the selection and arrangement of the material, in addition to a set of introductions. While not a synthetic treatment of late Ottoman economic history, this volume will probably retain its reference value for a long time to come.

A synthesis of nineteenth-century Middle Eastern economic history, with a strong emphasis on the Ottoman Empire's Arab provinces but not excluding Anatolia, is due to Roger Owen (Owen, 1981). Owen's regional speciality is Egypt, on whose cotton production and trade he had previously published what remains a classic monograph (Owen, 1969). In *The Middle East in the World Economy*, the author devotes most of his chapters to different regional economies, one set of analyses focusing on the period from 1850 to 1880 and a second one on the years from 1880 to the beginning of World War I. For the years preceding 1850, when statistical data are at a premium, Egypt, the Syrian provinces and Iraq are accorded subsections in a common chapter. Notable is the emphasis placed on Iraq, a province which in most discussions of Ottoman history, has been grievously neglected. Working from materials in European archives, Owen's focus is on the region's incorporation into the European-dominated world economy, with a special emphasis on financial control. The Ottoman and Egyptian bankruptcies, with the foreign control they occasioned, form pivotal points in Owen's account.

Balkan historians have also paid their tribute to economic history, and a notable example is the comprehensive work by John R. Lampe and Marvin R. Jackson (Lampe and Jackson, 1982). For our purposes, the first 150 pages authored by Lampe are directly relevant, although the later sections, concerning the economies of the newly independent Balkan states, also contain some relevant information. The authors insist on the geographic unity of the Balkans, which they do not regard as a Mediterranean entity (as had been done by Braudel, 1966, vol.I., pp. 22–93). Rather the geographical unity of southeastern Europe is assured by mountain ranges and above all, the Danube. Viewing the Danube as a unifying factor is due to the nineteenth-century focus of the book; in earlier periods, there was no through traffic on this river (McGowan, 1987). The geographical unity of southeastern Europe provides the justification for a comparative study of Balkan economies in the pre-independence period. From the vantage point of an economic historian, the Ottoman and Habsburg régimes are compared in a manner reminiscent of Barbara Jelavich's 1983 study. As the two books were written at the same time, this similarity of approach may be ascribed to the 'temper of the times'. Moreover, the willingness of the two authors to acknowledge the 'more complex and commercial nature' of the Ottoman Empire, can be ascribed to an at least indirect acquaintance with the more recent findings of Ottomanist historians (Lampe and Jackson, 1982, p.9).

PRESENTING OTTOMAN HISTORY AS A TOTALITY: THE 1980s

Up to the mid-1980s, Ottoman general histories in one volume had rarely been attempted, if one disregards a few short texts for popular consumption. One-volume histories are largely directed at outsiders to the profession. Thus the notable lack of interest on the part of scholars and publishers may be regarded as a symptom of the introversion characteristic of most Ottomanists during this period. This orientation was, however, to change after 1985 or so.

One of these attempts at synthesising Ottoman history will only be briefly touched upon here, as the bulk of the volume is dedicated to the republican period. But it is too interesting to ignore totally (Keyder, 1987). Keyder is by training an economic historian of modern Turkey, who in a perspective inspired by the work of Immanuel Wallerstein, discusses nineteenth- and early twentieth-century Ottoman history under the headings 'Before capitalist incorporation', 'The process of peripheralisation', 'The Young Turk restoration' and 'The missing bourgeoisie'. Dwelling on the continuities between Byzantine and Ottoman rule, Keyder takes a stand unusual among Ottomanist historians. He posits such continuities not only on the level of peasant material culture (where they are less in dispute) but on the level of the state–peasantry relationship as well.

In Keyder's perspective, both the 'classical' Byzantine state and the Ottoman sultanate of the sixteenth century were characterised by a special relationship between the ruler and the peasantry. Both the Emperor and the Sultan were supposed to protect the villagers from encroachment on the part of local magnates, so that the bureaucrats serving their respective masters could fill the state coffers with peasant taxes (Keyder, 1986, pp. 10–11). However, both empires ultimately failed to realise this goal. Keyder sees a parallel between the magnates of later Byzantine history and the notables who dominated the Ottoman provinces of the eighteenth or nineteenth century (Keyder, 1986, pp. 9–12). Thus down to the end of the Ottoman empire we are confronted with alternate periods of 'centralisation' and 'decentralisation'. Throughout these long political struggles the class basis of the state, first Byzantine and then Ottoman, did not change significantly.

Most importantly, at least during the Ottoman period, none of these oscillations was able to change the fundamental character of Anatolian society as a society of smallholding peasants. That there was a hiatus in peasant settlement in much of Anatolia and the Balkans, and often a period of nomad occupation intervened before a 'new' peasantry established itself in the region, is not of special importance for Keyder's argument. Only in the nineteenth century was the Ottoman bureaucracy confronted with a serious challenge from another social class, namely the emerging bourgeoisie. But historical circumstances determined that this bourgeoisie of the years around 1900 was largely Greek and Armenian, and was eliminated from Anatolia and Istanbul in the course of World War I and its aftermath. As a result, the republican successors of the Ottoman bureaucracy were able to prolong their rule by a few decades. Only a totally changed conjuncture, after the end of World War II, forced them to share power with a second, and this time Muslim, bourgeoisie.

Keyder's work attempts to combine history with political economy and sociology, and thus constitutes quite a challenge to the routines of the Ottomanist historical profession. However during the 1980s, 'straight' historians also attempted syntheses of their own. In 1989–90, there appeared the first printing of a multi-volume history of Turkey in Turkish, edited by Sina Akşin and authored by a sizeable group of scholars. The first volume is concerned with the Turks prior to the Ottoman Empire, and contains a long article by Halil Berktay on historiography. Ümit Hassan has authored a 'chronology of political events' and Ayla Ödekan an overview over the visual arts. Ödekan's contributions are prominent in later volumes as well. This strong emphasis on historiography and the fine arts shows the authors' wish to move away from the standard format of 'pure' political history.

The second volume covers the 'classical period' of Ottoman history from 1300 to 1600. In the third volume, dealing with the period from 1600 to 1908, we encounter a lengthy piece, authored by the editor himself, on nineteenth-century political thinking. By far the most voluminous of the series, the fourth volume deals with the collapse of the empire, and the entire history of the republic, not excluding the *coup d'état* of 1980. A new printing (1995) contains chapters on economic history in volumes II and III, which had previously been missing, and most importantly, a fifth volume devoted entirely to contemporary history. As a novel departure, this series was not sponsored by the Turkish Historical Commission or one of the universities, as had been customary through the 1970s. Put out by a private publisher, these volumes should be regarded as an explicitly non-governmental venture.

OTTOMAN HISTORY AS VIEWED FROM THE OUTSIDE: A FEW EXAMPLES[5]

So far our overview has been confined to members of the Ottomanist profession. But Ottoman history has proven itself a net importer of models and ideas, and a short note will thus be devoted to a few works which have been a source of inspiration to the present author and other Ottomanist historians. A great debt is owed to Fernand Braudel. In his pathbreaking works on the early modern world, Braudel had always emphasised that Ottoman history needed to be allotted a major space not only in any treatment of the Mediterranean orbit, but also of world history (Braudel,

---

[5]   This selection is so tiny that it cannot avoid being highly subjective; other Ottomanists asked for their 'favourites' would probably have given different answers.

1966, 1979). Thus in the first version of his work on the Mediterranean, this leading historian asked questions about Ottoman population and trade, which Ömer Lütfi Barkan, in his work published during the 1950s and 1960s, attempted to answer (Braudel, 1949). In Braudel's later study of economic life in the entire northern hemisphere, Istanbul, Aleppo and the trade routes passing through the Ottoman Empire are also given considerable attention. Here the author links the Ottoman state's continued control of these routes to its ability to defend itself against European 'incorporation', down to the beginning of the nineteenth century (Braudel, 1979, vol. III, pp. 410–15).

Needless to say, since Braudel's work on world history ended in the late 1970s, it cannot reflect current scholarship. Present-day 'culturalists' from the late 1970s onward (compare Hess, 1978) have been critical of Braudel's assumptions concerning a supposed unity of the Mediterranean, emphasising instead the politico-cultural split between the Christian and Islamic worlds. Generally speaking, ten to twenty years after his death, the reputation of a major writer or scholar is often at a low ebb; he is no longer a producing member of the literary or scholarly community, and has not been dead long enough to be considered a classic. In any instance, Braudel has made a contribution to Ottoman history over and above the relatively limited number of pages he has specifically devoted to the subject, for he has been instrumental in introducing the study of Ottoman history as a subject to economic historians in general.

Perry Anderson's *Lineages of the Absolutist State* constitutes another important book by a non-Ottomanist which attempts to include Ottoman history (Anderson, 1979). By its wide influence, it has contributed substantially toward making our field better known. Anderson is concerned with the different developments which led to royal absolutism in early modern Europe, or in a few rare cases, prevented its emergence. In the section dealing with the Ottoman Empire, he has marshalled a number of convincing arguments against the concept of the 'Asiatic Mode of Production'. But when Anderson discusses the Ottoman Empire in detail, this concept manages to creep in by the back door. This, in the opinion of the present author, is at least partly due to Anderson's insistence on making the rule of Ottoman Sultans appear fundamentally different from European absolutism. But given recent research on Ottoman 'magnates', the difference between the two systems, while significant, does appear much less cogent than it did in the 1950s or 1960s. Anderson, quite against his own intentions, finds himself perpetuating the old story of the 'peculiarity' of the 'immutable Orient' (Abou-El-Haj, 1991, pp. 3–5).

But it would be unfair to assign Anderson the sole responsibility for this state of affairs. He has used the best authorities on Ottoman history available at the time of writing. If the picture that he derived from them is that which he has relayed, and there is no reason to doubt his accuracy and fairness, then it is these studies which are at fault. In the opinion of the present author, many Ottomanists have focused too much on the state apparatus and its conservative policies, and neglected the dynamic factors in Ottoman society. If things had been different, the 'Asiatic Mode of Production' would not have maintained its hold for such a long time.

Among recent books on non-Ottoman Middle Eastern history, one of the most challenging is doubtlessly the work of R. Stephen Humphreys (Humphreys, revised edn 1995). Basically concerned with 'mediaeval' history down to 1500, the author includes the Ottoman history of Syria and Egypt when discussing questions of slow historical movement (Braudel's *longue durée*), such as rural history or the development of urban topography. On the most basic level, Humphreys' work can be used as a topically organised bibliography with extensive comments. But it is included here because in reality, it is very much more. In each section, Humphreys sketches the outlines of the problem to be treated and sometimes discusses the historiographical context in which individual contributions should be interpreted. At times, one might wish that he were less tolerant of the basic assumptions of, for example, French mandate historiography on Syria. In my view, a touch of Edward Said's iconoclasm would have been in order here. But even so, for both beginners and experienced practitioners of Ottoman history, this is a book which encourages new departures.

FROM 1989 TO THE PRESENT DAY: GENERAL HISTORIES

A recent attempt at synthesising Ottoman history has recently been undertaken by Halil Inalcık with Donald Quataert. These two authors have edited, and largely written, a 1,100 page volume on the economic and social history of the Ottoman Empire (Inalcık with Quataert eds., 1994, paperback version in two volumes, 1997)[6]. To this volume, Inalcık has contributed an long account of developments down to the end of the sixteenth century, which in the paperback version, constitutes the first volume. The discussion of the nineteenth century is due to Donald Quataert, who, during the period in which this book was put together, has also produced an important monograph on manufacturing in the nineteenth-century Ottoman Empire

[6] Page numbers are given according to the one-volume edition.

(Quataert, 1993). The remaining sections of the Inalcık–Quataert volume have been written by other scholars, with Bruce McGowan treating the eighteenth century. The appendix on monetary history, by Şevket Pamuk, has also formed the starting point for a more extensive monograph, to appear in the near future.[7]

In the introduction to the whole work, Inalcık and Quataert stress the links of the Ottoman Empire to the present-day world. As appropriate in a volume directed at a scholarly audience, historiographical links between Ottomanists and world historians are given special prominence. Not only is the development of Ottoman socio-economic history linked to the Braudelian revolution, the authors also highlight the convergence of early modern commercial history based on Ottoman sources with work done by Hungarian, Roumanian and Polish scholars. Frequent use of categories developed by non-Ottomanists forms another manner of placing the Otto-man Empire squarely on the world historical map. Inalcık has made ample use of the work of A. V. Chayanov on the operation of Russian peasant farms, in order to make sense of the fragmentary information available on Ottoman peasants (English translation, Chayanov, 1966). By highlighting the role of the family farm, Inalcık has managed to transcend the limitations of his 1973 work, with its all but exclusive focus on trade and administration; however, the crafts have been virtually ignored. Given this image of society, Ottoman concern with provisioning (pp. 179–187) takes on special import-ance. If towns were centres of production only in a minor way, and did not provide anything to the surrounding villages, obviously they could be provisioned only by administrative fiat.[8]

In his contribution on the nineteenth century, Donald Quataert has entered the debate on the role of manufacturing in the context of a world economy dominated by a few fast-industrialising nations. In this context Quataert dwells on the important Ottoman internal market, and points to the danger of regarding as significant only those branches of manufacture whose products were exported to Europe. But the survival or revival of manufactures had its price; as Quataert has stated even more forcefully in his monograph on Ottoman craft industries, these manufactures often were only able to subsist through the exploitation of low-waged labour (Quataert, 1993, fly leaf and p. 98).

While Quataert's image of Ottoman manufacturing in an era of European expansion is thus somewhat revisionist in approach, McGowan's treatment of the eighteenth-century Ottoman polity is more traditional. For

---

[7] The seventeenth century has been treated by the present author: no comment.

[8] Inalcık's discussion is largely limited to the later fifteenth and the sixteenth century.

McGowàn, Ottoman decline constitutes a central phenomenon, not merely economically and politically, but also as a matter of world view. Fortresses appear not merely as a response to practical needs, but as the expression of a 'defensive outlook upon the world' (p. 639). In the same fashion, the building of great mosques ceased because the Ottoman ruling group had lost its self-confidence. In the Preface to the entire volume, we find a comment on the divergence of McGowan's assessment from that of the other contributors. In my view, this pluralism is a good sign.

A further multi-author account of Ottoman history recently has been produced in Turkey. The Istanbul-based Research Centre for Islamic History, Art and Culture (IRCICA) is currently sponsoring a multi-volume work on Ottoman history, of which volume 1 appeared in 1994. Edited by Ekmeleddin Ihsanoğlu, historian of Islamic science, this first volume is devoted to political, institutional, military, legal and socio-economic history (Ihsanoğlu, 1994; a second volume appeared in 1998). Individual contributions, and sometimes even sections of contributions, can be read independently of one another. Contributors belong mostly to the 'middle generation' of Turkish historians, 'leavened' by a few younger ones such as Feridun Emecen. Footnotes and bibliography show that most of the contributors, apart from their archival work, also interact with their colleagues operating outside of Turkey.

Political history is divided into two major sections, with the peace of Küçük Kaynarca constituting the turning point (1774). Many present-day historians would accept this date, rather than earlier ones also often suggested, as the beginning of the empire's dissolution. Up to 1774, the story is told by Emecen, mainly known for his work on sixteenth- and seventeenth-century topics. From there to the end of the empire, the narrator is Kemal Beydilli, who has worked on topics somewhat outside the mainstream of Turkish academic historiography. Apart from studies on the role of non-Muslim minorities, Beydilli has authored a fascinating book on late eighteenth and early nineteenth-century Ottoman education (Beydilli, 1984, 1995). This background imparts the narration a 'flavour' somewhat different from typical chapters on the nineteenth century which usually are commissioned from specialists on the Tanzimat.

However, the later nineteenth century is also treated *in extenso*, with a stimulating chapter on bureaucratic change by Ilber Ortaylı. M. Âkif Aydın discusses legal history, including the difficult question of how Islamic religious law and the Sultan's capacity to rule by decree (*kanun*) were harmonised. Mübahat Kütükoğlu's extensive treatment of economic structure includes public finance, monetary matters, transportation and craft industries. There is ample visual documentation, in part from the photographic collection available in the IRCICA archives. Some very little known miniatures have also been included. When selecting pictures by European artists, care equally has been taken to avoid those that are too well known.

At the time of writing, the most recent contribution to our corpus is a one-volume (406 pp.) history of the Ottoman Turks by the American demographic historian Justin McCarthy (McCarthy, 1997). It is intended for the general reader, in this particular case, English rather than American. Unfortunately, the publisher has opted against any kind of literature list; the footnotes contain references only to those works cited *verbatim*. The narrative begins with the Seljuks and Byzantines, and continues with political history both evenemential (chapters 2 and 3) and institutional (chapter 4). Institutional history encompasses such diverse themes as the theory of government, pious foundations, merit and advancement in official hierarchies, the minorities, and economic organisation.

Political history is then taken up again with a chapter on the period of 'Destabilisation', which in McCarthy's view commences early, namely with the death of Süleyman the Magnificent in 1566. The following, relatively brief chapter on political history is devoted to the interplay between European imperialism and the nationalism of the Ottoman subject peoples in the nineteenth century. Subsequently, the political narrative is again interrupted, for an exposition of our rather limited information about the natural environment, micro-level social organisation and intrapersonal relations. Unfortunately, these aspects of Ottoman life are depicted as 'stills' from a not always clearly identified time period. That the term 'Turks' is sometimes used where 'Ottoman' would have been appropriate constitutes a minor stumbling block. The story of political events is then resumed in a chapter on nineteenth-century 'modernisation'.

At this point McCarthy has arrived at the topic on which he has done most of his original research, namely the human and demographic consequences of war and nationalism, to which recent events, first in Bulgaria and then in Bosnia, have given special poignancy. As we have seen in the course of our discussion, most authors dealing with war and nationalism have tended to neglect the sufferings of the Muslims while stressing those of the Empire's Christian subjects. By contrast, the plight of Muslim refugees constitutes one of the main focuses of McCarthy's book.

EARLY OTTOMAN HISTORY IN THE 1990s

Recent years have witnessed a continuing interest in the early centuries of the Ottoman Empire's existence. Colin Imber has produced an evenemential history of the period down to the death of Mehmed II in 1481 (Imber, 1990). Imber's main interest is in the chronology of events, a difficult problem with respect to this early epoch. Fifteenth-century historical texts by Ottoman authors are vague and often erroneous on chronology, and Byzantine and European sources are also less than helpful. Before embarking on the story itself, the author has supplied a useful survey of the available sources, which clearly spells out what the relevant texts do and do not contain. By a piece of bad luck, Imber's book and the accounts by Vatin and the Beldiceanus on early Ottoman history appeared at almost the same time, so that neither party could benefit from the other's work (in Mantran ed., 1989).

Imber prefaces his book with a quote from Sherlock Holmes: 'It is a capital mistake to theorise before one has data' (fly leaf). Imber thus intends to provide the secure foundations upon which any more interpretative account must rest. But this leaves us with the problem that interpretation and fact-finding often go hand-in-hand, rather than neatly following upon one another. To add to our predicament, we are unlikely ever to know much more about the origins of the Ottoman state than Imber and his fellow historians have told us. Thus one may understand the author to mean that attempts to make sense of this early period of Ottoman history will remain forever futile.

We have already discussed the elegant study of Cemal Kafadar (chapter 6), so that now, a brief reference must suffice (Kafadar, 1995). Kafadar is largely concerned with the manner in which facts and intellectual constructs have been discussed by twentieth-century historians. Especially appealing, at least to the present author, is his balanced position in the debate concerning an idea first propounded by Paul Wittek (Wittek, 1938). In Wittek's perspective, the Ottoman Empire owed its peculiar expansive power to its position on the frontier to the infidel world. Numerous immigrants from other Anatolian principalities therefore arrived in the fledgling *beylik*, with the intention of waging *gaza* (Holy War, the fighters themselves are called *gazi*) against Byzantines, Serbs and Hungarians.

This assumption was widely accepted among Ottomanist historians and became part of standard accounts. But from the 1970s onward, several attacks were launched against this interpretation, suggesting alternative sources of early Ottoman power such as the involvement of Ottoman mercenaries in Byzantine throne disputes, or the drive for booty on the part of nomad warriors (Lindner, 1983, pp. 1–50; Imber, 1990, p. 32). In response, Kafadar points out that the notion of a pure 'warrior for the faith', doing incessant battle for his lofty ideals alone, is a 'straw man' and not a real person (Kafadar, 1995, p. 57). While fifteenth and sixteenth-century Otto-man sources frequently held up such figures as models for their readers, their claims should obviously not be taken at face value. *Gaza* ethos could be combined with more worldly motivations, and Kafadar points out that the drive for booty and commitment to the faith could cohabit in one and the same person (Kafadar, 1995, pp. 37–8).

A CONTINUING EFFORT AT SYNTHESIS: THE 'OTTOMAN LEGACY' AS A RESEARCH PROBLEM

The brief overview presented here is not complete by any means. If during the coming years, as many books on 'large chunks' of Ottoman history continue to be published as we have seen recently, it will be out of date very soon. Among the different viewpoints represented in this litera-ture, we can pick up one feature common to many recent works, namely the debate on the legacy of the Ottoman empire to its successors[9]. However, it has recently been pointed out that, Turkey apart, much of this legacy exists in the realm of perception, rather than in that of 'objective realities' (Lory, 1985; Todorova, 1996). For if we ignore the (very important) sector of daily routines and the words associated with them, most Balkan states shortly after autonomy/independence tried very hard to get rid of all practices perceived as 'oriental'. By contrast, the lines of continuity linking the Turkish bureau-cracy of republican times with the nineteenth-century Ottoman past have recently been shown up in a perceptive text by Ilber Ortaylı (Ortaylı, in Ihsanoğlu ed., 1994).

When considering the Ottoman legacy, another important realm of debate is the role of the Greek Orthodox church, which, in its sixteenth- or even early nineteenth-century shape, was an Ottoman institution as much as anything else. In the context of nation-building, the role of this 'ottomanised' church hierarchy has been evaluated in contrary fashions by Greeks, Bulgarians, and Serbs. But on other aspects of the 'Ottoman legacy', at least certain Greek, Bulgarian, Serbian and Turkish scholars have been able to find a certain amount of common ground. At least *some* debates now take place on *some* issues without the participants being necessarily aligned

---

[9] Compare among others Lampe and Jackson (1982), Jelavich (1983), Todorova (1996).
    On the problem of the Ottoman legacy in general, see particularly the volume edited by L. Carl Brown, of which Todorova's article forms a part (Brown, 1996; Todorova, 1996). Together with Cyril Black, Brown has also edited a volume on modernisation in the (former) Ottoman Empire, another example of what might be called 'post-Ottoman comparative studies' (Brown and Black eds., 1992). For a further example compare Barkey and Von Hagen (1997).

according to national criteria (for a good introduction to the entire problématique, compare Hering, 1989, see also Papoulia, 1989).

Thus there seems to be a widespread agreement that the 'Ottoman
legacy' belongs more into the realm of perception than into that of 'hard',
'objective' realities. A recent book by Michael Palairet has now proposed
that from a economic point of view, this severing of links was an extremely
unfortunate development (Palairet, 1997). In Palairet's perspective, once
Mahmud II had centralised the government apparatus and done away with
roving bandits, the Ottoman centre's regular demand for taxes and military
supplies stimulated the development of protoindustries, of which the Bulgarian wool manufactures are probably the best known. With the provincial
Ottoman elites expelled, more land became available for peasant subsistence.
Moreover, taxes were often drastically reduced. Certain governments, especially in Serbia, even actively discouraged peasant involvement with the
market. As a result, reversion to subsistence economies was widespread.
Protoindustries collapsed, while many towns, having lost their political and
economic functions, declined. If Palairet's account is at all realistic, national
independence was a misfortune rather than a stimulant to Balkan economies, and in many instances, European capitalists showed only moderate
interest in 'incorporating' remote regions of limited productivity into the
'world system'. In Palairet's view, elites desiring the urbanisation and indus-
trialisation of Serbia, Bulgaria or Bosnia would have done better to remain
within the Ottoman orbit.

But let us return to the Ottoman legacy in the broader sense of the
term. When discussing this issue, which involves examining the contacts of
Muslims and non-Muslims living in the Balkans under Ottoman rule, two
possible historical approaches have recently been suggested (Todorova,
1996). Both will produce valid results as long as they are used on the
appropriate topics, and those who adopt them take care not to overstate
their respective cases. Some scholars start out from the assumption that
Balkan Christians lived fairly isolated lives, with little interference from the
Ottoman authorities as long as taxes were regularly paid. These Christian
subjects of the Sultan thus developed their own provincial culture, and only
when some of them converted did they move out of this charmed circle and
enter the dominant culture. After independence, with local Muslims leaving
the country or at least losing their political influence, the thin veneer of
official Ottoman culture disappeared, to reveal the autochthonous Christian
substratum below. In many places, such as Serbia and Bulgaria, this substratum was to all intents and purposes a purely peasant culture.

Todorova has suggested that this assumption of Muslim–Christian separateness can be useful when treating certain topics (Todorova, 1996). Thus a biographer of the Bulgarian monk and eighteenth-century proto-nationalist Paisi Chilandarskij may find it appropriate, for Chilandarskij did live out his life without major references to Ottoman written culture. But Mount Athos with its age-old privileges, home to Chilandarskij for much of his life, constituted a rather special world. Most educated non-Muslims of Ottoman background, unless they chose Paris, Venice or Vienna as the scenes of their activities, could not easily avoid contact with at least the local authorities. Beyond the lowest level, however, all functionaries were Muslims, even though these Muslims were not necessarily Turks.

Thus, there are many cases in which the assumption that Balkan Muslims and their Christian neighbours inhabited separate worlds is decidedly unhelpful. To take just one example, let us assume a researcher planning to work on the eighteenth-century historian, musician and short-term Moldavian governor Demetrius Cantemir. This multi-faceted scholar and artist designed houses in the style current among Istanbul courtiers, and filled the footnotes to his history of the Ottoman Empire with stories from the folklore of the capital. Such a person can only be understood in a context encompassing both Islamic and Christian civilisation (Cantemir, ed. Dutu and Cernovodeanu, 1973). On a much more modest plane, the Serres chronicler and priest Synadinos also must be placed in a context transcending the divisions of religion (Odorico et al., 1996; Todorova, 1996).

Beyond this and other specific cases moreover, historians of Balkan culture will often come to the conclusion that Muslims and Christians did not live alongside each other for several centuries without some intellectual and personal interchange. Given the dominant character of Ottoman imperial civilisation, such contact meant that assumptions typical of courtiers and Muslim townsmen 'filtered down' to the empire's non-Muslim subjects. Surviving in many Balkan towns, domestic architecture amply demonstrates this effect. But movements in the opposite direction were not totally out of the question either, to witness the numerous terms for things maritime which have passed into Ottoman from Greek (Kahane, Kahane and Tietze, 1958). In the present-day context we have become more sensitive to the concerns of the people who made such cultural transfers possible. Crossing confessional boundaries was a serious and sometimes risky business (Todorova, 1993, 1996; Faroqhi, 1995, pp. 95–117). Yet without such movements, Ottoman civilisation would have been much less colourful.

SUGGESTED READINGS

Castellan Georges (1991). *Histoire des Balkans* (Paris: Fayard) (evenemential history, with occasional tendencies toward the *chronique scandaleuse*).

Hösch, Edgar (3rd edn 1995). *Geschichte der Balkanländer von der Frühzeit bis zur Gegenwart* (Munich: C.H. Beck) (the Austrian impact upon the Balkans, particularly in the nineteenth century).

Lewis, Geoffrey (3rd edn, 1965). *Turkey* (London: Ernest Benn Ltd.) (general book on modern Turkey, with brief historical introduction).

Mantran, Robert (ed.) (1989). *Histoire de l'Empire Ottoman* (Paris: Fayard) (good overall narrative treatment; the section on the Arab provinces highly recommended).

Matuz, Josef (1985). *Das Osmanische Reich, Grundlinien seiner Geschichte* (Darmstadt/ Germany: Wissenschaftliche Buchgesellschaft) (by a specialist on diplomatics; emphasis on German involvement in the late Ottoman Empire).

Werner, Ernst (3rd edn 1978). *Die Geburt einer Grossmacht − die Osmanen (1300–1481)* (Berlin-East: Akademie Verlag) (by a scholarly East German Marxist, one of the first to point out that a drive for booty and ideological motives can coexist in the same person).

8

CONCLUSION

FURTHER DESIDERATA

Obviously the discussion of sources, both primary and secondary, as attempted in the present volume does not nearly exhaust our subject. Some readers will regret that miniatures, mosques, palaces and photographs have not been discussed, and it is true that this type of source has been gaining in importance with every passing year. During the last two decades or so, many historians of Ottoman art have given up the purely descriptive approach favoured in the 1960s or 1970s. Architectural historians have also abandoned the exclusive concern with building structure typical of that time.

At present, quite a few researchers dealing with Ottoman images try to place the objects studied in a context, either political or social. Such an interest encourages forays into the territory otherwise occupied by historians. To mention but one example, the Ottoman dynasty, with no links to the prestigious rulers of the early caliphate or the mediaeval Middle East, attempted to legitimise itself by sumptuous public building: this phenomenon is of obvious interest to both political and art historians. Or else miniatures, fayence or carpets constitute luxury goods as well as works of art. Here the interest that 'straight' historians have recently been taking in consumption has tended to bring art historians into contact with their colleagues from neighbouring disciplines.

In a different vein, the critical attitude of post-colonial historians toward the creation of myths and images has made Ottomanists aware of the fact that no less than written sources, images must be carefully analysed before they can be put to use. In consequence, critical studies of image making, especially of photography, have become quite frequent (for a good example, see Beauge, Çizgen, [1992]). Unfortunately, an even cursory discussion of the questions raised by these new studies would have resulted in a chapter of some length, which could not be accommodated in the 100,000–word format demanded by the publisher. It may be possible to deal with this matter some time in the not too remote future, *insha'allah*.

Another type of historical source badly neglected in the present volume is *belles lettres*. Poetry constituted a major part of Ottoman literature, and it surely can yield information on cultural assumptions and aesthetic preferences, significant issues to the cultural historian. When studying the relations of poets and patrons, moreover, we can gain an understanding of how talented persons from outside the Ottoman elite might gain a foothold in the latter. This in turn constitutes a major research area for the political historian (see for example Fleischer, 1986, pp. 41–69). I have neglected poetry because of my lack of literary training, feeling rather intimidated by this ocean of verses and images, bordered only by the 'unreadable shores of love' (Holbrook, 1994). It is also regrettable that Ottoman saints' legends or storytellers' productions have so often been studied in a purely Ottoman context, without reference to the work undertaken by historians of comparative literature. For such 'simple forms' of narrative occur in many civilisations the world over, and it would be interesting to know where the Ottoman examples stand in this world-wide continuum. But if comparative literary studies incorporating Ottoman material come into being at some point in the future, we will need a trained comparativist to provide us historians with an intelligent summary.

By contrast, Ottoman novels, these children of the Tanzimat, have been studied quite extensively, and a summary of the findings can, albeit with some qualms, be given by a non-specialist (for a recent work, see Moran, 1983–1994). While novels are not meant to provide a photographic image of the society they depict, they do constitute an important source when attitudes and value judgments are being studied. But again, this issue could not be accommodated within the word limit given, and as some sections had to fall victim to the *bostancıbaşı*'s cord, I have eliminated discussions of those research areas in which I have least expertise. Hopefully a literary historian will take up the challenge in the future[1].

THE RICHNESS AND LIMITS OF OUR SOURCES

Given the richness and variety of Ottoman textual sources, there is work for many generations. If proof were needed, one might remind the

---

[1] The Head Gardener also was in charge of Palace security, and executions on the Palace grounds figured among his duties.

reader that only the first volume of Evliya's travelogue, along with selections from later volumes, has been edited in a satisfactory fashion (see chapter 5). Where the last fifty years of the Ottoman Empire are concerned, much source material is still in the possession of private persons, now more inclined to share letters and personal memories with the reading public than in the past. Authors both well known and obscure have produced family histories delving deep into the Ottoman past (for a recent example, see Devrim, 1994). Even greater are the masses of archival material; given its enormous bulk, most of it will doubtlessly remain unpublished. Yet future researchers will appreciate the work of document publication which has become so much more intensive during the last few years, with the Prime Minister's Archives, and, more recently, the Istanbul City Administration funding many of the projects (see chapter 2).

But no book can inform the researcher of all the things he/she is likely to find. In the course of his/her work, many a historian will discover groups of documents or narrative texts providing answers to questions uniquely his/her own. These may well become the speciality of the author in question. Thus the tax registers (*tahrir*) are associated with the names of Ömer Lütfi Barkan and Halil Inalcık. Ronald Jennings devoted his life to the study of Anatolian kadi registers, while Roderic Davison excelled in ingenious comparisons between nineteenth-century Ottoman and European sources. Many scholars will develop their *problématiques* in close conjunction with the sources about which they know most, and this intimate knowledge allows them to produce more sophisticated studies. But at the same time, this proceeding may result in 'blinkers', namely when specialists come to assume that certain problems are not worth treating because the sources they know best do not cover them. It is therefore good practice to change one's archive from time to time.

However it must be admitted that like any other corpus of sources, Ottoman records do have their gaps. Most Ottoman subjects were peasants or nomads, who being mostly illiterate, have left few direct testimonies. As previous discussion has shown (chapter 4), this means that our records concerning the overwhelming majority of the Ottoman population were written by outsiders, whose main aim, moreover, was the collection of taxes. That such people were not always given truthful information should be obvious. But even where non-elite urban society is concerned, we very rarely possess direct testimonies. More often than not, we use records set up by court scribes, who employed sets of standardised formulas, in order to find out something about the social organisation of even Istanbul or Bursa guildsmen, to say nothing about the inhabitants of more remote places. And while practitioners of women's history are doing an impressive job teasing out information on this neglected half of humanity, it must still be admitted that the sources currently available provide answers to only a limited number of the questions we might wish to ask.

Unfortunately, the gaps in Ottoman documentation can only in certain specific instances be closed with the help of European sources. This becomes especially obvious when we look at micro-history and the interaction of individuals, a subject which currently attracts ingenious young historians. In this field, Ottoman sources are not very loquacious, and additional evidence from outsiders would be valuable[2]. But here our hopes are largely disappointed, as only a small number of European observers were interested in Ottoman subjects as human beings. Sometimes, for instance when French or Venetian pilgrims paying a brief visit to Jerusalem were involved, such contact may in fact have been minimal, confined to a few purchases, and to payments for lodgings, road tolls and guides. But it remains noteworthy that most travellers have so little to say about even the limited contacts which they could not avoid making. Political and diplomatic concerns, the search for vestiges of Greco-Roman antiquity or else commercial opportunities, were much higher on the agenda of European visitors than the lives of both Muslim and non-Muslim Ottomans. As we have observed in the case of Gyllius (chapter 5), prolonged scholarly concern with the archaeology of late antique Constantinople could very well go together with a profound indifference, or even hostility, towards the inhabitants of contemporary Istanbul.

That very few foreign visitors knew Turkish or Arabic constituted an additional barrier. Moreover, the difference in religion meant that a serious dialogue was only possible if both the European visitor and his/her Ottoman interlocutor were somewhat exceptional people. We have encountered some of them, namely Lady Mary Montague on the one hand, and Kâtip Çelebi or Ali Ufki on the other. On both the Muslim and Christian shores of the Mediterranean, there may have been many sailors, fishermen and soldiers who knew much more about the world 'on the outside' than the typical scholar. Where the Ottoman side is concerned, the captivity report of Osman Ağa indicates as much (chapter 6). But not many Osman Ağas have committed their experiences to writing.

A fortiori, very few European visitors ever asked themselves how their actions might affect the people with whom they came into contact. Some visitors may have caused their hosts a lot of trouble, and remained

---

[2] See however Georgeon and Dumont (ed.), 1997 for an indication of what can be done even with the material at hand.

blissfully unaware of the fact. An extreme case is the writer and scholar Charles Doughty, who travelled the Syrian hajj route before 1888 (Doughty, 4th edn, 1979). Differently from most other foreign travellers, this explorer did learn Arabic and form close relationships with a few men he encountered in the Arabian oases. But from his friends, Doughty expected extremely difficult and dangerous things, without ever asking himself why these persons should take such risks on his behalf. Yet this was an excellent observer with considerable artistic talent, who spent a lengthy period in his chosen region. One can only imagine the troubles which less accomplished travellers must have caused to their interlocutors.

Under these circumstances, it is not surprising that many aspects of the world inhabited by the subjects of the Ottoman Sultan remain closed to us. How one confronts this situation is of course a personal matter; quite a few researchers have confessed to being very frustrated in the face of numerous unanswered queries. In my own experience, reading widely in European and/or Asian history is a good way of opening up new vistas and discovering new problems to investigate. Doubtlessly we only find answers to our questions by closely analysing primary sources; but novel questions are frequently developed by pondering historiographies concerning India, China or early modern Europe.

POLITICS AND VALUE JUDGMENTS

When reviewing the secondary literature in even the cursory fashion undertaken in the present book, we have encountered numerous value judgments. In the mind of any person, multitudes of such judgments are formed every day, most of them only half conscious. Whether they will find expression in a book or article depends on the aims an author has set him/herself. A motif common to quite a few Ottoman and European writers was to express criticism of one's own society by a description of foreign parts. We have seen that Busbecq admired the devotion of the Ottoman ruling class to the Sultan, wishing that the Habsburg rulers could command similar allegiance from their often obstreperous nobilities. Evliya was impressed by the flourishing towns of the infidels, and the good care they took of their churches; these features were emphasised presumably in order to encourage emulation among his readers (chapters 5 and 6). This attitude has the advantage that the travelogue writer will regard the foreign society described with a sympathetic eye. But when taken to extremes, relaying a realistic image of the foreign culture becomes a secondary consideration. In the writer's mind, the culture and society he/she has (supposedly) encountered exist only as a means of expressing opinions concerning the home society.

Value judgments usually hit the eye mainly when we do not, or no longer, share them. Post-colonial historiography has rightly dwelt on the role of European travel accounts in symbolically appropriating non-European sections of the world (chapter 5)[3]. With the loss of what had once been Christian territory to the Muslims forming a major issue in the writers' minds, western visitors to the Ottoman Empire were prone to denigrate what they saw. By implication, a Christian/European government of Istanbul or Palestine would perform better than 'the infidels'. As scholarly preoccupation with the Middle East, in Europe and later in the United States, was so often a corollary of imperialist and expansionist designs, denigration of Ottoman rule was expressed with particular force in the scholarly literature.

But this is not the whole story; for a whole complex of positive emotions was also involved. From the later 1920s onward, the Kemalist project of founding a Turkish national state aroused considerable sympathy and even enthusiasm among foreign historians and philologists. When from the middle 1930s onward, Turkish universities offered a refuge to scholars driven out of Nazi Germany and Austria, this sympathy was further strengthened. Many of these scholars left Turkey after World War II to take up prominent positions especially in US academia. Apart from the – preponderant – impact of the Cold War alliance, the experiences of these refugees may have gained the Turkish national project additional sympathies among American Ottomanists. Equally important for American scholars, if not more so, was the Peace Corps experience of the 1960s. Sizeable numbers of young men and women, at the impressionable period which follows college graduation, learned Turkish and spent some years in Anatolian small towns or villages. Even though the activities of certain Peace Corps members soon gave the project a bad name, many volunteers developed genuine sympathies for Turks and Turkey, often enough for life. In addition the numerous Turkish economists, sociologists and historians who have received their graduate training in the USA or Great Britain have also contributed to the integration of Turkish and non-Turkish Ottoman studies. That quite a few of these American-trained Turkish Ottomanists have subsequently become faculty members in universities of the USA or Canada, with PhD students of their own, has further strengthened the trend toward integration. Particular-

---

[3] We have however noted that when Evliya travelled in the world of the infidels, he shared this perception.

ly the former students of Halil Inalcık from his Chicago days, both Turks and Americans, continue to have a major impact on the present state of our field. But the most active role in this respect fell to the doyen of present-day Ottomanist historians himself: for over a decade, Halil Inalcık constituted a major presence on the American scholarly scene.

In the 1960s, the sympathies of non-Turkish, especially American, Ottomanists for the Turkish national project did not imply taking sides in the contemporary politics of that country. For at the time, all parties active on the Turkish scene, from extreme right to extreme left, ardently espoused the national project, and foreign scholars generally followed the same pattern. But the resurgence of Armenian demands in the 1970s, and the terrorism that accompanied it, acted as a divisive factor, encouraging reactions of 'standing up and being counted' among American Ottomanists. Some of the latter have shown rather obvious allegiance to Turkish official positions. A further parting of the ways can be observed from about 1980 onward, with an islamist party becoming a major force in Turkey. Now allegiance of foreign Ottomanists to the Turkish national republican project generally implies an espousal of secularist values, those whose sympathies are closer to the islamist side forming a distinct minority.

A further complication stems from the fact that many European scholars, and to a perhaps lesser degree, Americans as well, have developed considerable doubts about the validity of the national project in their own countries. To put it differently, for a scholar concerned about the violations of human rights suffered by foreigners in the European Community, it is not possible to support wholeheartedly nationalist views in any part of the globe. We thus are confronted with a somewhat paradoxical situation. A European conservative, who normally assumes that people outside of western European culture should not be full members of the local community in Hamburg or Marseilles, may not have any qualms about supporting Turkish nationalist views with all their present-day implications. A liberal (in the broad sense of the word), who will espouse the right of Turkish or North African minorities to form part of the European scene, may well find the opinions of the small group of intellectual Turkish dissidents much more appealing (as an example, see the writings of Murat Belge, especially Belge, n.d.).

When writing about the origins of the Ottoman Empire or the story of Istanbul photography, these isues may be pushed into the background, but they are never eliminated entirely. Yet differently from what may be true of other fields, we cannot make out a clear dividing line between Turkish and non-Turkish Ottomanist historiography. In my view, it would be more appropriate to see our field as being made up of a number of clusters, each cluster containing a variety of related research activities. Some of these clusters may consist of a larger or smaller number of studies undertaken by Turkish, French or American scholars respectively; but rather than clear dichotomies of 'black and white', our field seems to contain multiple shades of gray.

HISTORIOGRAPHY AND NOSTALGIA

But as in human affairs, there is no rule without exception, there is one issue on which Turkish and non-Turkish Ottomanists do tend to diverge, and which concerns emotional attitudes to the Ottoman past. Halil Berktay has pointed out that the 'Jacobin' phase of the Turkish republic, with its outspoken rejection of the Ottoman heritage, was soon followed by the 'appropriation' of Ottoman history for the purposes of the new state (Berktay, 1991). In this later phase, scholars such as Ömer Lütfi Barkan viewed the Turkish Republic as the legitimate heir to the Ottoman Empire. Extremists such as Ismail Hami Danişmend went much further, denouncing the impact of the fifteenth- and sixteenth-century dignitaries recruited through the 'levy of boys' (devşirme). Allegedly and anachronistically, these men had prevented the Ottoman Empire from functioning as a Turkish national state (Danişmend, 1971).

After 1980 however, with the rise of different versions of the nostalgia culture, a more diffuse view of the Ottoman Empire as a symbol of the 'good old days' has become widespread among Turkish historians. Public opinion in Turkey tends to share this attitude, and it must be admitted that this harking back to a supposedly 'cleaner' and 'healthier' past, no matter how unrealistic, is typical of present-day European attitudes as well. Turkish historians sharing the nostalgia culture will exhibit a tendency to see Ottoman society, even in the eighteenth or nineteenth century, as largely harmonious. Of course, there are more or less sophisticated versions of this *laudatio temporis acti*.

While attitudes of this kind are not very suitable for exportation, non-Turkish historians of the Ottoman Empire, including many Balkanists, have produced their own myths. Many of them remain attached to a image of Ottoman 'greatness', lasting through the age of Süleyman the Magnificent, followed by a long period of 'decline' (see chapter 8). A full discussion of these attitudes would easily fill a book, and there are historians better qualified for this undertaking than myself (for some valuable arguments, see Abou-El-Haj, 1991, pp. 6–11). But even formulating such visions and nostalgias in a few bald lines, which is all we can do in the present context, hopefully will make us more aware of the irrationalities involved, and induce a degree of scepticism.

EXPLORING NEW HORIZONS

Before concluding this exploration of sources used by Ottomanist historians, we will take a brief look at research topics which may be of interest to present and future scholars. This section is intended as a set of suggestions, and not as a prediction of trends. For trends in Ottomanist historiography, as in other fields, depend first and foremost on political developments. Yet the events of 1989 have left us with the experience that even sophisticated political forecasting is anything but foolproof. Moreover the concern with 'culture', which for the last two decades has had such an impact on historical writing, may also not last for ever, an expectation based on the simple experience that most intellectual trends do not continue for much longer than twenty or thirty years. With two major unknowns and but one equation, predictions seem impossible. Nor can we tell to what extent 'saving-moneyism', the 'Europe-as-a-beleaguered-fortress' mentality and other equally detrimental tendencies will allow research into Ottoman history to continue in the 'core countries of the capitalist world system'.

But quite a few Ottomanist historians do tend to like their field, and may develop ways and means of working around such difficulties. History can be practiced with limited amounts of money. This constitutes a distinct advantage, in spite of the unfortunate corollary that legislators and university authorities will think that historical research can be conducted without any funding at all. Presumably a major impulse will come from the new sections in the Ottoman archives which are being opened every year. This will affect nineteenth-century specialists first and foremost; for in the Ottoman Empire as in many other countries, the reorganisation of the bureaucracy during that period led to an enormous increase in the quantity of records produced. This statement remains valid, even though the new-style officials saw themselves less and less as scribes producing well-crafted documents and increasingly as servants of the state implementing certain policies (Findley, 1980, 1989). Archival records reflect the decision-making process within officialdom, both at the Sultan's court and the Sublime Porte, the official name for the Grand Vizier's office. The opening of the Yıldız archives permits us to see how this process was modified during the neo-absolutist reign of Sultan Abdülhamid II. Their detailed examination will doubtlessly disperse many myths concerning the politics of that period, which both enemies and defenders of the Hamidian régime have produced in abundance (Deringil, 1998).

THE EIGHTEENTH CENTURY AS A POTENTIAL 'GROWTH AREA'

But to an early modernist, the real challenge comes from the archival sources concerning the eighteenth century. This is the great *terra incognita*, particularly for Anatolia, but also for Istanbul, and to a much lesser degree, the Balkans and the Arab provinces. Thirty to forty years ago, few people would have accepted that archival research into this period was urgently needed. After all, the second volume of Gibb and Bowen's comprehensive work had recently come out, and was only very marginally based on unpublished archive materials (Gibb and Bowen, 1957). To most scholars subscribing to the 'decline' paradigm, it seemed much more relevant and also more gratifying to study the Ottoman 'golden age' of the fifteenth and sixteenth centuries. Or else researchers preferred the pre-history of the Turkish national state, namely the post-Tanzimat years. This lack of interest among historians also explains why archivists, who do not operate in a vacuum, did not feel especially motivated to catalogue eighteenth-century materials.

However, during the last twenty years or so, the outlook of many scholars has changed. It was first understood that eighteenth-century records had potential significance for the economic historian, after Mehmet Genç had discovered the workings of the life-time tax farm (Genç, 1975). By demonstrating that the down payments by newly entering tax farmers reflected market trends, Genç opened the way to an albeit limited quantitative analysis of the Ottoman internal market. Moreover Genç, Fukazawa, Raymond and Panzac have all shown that in spite of demographic crises in certain parts of the Balkans, other sectors of the Ottoman economy continued to thrive and expand sometimes well into the 1760s (Fukazawa, 1987; Raymond, 1973–74; Panzac, 1982). Admittedly this relatively optimistic view of the eighteenth century's first sixty years is not shared by all specialists (McGowan, 1994). But it is an encouraging development that at least some Ottomanist historians no longer regard the eighteenth century as a period of unmitigated economic decline.

Moreover, now that 'privatisation' has become the watchword of politicians and economists, the reputation of tax farmers, less than savoury ever since the French Revolution, also has tended to improve. A recent study has stressed the possibilities of long-term tax-farming contracts in binding eighteenth-century provincial elites to the centre. As the latters' material well-being depended on their share in the Ottoman financial enterprise, these notables saw no reason to break away from the Empire (Salzmann, 1993). Moreover tax-farming also constitutes a subject of interest to historians of the non-Muslim minorities. For Armenian *sarrafs* in the eighteenth and early nineteenth centuries served as the indispensable adjuncts to tax-farming Muslim dignitaries. Often enough, these *sarrafs* controlled impressive sums of money; however the execution of a notable or vizier often also entailed the death of his *sarraf*. As tax-farming, in spite of its negative impact upon the well-being of the taxpayers, is thus now credited with some positive aspects, it will be psychologically easier for aspiring historians to subject themselves to the extra drudgery involved in reading and understanding tax-farming records. And as the financial, political and economic apparatus of the eighteenth-century Ottoman state depended upon tax-farming, a great leap forward in our understanding of the period may well be the result.

DEMYSTIFYING CENTRALISM

In conjunction with eighteenth-century studies, some historians have begun to question the assumption, totally unchallenged until very recently, that state centralisation is at all times a hallmark of political development. Notions of linear progress have been abandoned in most fields of history. But strangely enough, it has taken time for this trend to be fully accepted by some political scientists. However, in recent years, federative structures developing in the European Community, where a decentralising as well as a centralising component is very much in evidence, seem to have made an impression on students of politics. More scholars are now willing to accept that decentralised structures may have their legitimate place in political life. As a corollary some historical sociologists will admit that centralisation has its costs, for instance in terms of rising political violence and sharply increased taxation. We have encountered Charles Tilly, one of the 'grand old men' of current historical sociology (see chapter 1), whose work on early modern France stresses exactly these aspects (Tilly, 1985).

More recently the topic of decentralisation has been taken up by Ottomanists as well, but with a characteristic difference; demystifying Louis XIV still seems psychologically easier than doing the same to Süleyman the Lawgiver or Mehmed the Conqueror (on Louis XIV, see Burke, 1992). Thus Karen Barkey has argued in favour of a sixteenth- and seventeenth-century central government incorporating rebels into the governmental structure (Barkey, 1994). This policy enabled the Ottoman central administration to maintain itself while using force only to a limited extent, much less than was current in, for instance, seventeenth-century France. Attempted integration on the part of the central power may be regarded as a concession to separate political authorities emerging in the Ottoman provinces, as opposed to the punitive measures resorted to regularly by Richelieu or Louis XIV. By thus neutralising potential contenders for power, the Otto-man administration saved its subjects a great deal of suffering, as well as husbanding resources which could be used in foreign wars.

     This new scepticism with respect to the virtues of centralisation has special relevance where the eighteenth-century Ottoman Empire is con-cerned. Many scholars do not any more consider the emergence of locally based powerholders as evidence for protonationalist movements in the provinces (for an early example of this trend, compare Barbir, 1979–80). Previously, the assumption had been that 'nations' continued to exist in Bulgaria, Greece or Syria after the Ottoman conquest. These putative nations, so to speak, waited in the wings of the historical stage for the strength of the central state to decline, in order to reemerge in force. But now this assumption of national continuity is being strongly contested. In consequence, its corollary, namely the 'decline' of the Ottoman central state in the eighteenth century, also appears a less compelling assumption (Ander-son, 1983). That this approach is not reflected in many manuals, even those of fairly recent vintage, will be apparent to all readers of chapter 7. But manuals – including, in all probability, the present one – often do not reflect the very latest tendencies of research.

     Some historians have suggested that throughout pre-Ottoman and Ottoman history centralisation and its opposite have been cyclical phenom-ena. Of course, this assumption implies that no absolute value should be attached to centralisation (Keyder, 1987). Other scholars have stressed the potential for resistance to political crises which the Ottoman state derived from its flexibility and willingness to resort to decentralisation whenever necessary (Togan, 1992; Salzmann, 1993). Particularly Salzmann's article, closely argued and published in a journal read by non-Ottomanists, may well induce a number of historians to abandon the equation of state central-isation with political progress.

ON THE VIRTUES OF COMPARISON
     In the arguments outlined above, we find a good deal of implicit and explicit historical comparison. History has not gone as far as literary studies, where comparison has become the key to theoretical thinking on the phenomenon of literature itself. But even so, certain well-studied historical processes outside of the Ottoman world have come to inspire Ottomanist historians. This applies, for instance, to the post-Roman, 'Dark Age' phenomena of migration and state formation, which the recent coop-eration between social anthropologists, archaeologists and historians have

helped us view in a new light. Mediaevalists have gained a new understanding of the formation of fairly ephemeral states by migrant peoples, dominating previously established sedentary populations. This knowledge may have
some relevance for historians trying to unravel the complex and little known
processes governing the formation of fourteenth-century Anatolian principalities, the Ottoman not excluded (Berktay, 1990). Whether one wishes to
regard these phenomena as examples of the transition from a 'warrior
democracy' to a feudal society is a matter of personal choice (Kaser, 1990, p.
163). But the results gained by Europeanist mediaevalists can also be helpful
in other matters. Thus the use of pre-existing scribal traditions by a newly
established ruling class has been well studied for mediaeval Europe; *mutatis
mutandis* this phenomenon is relevant to Ottomanist historians as well. Thus
the Great Seljuk rulers adopted Iranian scribal traditions, which were then
transferred to recently conquered Anatolia. In their turn, the Ottomans
inherited the scribal traditions practiced by the Seljuks of Rum. Moreover
in the eleventh or twelfth century, the Byzantine example, particularly in
the financial realm, was probably of more importance to Anatolian state-
builders than it was to be in later times. To understand these selective
adoptions of foreign traditions, and their ultimate synthesis, the burgeoning
research on mediaeval Europe may well be helpful to the historian of early
Ottoman Anatolia.

But researchers interested in Ottoman–European comparisons now
pay more attention to the sixteenth and seventeenth centuries. Admitting
that such comparisons are feasible constitutes something of a novelty. Ever
since Montesquieu, there had existed a strong tendency among European
and American scholars to regard the difference between Ottoman and
European political systems as absolute. In the wake of Max Weber, Europeanists regarded the lack of an aristocracy dominating the countryside, and
of autonomous cities, as characteristics setting the Ottoman social formation
totally apart from its European counterparts.[4] But research undertaken
during the last few decades has shown that the differences between conti-
nental Europe and the Ottoman world were less clear-cut than had once
been assumed. After all, absolute monarchies of the sixteenth and seventeenth centuries did away with urban self-government in many parts of
Europe. Thus what had been considered a major characteristic of European
society has turned out to have been an ephemeral and limited phenomenon
(Braudel, 1979, vol. 1, pp. 457–458). On the other hand, it is well-known at
least to specialists that the Ottoman political class of the seventeenth and

[4] Turkish historians have rarely considered these features as being of major importance.

eighteenth centuries functioned very much like an aristocracy, even though it did not possess the personal security enjoyed by European noblemen and gentry (Abou-el-Haj, 1991, pp. 48–58).

Moreover Ottomanist historians have come to realise that the lack of formal urban institutions did not mean that town elites had no way of articulating their specific interests. Nor do these researchers any longer assume that Ottoman towns merely consisted of amorphous masses of isolated quarters and guilds. As a result, the Ottoman Empire and, for example, absolutist France are now perceived by some scholars not as incommensurable entities, but as societies which though different, share certain common features. Given the narrowing gap between the different historiographies, studies have begun to appear in which comparison is a major theme (Barkey, 1994; Salzmann, 1995).

A further debate concerns the manner in which we should evaluate the interest which some members of the Ottoman elites showed toward intellectual tendencies of eighteenth- and nineteenth-century Europe. Current interpretations focus on the military defeats which the Ottoman Empire suffered in the last decades of the seventeenth century, and, in an even more massive form, during the second half of the eighteenth. In order to remedy this situation, Ottoman elites sponsored the training of new-style military men, along with the technical cadres which were to make armies function more effectively. But it soon emerged that such training was not effective if students did not familiarise themselves with the theoretical underpinnings of the techniques they were to use, such as the mathematical foundations of ballistics. As a result, students in military colleges, but soon those in civilian professional schools as well, began to learn French in order to read a wider array of textbooks. With time the knowledge of this language became an avenue toward acquaintance with non-technical subjects as well.

However, so the model narrative continues, for many years theological and philosophical assumptions militated against the new style of scientific thinking. Thus the assumption that laws of nature operate without exception, to many people seemed to contradict the almightiness of God, who can do whatever he wishes (Mardin, 1962, p. 89). As the new learning was unable to acquire a secure status in the established world view, still strongly dominated by religion, some intellectually minded Ottomans in the years around 1900 gravitated toward agnosticism. But apart from a small elite, the insecure religious status of the new learning did not allow it to put down very secure roots in late Ottoman society.

Many features in this model certainly correspond to observed reality. However, a comparison with the different movements of intellectual renewal recognised by Europeanist historians of the mediaeval and early modern periods suggests a somewhat different interpretation. In the Carolingian period around 800 CE, in the twelfth century and again in the fifteenth, major cultural shifts in western Europe were achieved and/or legitimised by reference to what had become a foreign culture, namely the classical antiquity of Rome and later also Greece. Certainly, texts and images from this foreign culture were interpreted by the standards of the day. But especially the understanding of Roman literary culture, limited though it may have been, made it possible to conceive alternatives to the largely oral culture of the early middle ages, when books were valued more as liturgical objects than items to be read. Equally in the eighteenth century, models derived from real or invented Chinese history allowed French political thinkers to formulate notions of an enlightened secular monarchy.

When used in this fashion, texts from a foreign cultural tradition can be of help in developing new ideas, which would be difficult to legitimise within the universe of a single culture. Reference to Greece, Rome or China allowed European intellectuals to envisage a world rather different from the one they inhabited. At least in my view, it is perfectly possible that something similar happened in late nineteenth- and early twentieth-century Ottoman elite culture. One might surmise that by reading Victor Hugo or practising figurative painting, educated Ottomans were trying to enlarge the compass of their own intellectual world, and as a first step toward that purpose, adopted sizeable sections of contemporary French culture.

But this cultural project was constantly frustrated by the political situation. With the Ottoman Empire in retreat everywhere, the wholesale adoption of the adversary's culture came to look rather like treason in the public eye, and those engaged in this project were constantly under pressure. Needing to justify themselves at every step, they may have found it difficult to maintain the single-mindedness and spontaneity that is an important ingredient in any cultural enterprise. In concrete terms, the catastrophic political situation made it impossible for people with close ties to the Ottoman ruling class to say something like 'I don't care what happens in the outside world, I am painting' (or 'engaging in mathematical speculation', or 'editing an ancient text'). After all European culture was being promoted within Ottoman society as a prerequisite for resistance against European political encroachment, in other words, in order to 'save the state'. But although large slices of European culture were being adopted, the Ottoman state was very obviously not being saved, quite to the contrary. Given this situation, the proponents of the new learning and new-style arts were forced to make so many concessions that they found it difficult to function effectively (Mardin, 1971).

This understanding of post-Tanzimat cultural change is probably not being shared by the majority of the Ottomanist community. Thus in an introductory survey, a brief summary must suffice. Other models of post-Tanzimat cultural change may be developed. But historians wishing to transcend the idea that Ottoman cultural reform was nothing but a response to Great Power encroachment, and nationalism among the subject peoples, will probably start out from ideas developed by historians with a comparative bent.

Moreover we are only beginning to explore the possibilities of comparison between the Ottoman Empire and extra-European civilisations. This is largely due to the fact that whenever Ottomanists have some understanding of the history of a non-Ottoman society, this knowledge normally refers to Europe. But now, as more and more Japanese scholars concern themselves with Ottoman history, links are developing to historians studying the Far East. Ottoman interest in things Japanese goes back to the beginning of the century, when the Japanese victory over Russia alerted the Ottoman elites to the possibility that a 'modernised' Asian society might win out against Russia. But this brief flurry of interest did not result in a serious study of Japanese history by Ottomanist historians, either Turkish or foreign. It was only in 1964 that an American project, in which Halil Inalcık participated, attempted a systematic comparison of Ottoman and Japanese nineteenth- and twentieth-century history. Given the temper of the times, the successes and failures of 'modernisation' formed the major focus (Inalcık, 1964). In 1984, when the 'modernisation' paradigm no longer dominated the scene, and Japanese history had begun to establish itself as a recognised discipline in Turkey, there appeared an issue of the journal *Toplum ve Bilim*, at the time edited by Huri Islamoğlu-Inan. This publication was devoted to the image of Japan in the Ottoman Empire and Turkey. Recently Selçuk Esenbel has attempted some sophisticated comparisons between the cultural practices of the elites of Meiji Japan and the Ottoman Empire (Esenbel, 1994, 1996). All this is no more than a beginning, but hopefully in the long run, further comparative ventures will emerge.

However, it would seem that Ottomanist historians can draw at least as much, if not more, inspiration from the history of China. It is rather a pity that the small band of Turkish historians with a knowledge of Chinese have tended to concern themselves with Central Asia, rather than with comparative studies. Only very few attempts have been made to compare developments characterising this or that period of Chinese history with the dynamics typical of the Ottoman realm (Togan, 1992). Yet it would seem that some of the categories used by Chinese historians, but virtually unknown to the practitioners of our discipline, such as inclusiveness (of outsiders) versus exclusiveness, should be taken into consideration by Ottomanist historians as well (for an attempt in this direction, see Barkey, 1994). Certain thorny topics in Ottoman history, such as the military rebellions of the late sixteenth and early seventeenth centuries, will probably benefit from study within a comparative perspective (Faroqhi, 1995; for a broadly-based study of revolution and rebellion, including France, China and the Ottoman Empire, see Goldstone, 1991).

A further topic worth pursuing is the comparative study of Russian and Ottoman histories. As a result of the Cold War, very few Ottomanists have ever worked on the rich materials relevant to our discipline found in the Russian archives. Russian historians of the Ottoman Empire also have been denied access to the sources available in Turkey. As a result, few Ottomanist historians have been motivated to learn Russian, so that even now, with opportunities for cooperation increasing, it will take time before they can be pursued. On the other hand, Ottoman-Russian history potentially is a rich field, not only because of the – largely conflictual – common history of the two empires between the late seventeenth and the twentieth century. For even a casual observer will note certain parallels in socio-political organisation, such as the strong position of the ruler, the parallel roles of strelitzi and janissaries, and particularly, the numerous features shared by Ottoman *timar* holders and the so-called middle service class of seventeenth-century Czarist Russia (Hellie, 1971). At the same time, there also existed marked contrasts between the two societies. Thus peasant dependence was, for the most part, much more extreme in Russia than in the Ottoman Empire.

It is possible to go on at length in this vein. Sketching future research is not really very difficult – the problems only emerge when one actually sets to work. But at least to me, Ottoman history has provided the occasion for many a fascinating quest.

SUGGESTED READING

Berktay, Halil (1991).'Der Aufstieg und die gegenwärtige Krise der nationalistischen Geschichtsschreibung in der Türkei', *Periplus*, 1, 102–125 (fascinating, though published in a small journal, and in German to boot).
Davison, Roderic H. (1990). *Essays in Ottoman and Turkish History, 1774–1923,*

The Impact of the West (Austin: University of Texas Press) (collected articles by a connoisseur of the Tanzimat period).

Esenbel, Selçuk (1994). 'The Anguish of Civilised Behaviour: The Use of Western Cultural Forms in the Everyday Lives of The Meiji Japanese and the Ottoman Turks During the Nineteenth Century', *Japan Review*, 5, 145–185 (full of fascinating insights).

Finn, Robert P. (1984). *The Early Turkish Novel, 1872–1900* (Istanbul) ISIS: (informative).

Genç, Mehmet (1984). 'XVIII. Yüzyılda Osmanlı Ekonomisi ve Savaş', *Yapıt, Toplumsal Araştırmalar Dergisi*, 49 (4), 51–61; 50 (5), 86–93; French version (1995): 'L'économie ottomane et la guerre au XVIIIᵉ siècle', *Turcica*, XXVII, 177–196 (a classic, 'required reading').

Kaser, Karl (1990). *Südosteuropäische Geschichte und Geschichtswissenschaft, eine Einfürung* (Vienna, Cologne: Böhlau) (brilliant though sometimes erratic comments from a specialist on southeastern Europe).

Mardin, Şerif (1962). *The Genesis of Young Ottoman Thought, A Study in the Modernization of Turkish Political Ideas* (Princeton University Press) (still the best intellectual history of the period; a classic).

Moran, Berna (1983–1994). *Türk Romanına Eleştirel bir Bakış*, 3 vols. Istanbul: Ileştim) vol 1: *Ahmet Mithat'tan A. H. Tanpınar'a* (by a literary historian mainly interested in modern Turkey; comparisons with French and Russian novels).

Necipoğlu, Gülru (1991). *Architecture, Ceremonial and Power, The Topkapı Palace in the Fifteenth and Sixteenth Centuries* (Cambridge MA: The Architectural History Foundation and MIT Press) (fundamental for anyone concerned with the links between political and art history in the Ottoman realm).

Salzmann, Ariel (1993). 'An Ancien Régime Revisited: 'Privatization' and Political Economy in the Eighteenth-Century Ottoman Empire', *Politics and Society*, XXI. 4, 393–423 (innovative and thought-provoking).

Tilly, Charles (1985). 'War Making and State Making as Organized Crime', in *Bringing the State Back In*, ed. Peter Evans, Dietrich Rueschemeyer and Theda Skocpol (Cambridge: Cambridge University Press), pp. 169–91 (worth pondering, for Ottomanists and others).

REFERENCES

Works not cited in the main text but only recommended as 'suggested reading' have not been included.

WORKS OF REFERENCE

(Dictionaries, encyclopedias, archive and library catalogues).

Abrahamowicz, Zygmunt (1959). *Katalog Dokumentów Tureckich, Dokumenti do Dziejów Polski i Krajów Osciennych w Latach 1455–1672* (Warsaw: Polska Akademia Nauk).

Akgündüz, Ahmet *et alii* (eds.) (1988–89). *Şeriye Sicilleri*, 2 vols. (Istanbul: Türk Dünyası Araştırmaları Vakfı).

Altan, Mustafa Haşim, J. McHenry and Ronald Jennings (1977). 'Archival Materials and Research Facilities in the Cyprus Turkish Federated State: Ottoman Empire, British Empire, Turkish Republic', *International Journal of Middle East Studies*, 8, 29–42.

Artuk, Ibrahim and Cevriye Artuk (1971, 1974). *Istanbul Arkeoloji Müzeleri, Teşhirdeki Islâmî Sikkeler Kataloğu*, 2 vols. (Istanbul: Milli Eğitim Bakanlığı).

Babinger, Franz (1927). *Die Geschichtsschreiber der Osmanen und ihre Werke* (Leipzig: Otto Harrassowitz).

(1982). *Osmanlı Tarih Yazarları ve Eserleri*, tr. by Çoşkun Ücok (Ankara: Kültür ve Turizm Bakanlığı).

Belge, Murat (1985). *Tanzimat'tan Cumhuriyet'e Türkiye Ansiklopedisi*, 6 vols. (Istanbul: İletişim).

Benningsen, Alexandre *et al.* (1978). *Le Khanat de Crimée dans les Archives du Musée du Palais de Topkapı* (Paris, The Hague: Mouton and EHESS).

Blaškovič, Josef, Karel Petraček and Rudolf Vesely (1961). *Arabische, türkische und persische Handschriften der Universitätsbibliothek in Bratislava* (Bratislava: Die Universitätsbibliothek in Bratislava).

Blochet, E. (1932–33). *Bibliothèque Nationale, Catalogue des manuscrits turcs* (Paris: Bibliothèque Nationale).

Bonine, Michael, Eckart Ehlers *et al.* (1994). *The Middle Eastern City and Islamic Urbanism, An Annotated Bibliography of Western Literature* (Bonn: Ferdinand Dümmlers).

Bursalı Mehemmed Tâhir (1333–34/1914–16 to 1343/1924–25, reprint 1971). *ʿOsmanlı Müʾellifleri (A Biographical Dictionary of the Ottoman Literature)*, 3 vols. (Istanbul: Matbaa-yı Amire; reprint: Westmead/England.: Gregg International Publishers Ltd).

Collective work (1938–40). *Topkapı Sarayı Müzesi Arşivi Kılavuzu*, 2 fasc., down to and incl. letter ʿHʾ (Istanbul: T.C. Maarif Vekilliği).

(1943). *Istanbul Kütüphaneleri Tarih-Coğrafya Yazmaları Katalogları* (Istanbul: T.C. Maarif Vekilliği).

(1963–1977). *XIII. Yüzyıldan beri Türkiye Türkçesiyle Yazılmış Kitaplardan Toplanan Tanıklarıyla Tarama Sözlüğü* (Ankara: Türk Dil Kurumu).

(1968). *Redhouse Yeni Türkçe-Ingilizce Sözlük, New Redhouse Turkish-English Dictionary* (Istanbul: Redhouse Press).

(1976–1990). *Türk Dili ve Edebiyatı Ansiklopedisi, Devirler, Isimler, Eserler, Terimler* (Istanbul: Dergâh Yayınları).

(1979–). *Türkiye Yazmaları Toplu Kataloğu. The Union Catalogue of Manuscripts in Turkey* (Ankara: T.C. Kültür ve Turizm Bakanlığı).

(1981–84). *Yurt Ansiklopedisi, Türkiye Il Il: Dünü, Bugünü, Yarını*, 11 vols. (Istanbul: Anadolu Yayıncılık AŞ).

(1988–). *Türkiye Diyanet Vakfı Islam Ansiklopedisi* (Istanbul: Türkiye Diyanet Vakfı).

(1992). *Başbakanlık Osmanlı Arşivi Rehberi* (Ankara: Başbakanlık, Devlet Arşivleri Genel Müdürlüğü).

(1993–1995). *Dünden Bugüne Istanbul Ansiklopedisi*, 8 vols. (Istanbul: Kültür Bakanlığı and Tarih Vakfı).

(1995). *Başbakanlık Osmanlı Arşivi Katalogları Rehberi* (Ankara: T.C. Başbakanlık, Devlet Arşivleri Genel Müdürlüğü).

Cresti, Federico and Salvatore Bono (1988). *Documenti sul Maghreb dal XVII al XIX seculo, Archivio Storico della Congregazione 'De Propaganda Fide', 'Scritture Riferite nei Congressi-Barbaria'* (Perugia: Università degli Studi).

Danişmend, Ismail Hami (1971). *Izahlı Osmanlı Tarihi Kronolojisi*, 5 vols. (Istanbul: Türkiye Yayınevi).

Deniz Kuvvetleri Komutanlığı (ed.) (1966). *Piri Reis Haritası* (Istanbul: Seyir ve Hidrografi Dairesi).

Devellioğlu, Ferit (1962). *Osmanlıca-Türkçe Ansiklopedik Lugat, Eski ve Yeni Harflerle* (Ankara: n.p.).

Droulia, Loukia (ed.) (1993). *On Travel Literature and Related Subjects: References and*

Approaches (Athens: Institute of Neohellenic Research, National Hellenic Research Foundation).

Duman, Hasan (1406/1986). *İstanbul Kütüphaneleri Arap Harflı Süreli Yayınları Toplu Kataloğu 1828–1928 ...* (Istanbul: IRSICA).

Džaja, Srecko, Günther Weiß, Mathias Bernath and Karl Nehring (1995). *Austro-Turcica 1541–1552, Diplomatische Akten des habsburgischen Gesandtschaftsverkehrs mit der Hohen Pforte im Zeitalter Süleymans des Prächtigen* (Munich: R. Oldenbourg).

Elker, Salâhaddin (1953). *Divan Rakamları* (Ankara: Türk Tarih Kurumu).

The Encyclopedia of Islam (1913–1934). ed. by M.T. Houtsma, T.W. Arnold, R. Basset, R. Hartmann *et alii* , 4 vols. (Leiden: E.J. Brill).

The Encyclopedia of Islam (2nd edn, 1960–). ed. by H. A. R. Gibb *et alii* (Leiden: E.J. Brill).*(EI)*

Flemming, Barbara (1968). *Türkische Handschriften, Teil 1* (Wiesbaden: Franz Steiner).

Flügel, Gustav (1865–67). *Die arabischen, persischen und türkischen Handschriften der kaiserlich-königlichen Hofbibliothek zu Wien* (Vienna: K. K. Hof- und Staatsdruckerei).

Gölpınarlı, Abdülbaki (1967–1972). *Mevlânâ Müzesi Yazmalar Kataloğu*, 3 vols. (Ankara: Milli Eğitim Bakanlığı).

Götz, Manfred (1968). *Türkische Handschriften, Teil 2* (Wiesbaden: Franz Steiner).

(1979). *Türkische Handschriften* (Wiesbaden: Franz Steiner).

Günday, Dündar (1974). *Arşiv Belgelerinde Siyakat Yazısı Özellikleri ve Divan Rakamları* (Ankara: Türk Tarih Kurumu).

M.S.B. Harita Genel Müdürlüğü (1977). *Yeni Türkiye Atlası* (Ankara: Harita Genel Müdürlüğü).

Ihsanoğlu, Ekmeleddin, Ramazan Şeşen, Cevat Izgi and Cemil Akpınar (1406/1986). *Catalogue of Manuscripts in the Köprülü Library* (Istanbul: IRSICA).

Ihsanoğlu, Ekmeleddin, Nimet Bayraktar and Mihin Lugal (1995). *Bibliography on Manuscript Libraries in Turkey and the Publications on the Manuscripts Located in these Libraries* (Istanbul: IRSICA).

Inal, Ibnülemin Mahmud (1930–42). *Son Asır Türk Şairleri*, 14 issues (Istanbul: Devlet Basimevi).

Inal, Ibnülemin Mahmud Kemal (2nd edn 1955). *Osmanlı Devrinde Son Sadrazamlar*, 4 vols. (Istanbul: Maarif Basımevi).

İslam Ansiklopedisi, İslam Alemi Tarih, Coğrafya, Etnografya ve Biyografya Lugatı (1949–1986). Collective work (Istanbul: Milli Eğitim Bakanlığı). *(IA)*

Iz, Fahir and Günay Kut (1985–86), 'XV. Yüzyılda Nazım,' in *Başlangıçından Günümüze Kadar Büyük Türk Klâsikleri, Tarih-Antoloji-Ansiklopedi*, 2 vols. (Istanbul: Ötüken and Söğüt), vol. 2, pp. 109–260.

Kahane, Henry, Kahane, Renée and Tietze, Andreas (1958). *The Lingua Franca of the Levant, Turkish Nautical Terms of Italian and Greek Origin* (Urbana: University of Illinois Press).

Karatay, Fehmi Edhem (1961). *Topkapı Sarayı Müzesi Kütüphanesi, Türkçe Yazmalar Kataloğu*, 2 vols. (Istanbul: Topkapı Sarayı Müzesi).

Kiefer, J.D. and T.X. Bianchi (1835). *Elsine-i turkiye ve frānseviyenin lughatı*, 2 vols. (Paris: n.p.).

Kornrumpf, Hans-Jürgen with Jutta Kornrumpf (1973). *Osmanische Bibliographie mit besonderer Berücksichtigung der Türkei in Europa* (Leiden, Cologne: E. J. Brill).

Kreiser, Klaus (1988). *Historische Bücherkunde Südosteuropa*, vol. II: *Neuzeit*, Teil 1: *Osmanisches Reich, Makedonien, Albanien* (München: Oldenbourg).

Mantran, Robert (1961). *Inventaire des documents d'archives turcs du Dar el-Bey* (Tunis, Paris: Université de Tunis, PUF).

Meninski, Franciscus a Mesgnien (2nd edn 1780). *Lexicon Arabico-Persico-Turcicum*, 4 vols. (Vienna: Joseph de Kurzböck).

Ministry of Culture and Tourism of the Turkish Republic (1988). *Kitab-ı Bahriye - Piri Reis*, 4 vols. (Ankara, Istanbul: The Historical Research Foundation, Istanbul Research Center).

Özkırımlı, Attila (1982). *Türk Edebiyatı Ansiklopedisi* (Istanbul: Cem Yayınevi).

Özege, Seyfettin (1971–79). *Eski Harflerle Basılmış Türkçe Eserler Kataloğu*, 5 vols (Istanbul: Nihal Kütüphanesi).

Özendes, Engin (2nd edn 1995). *Osmanlı İmparatorluğunda Fotoğrafçılık (1839–1919), Photography in the Ottoman Empire . . .* (Istanbul: İletişim Yayınları).

Özön, Mustafa Nihat (1971). *Osmanlıca-Türkçe Sözlük* (Ankara: Bilgi).

Pakalın, Mehmet Zeki (reprint 1971). *Osmanlı Tarih Deyimleri ve Terimleri Sözlüğü*, 3 vols. (Istanbul: Milli Eğitim Bakanlığı).

Pearson, J.D. with Julia Ashton (1958). *Index Islamicus 1906–1955, A catalogue of articles on Islamic studies in periodicals and other collective publications* (Cambridge: W. Heffer & Sons) (continued in several vols., see also Roper, C. T.)

Pedani Fabris, Maria Pia (1994a). *I 'Documenti turchi' dell'Archivio di Stato di Venezia* (Roma: Ministero per i beni culturali e ambientali, Ufficio centrale per i beni archivistici).

Petritsch, Ernst Dieter (1991). *Regesten der osmanischen Dokumente im Österreichischen Staatsarchiv, Mitteilungen des Österreichischen Staatsarchivs*, Suppl. 10/1 (Vienna: Österreichisches Staatsarchiv).

Redhouse, James (1890, reprint 1921). *A Turkish and English Lexicon* (Istanbul: Matteosian).

Reychman, Jan and Ananiasz Zajaczkowski (1968). *Handbook of Ottoman-Turkish Diplomatics*, tr., revised, indexed and ed. Andrew S. Ehrenkreutz, Fanny Davis and Tibor Halasi-Kun (The Hague, Paris: Mouton).

Rieu, Charles (1881). *Catalogue of the Turkish Manuscripts in the British Museum* (London: Trustees of the British Museum).

Roper, G.J. and C.H. Bleaney (1996). *Index Islamicus. A bibliography of books, articles and reviews on Islam and the Muslim world published in the year 1994 with additions from 1993* (London . . .: Bowker-Saur).

Samy-Bey-Fraschery, Ch. (= Şemseddin Sami) (1885). *Dictionnaire turc-français* (Istanbul: Mihran).

(1889). *Ḳāmūs ül ʿĀlam, Dictionnaire universel d'histoire et de géographie*, 6 vols. (Istanbul: Mihran).

Sohrweide, Hanna (1974). *Türkische Handschriften und einige in den Handschriften enthaltene persische und arabische Werke* (Wiesbaden: Franz Steiner). (1981). *Türkische Handschriften, Teil 5* (Wiesbaden: Franz Steiner).

Süreyya, Mehmed (1308/1890–91 to 1315/1897). *Sicill-i ʿOsmânî (The Ottoman National Biography)*, 4 vols. (Istanbul: Matbaa-yı Amire; reprint: Westmead/England.: Gregg International Publishers Ltd).

Temimi, Abdeljelil (1979). *Sommaire des régisters arabes et turcs d'Alger* (Tunis: Revue d'histoire magrébine).

Türkiye Ekonomik ve Toplumsal Tarih Vakfı (4. printing, 1996). *Istanbul Kültür Kurumları Rehberi* (Istanbul: T.C. Kültür Bakanlığı and Türkiye Ekonomik ve Toplumsal Tarih Vakfı).

Turner, Jane (ed.). *The Dictionary of Art*, 34 vols. (London: Macmillan).

Unat, Faik Reşat (1968). *Osmanlı Sefirleri ve Sefaretnameleri*, ed. Bekir Sıtkı Baykal (Ankara: Türk Tarih Kurumu).

Uzunçarşılı, Ismail Hakkı, Ibrahim Kemal Baybura and Ülkü Altındağ (1985–86). *Topkapı Sarayı Müzesi Osmanlı Saray Arşivi Katalogu, Fermanlar*, 2 fasc. (Ankara: Türk Tarih Kurumu).

Yazır, Mahmud (1942). *Eski Yazıları Okuma Anahtarı* (Istanbul: Vakıflar Umum Müdürlüğü).

Zenker, Jules Théodore (1866). *Dictionnaire turc-arabe-persan*, 2 vols. (Leipzig: Wilhelm Engelmann), (explanations given in both French and German). (reprint 1994). *Türkisch-Arabisch-Persisches Handwörterbuch*, 2 vols. (Hildesheim/Germany, New York: Georg Olms).

WORKS CITED

Abdel Nour, Antoine (1982). *Introduction à l'histoire urbaine de la Syrie ottomane (XVIᵉ-XVIIIᵉ siècle)* (Beirut: Université Libanaise).

Adanır, Fikret (1989). 'Tradition and Rural Change in Southeastern Europe,' in *The Origins of Backwardness in Eastern Europe*, ed. Daniel Chirot (Berkeley: University of California Press), pp. 131–176.

(1998). 'The Ottoman Peasantries, c.1360–c.1860,' in *The Peasantries of Europe from the Fourteenth to the Eighteenth Centuries*, ed. Tom Scott (London, New York: Longman), pp. 269–312.

Abou-El-Haj, Rifaʿat A. (1991). *Formation of the Modern State, The Ottoman Empire, Sixteenth to Eighteenth Centuries* (Albany NY: SUNY Press).

Aigen, Wolffgang (1980). *Sieben Jahre in Aleppo (1656–1663), Ein Abschnitt aus den 'Reiß-Beschreibungen' des Wolffgang Aigen*, ed. Andreas Tietze (Vienna: Verlag der wissenschaftlichen Gesellschaften Österreichs).

Akarlı, Engin (1988). 'Provincial Power Magnates in Ottoman Bilad al-Sham and Egypt, 1740–1840', in *La vie sociale dans les provinces arabes à l'époque ottomane*, ed. Abdeljelil Temimi (Baghouan: CÉROMDI), vol. 3, 41–56.

Akbayar, Nuri (1985). 'Osmanlı Yayıncılığı', in *Tanzimat'tan Cumhuriyet'e Türkiye Ansiklopedisi*, 6 vols. (Istanbul: İletişim) VI, pp. 1680–96.

Akdağ, Mustafa (1959, 1971). *Türkiye'nin İktisadî ve İçtimaî Tarihi*, 2 vols. (Ankara: Ankara Üniversitesi Dil ve Tarih-Coğrafya Fakültesi).

(1963). *Celâlî İsyanları (1550–1603)* (Ankara: Ankara Üniversitesi Dil ve Tarih Coğrafya Fakültesi).

Aksan, Virginia (1993). 'Ottoman Political Writing, 1768–1808', *International Journal of Middle East Studies*, 25, 53–69.

(1994) 'Is There a Turk in the Turkish Spy?', *Eighteenth-Century Fiction*, 6, 3, 201–13.

(1995). *An Ottoman Statesman in War and Peace, Ahmed Resmi Efendi 1700–1783* (Leiden: E. J.Brill).

Akşin, Sina (ed.) (1990–1995). *Türkiye Tarihi*, vol. I: *Osmanlı Devletine kadar Türkiye*, vol. 2: *Osmanlı Devleti 1300–1600*, vol 3: *Osmanlı Devleti 1600–1908*. vol. 4: *Çağdaş Türkiye 1908–1980*, vol 5: *Bügünkü Türkiye 1980–1995* (Istanbul: Cem Yayinevi).

Albèri, Eugène (ed.) (1840–45). *Relazioni degli ambasciatori veneti durante il secolo XVI*, Series III: *Relazioni dell'Impero Ottomano*, 3 vols. (Florence).

Anastassiadou, Meropi (1993). 'Les inventaires après décès de Salonique à la fin du XIXᵉ siècle: source pour l'étude d'une société au seuil de la modernisation', *Turcica*, XXV, 97–136.

(1997). *Salonique, 1830–1912, Une ville ottomane à l'âge des Réformes* (Leiden: E. J. Brill).

Anderson, Benedict (1983). *Imagined Communities, Reflections on the Origin and Spread of Nationalism* (London, New York: Verso).

Anderson, Perry (2nd edn 1979). *Lineages of the Absolutist State* (London: Verso).

Artan, Tülay (1993). 'From Charismatic Leadership to Collective Rule: Introducing Materials on the Wealth and Power of Ottoman Princesses in the Eighteenth Century', *Toplum ve Ekonomi*, IV, 53–94.

Aşçıdede Halil Ibrahim (1960). *Geçen Asrı Aydınlatan Kıymetli bir Eser: Hatiralar*, ed. Reşad Ekrem Koçu (Istanbul).

ʿĀšıqpašazāde (1929). *Die altosmanische Chronik des Āšıqpašazāde, auf Grund mehrerer neuentdeckten Handschriften . . .*, ed. Friedrich Giese (Leipzig: Harrassowitz).

Atasoy, Nurhan and Julian Raby (1989). *Iznik, the Pottery of Ottoman Turkey* (Istanbul and London: Institute of Social Sciences of Istanbul University, Alexandria Press).

Babinger, Franz (ed.) (1931). *Das Archiv des Bosniaken Osman Pascha, nach den Beständen der Badischen Landesbibliothek zu Karlsruhe . . .* (Berlin: n.p.).

Barbir, Karl K. (1979–80). *Ottoman Rule in Damascus, 1708–1758* (Princeton: Princeton University Press).

Barkan, Ömer Lütfi (1939). 'Türk-Islam Hukuku Tatbikatının Osmanlı Imparatorluğunda Aldığı Şekiller I: Malikâne-Divanî Sistemi', *Türk Hukuk ve İktisat Tarihi Mecmuası*, 1, 119–85.

(1939–40). 'XV ve XVI Asırlarda Osmanlı İmparatorluğunda Toprak İşçiliğinin Organizasyonu Şekilleri,' *İstanbul Üniversitesi İktisat Fakültesi Mecmuası* I, 1, 29–74; I, 2, 198–245; I, 4, 397–447.

(1940–41). 'Türkiye'de İmparatorluk Devirlerinin Büyük Nüfus ve Arazi Tahrirleri ve Hakana Mahsus İstatistik defterleri', *İstanbul Üniversitesi İktisat Fakültesi Mecmuası*, I, 1, 20–59; II, 2, 214–247.

(1942). 'Osmanlı İmparatorluğunda bir İskân ve Kolonizasyon Metodu Olarak Vakıflar ve Temlikler', *Vakıflar Dergisi*, II, 279–386.

(1951). 'Tarihi Demografi Araştırmaları ve Osmanlı Tarihi', *Türkiyat Mecmuası*, X, 1–26.

(1953–1954). 'H. 933–934 (M. 1527–1528) Malî Yılına Ait bir Bütçe Örneği', *İstanbul Üniversitesi İktisat Fakültesi Mecmuası*, 15, 1–4, 251–329.

(1964). '894 (1488/1489) Yılı Cizyesinin Tahsilâtına Âit Muhasebe Bilânçoları', *Belgeler*, I, 1, 1–117.

(1966). 'Edirne Askeri Kassamı'na Ait Tereke Defterleri (1545–1659)', *Belgeler*, III, 5–6, 1–479.

(1975a). 'The Price Revolution of the Sixteenth Century: A Turning Point in the Economic History of the Near East', *International Journal of Middle East Studies*, VI, 3–28.

(1975b). "Feodal' Düzen ve Osmanlı Tımarı'", in *Türkiye İktisat Tarihi Semineri, Metinler / Tartışmalar . . .*, ed. Osman Okyar and Ünal Nalbantoğlu (Ankara: Hacettepe Üniversitesi), pp. 1–32.

Barkan, Ömer Lutfi and Ekrem Hakkı Ayverdi (eds.) (1970). *İstanbul Vakıfları Tahrîr Defteri, 953 (1546) Târîhli* (Istanbul: İstanbul Fetih Cemiyeti).

Barker, Thomas M. (1967). *Double Eagle and Crescent, Vienna's Second Turkish Siege and its Historical Setting* (Albany, N. Y.: SUNY Press).

Barkey, Karen (1994). *Bandits and Bureaucrats, The Ottoman Route to State Centralization* (Ithaca, London: Cornell University Press).

Barkey, Karen and Mark Hagen (eds) (1997). *After Empire. Multiethnic Societies and Nation-Building, The Soviet Union and Russian, Ottoman and Habsburg Empires* (Boulder/Col.: Westview Press).

Barozzi, Nicolo and Guglielmo Berchet (eds.) (1871–72). *Le relazioni degli stati europei lette al Senato dagli Ambasciatori veneziani nel secolo decimosettimo*, series Va Turchia, 2 vols. (Venice: Naratovich).

Bašeskiya, Mula Mustafa Ševki (1968). *Ljetopis (1746–1804)*, tr. Mehmed Mujezinovic (Sarajevo: Veselin Masleša).

Bayly, Christopher A. (1983). *Rulers, Townsmen and Bazaars, North Indian society in the age of British expansion, 1770–1870* (Cambridge: Cambridge University

Press).

(1989). *Imperial Meridian, The British Empire and the World 1780–1830* (London, New York: Longman).

Beauge, Gilbert and Engin Çizgen (n.d. [1992]). *Images d'empire, aux origines de la photographie en Turquie* (Istanbul: Institut d'Études Françaises d'Istanbul).

Beckingham, C. F. (1983). *Between Islam and Christendom, Travellers, Facts and Legends in the Middle Ages and the Renaissance* (London: Variorum Reprints).

Behrens-Abouseif, Doris (1994). *Egypt's Adjustment to Ottoman Rule, Institutions, waqf and Architecture in Cairo (16th and 17th Centuries)* (Leiden: E. J. Brill).

Beldiceanu, Nicoara (1980). *Le timar dans l'État ottoman (début XIVe – début XVIe siècle)* (Wiesbaden: Otto Harrassowitz).

Beldiceanu, Nicoara and Irène Beldiceanu-Steinherr (1978). 'Règlement ottoman concernant le recensement (première moitié du XVIe siècle)', *Südost-Forschungen*, 37, 1–40.

Beldiceanu-Steinherr, Irène (1976). 'Fiscalité et formes de possession de la terre arable dans l'Anatolie préottomane', *JESHO*, 19, 3, 233–313.

Belge, Murat (n.d.) *Türkiye Dünyanın Neresinde?* (Istanbul: Birikim).

Benedict, Peter (1974). *Ula, an Anatolian town* (Leiden: E.J. Brill).

Bennassar, Bartholomé and Lucile Bennassar (1989). *Les chrétiens d'Allah, l'histoire extraordinaire des renégats* (Paris: Perrin).

Bennet, Ferdinand, ed. Karpat, Kemal (1980). 'The Social, Economic and Administrative Situation in the Sancak of Kayseri in 1880: the Report of Lieutenant Ferdinand Bennet, British Vice-Consul of Anatolia (October, 1880)', *International Journal of Turkish Studies*, 1, 2, 107–25.

Benningsen, Alexandre and Chantal Lemercier-Quelquejay (1976). 'La Moscovie, la Horde Nogay et le problème des communications entre l'Empire ottoman et l'Asie centrale en 1552–1556', *Turcica*, 8, 2, 203–236.

Berkes, Niyazi (1969, 1970). *100 Soruda Türkiye İktisat Tarihi*, vol. 1: *Osmanlı Ekonomik Tarihinin Temelleri*, vol. 2 (no subtitle) (Istanbul: Gerçek Yayınevi).

Berktay, Halil (1983). *Cumhuriyet İdeolojisi ve Fuat Köprülü* (Istanbul: Kaynak Yayınları).

(1985). 'Tarih Çalışmaları,' in *Cumhuriyet Dönemi Türkiye Ansiklopedisi* (Istanbul: İletişim Yayınları), pp. 2456–2478.

(1991). 'Der Aufstieg und die gegenwärtige Krise der nationalistischen Geschichtsschreibung in der Türkei', *Periplus*, 1, 102–125.

(1992). 'The Search for the Peasant in Western and Turkish History/Historiography', in *New Approaches to State and Peasant in Ottoman History*, ed. Halil Berktay and Suraiya Faroqhi (London: Frank Cass), pp. 109–84.

Beşir Fuad'ın Mektupları (n.d.). ed. C. Parkan Özturan and Selâhettin Hilav (Istanbul: Aarba).

Beydilli, Kemal (1984). 'Ignatius Mouradgea D'Ohsson (Muradcan Tosuniyan)', *İstanbul Üniversitesi Edebiyat Fakültesi Tarih Dergisi*, 34, 247–314.

Beydilli, Kemal (1995). *Türk Bilim ve Matbaacılık Tarihinde Mühendishane, Mühen-*

dishâne Matbaası ve Kütüphânesi (1776–1826) (Istanbul: Eren).

Biegman, N. (1967). *The Turco-Ragusan Relationship* (The Hague: Mouton).

Binark, Ismet *et al.* (eds.) (1993). *3 Numaralı Mühimme Defteri (966–968/ 1558–1560),* 2 vols. (Ankara: Başbakanlık Devlet Arşivleri Genel Müdürlüğü).

(eds.) (1994). *5 Numaralı Mühimme Defteri (973/1565–66)* (Ankara: Başbakanlık Devlet Arşivleri Genel Müdürlüğü).

(eds.) (1996). *12 Numaralı Mühimme Defteri 978–979/1570–1572,* 3 vols. (Ankara: Başbakanlık Devlet Arşivleri Genel Müdürlüğü).

Black, Cyril and Brown, Carl E. (eds.) (1996). *Modernization in the Middle East, the Ottoman Empire and its Afro-Asian Successors* (Princeton: The Darwin Press).

Bostan, Idris (1992). *Osmanlı Bahriye Teşkilâtı: XVII. Yüzyılda Tersane-i Amire* (Ankara: Türk Tarih Kurumu).

Braudel, Fernand (2nd edn, 1966). *La Méditerranée et le monde méditerranéen à l'époque de Philippe II,* 2 vols. (Paris: Librairie Armand Colin) (1st edn in one volume, 1949).

(1979). *Civilisation matérielle, économie et capitalisme,* 3 vols. (Paris: Armand Colin).

Bremer, Marie Luise (1959). *Die Memoiren des türkischen Derwischs Aşçı Dede İbrāhīm* (Walldorf/Hessen: Verlag für Orientkunde Dr. H. Vorndran).

van Bruinessen, Martin M. (1989). *Agha, Scheich und Staat, Politik und Gesellschaft Kurdistans* (Berlin: Edition Parabolis).

Brummett, Palmira (1994). *Ottoman Sea Power and Levantine Diplomacy in the Age of Discovery* (Albany NY: SUNY Press).

Bryer, Anthony and Heath Lowry (eds.) (1986). *Continuity and Change in Late Byzantine and Early Ottoman Society,* (Birmingham, Washington: The University of Birmingham, Dumbarton Oaks).

Burke, Peter (1992). *The Fabrication of Louis XIV* (New Haven, London: Yale University Press).

Busbecq, Ogier Ghiselin de (1968). *The Turkish Letters of Ogier Ghiselin de Busbecq, Imperial Ambassador at Constantinople 1554–1562,* tr. Edward Seymour Forster (Oxford: Clarendon Press).

Cahen, Claude (1968, 2nd revised ed. in French, 1988). *La Turquie pré-ottomane* (Istanbul: ISIS).

Cantemir, Dimitrie (1973). *Dimitrie Cantemir, Historian of Southeastern European and Oriental Civilizations,* ed. Alexandru Dutu and Paul Cernovodeanu, preface by Halil Inalcık (Bucarest: Association Internationale d'Etudes du Sud-Est Européen).

Carter, Francis (1972). *Dubrovnik (Ragusa), a Classic City State* (London, New York: Academic Press).

Cervantes Saavedra, Miguel de (18th edn, 1997). *Novelas ejemplares,* ed. Harry Sieber, 2 vols. (Madrid: Catedra-Letras Hispanicas).

Cezar, Yavuz (1986). *Osmanlı Maliyesinde Bunalım ve Değişim Dönemi (XVIII. yydan Tanzimat'a Mali Tarih)* (Istanbul: Alan Yayıncılık).

Chambers, Richard L. (1973). 'The Education of a Nineteenth-Century Ottoman *ālim*, Ahmed Cevdet Paşa', *International Journal of Middle East Studies*, 4, 4, 440–464.

Chardin, Jean (1711). *Voyages de M. le Chevalier Chardin en Perse et en autres lieux de l'Orient* (Amsterdam).

Chaudhuri, K. N. (1985). *Trade and Civilisation in the Indian Ocean, An Economic History from the Rise of Islam to 1750* (Cambridge: Cambridge University Press).

Chayanov, A. V. (1966). *The Theory of the Peasant Economy* (Homewood, Ill.).

Clayer, Nathalie (1994). *Mystiques, état & société, les Halvetis dans l'aire balkanique de la fin du XVe siècle à nos jours* (Leiden: E. J.Brill).

Collective work (1957). *Kâtip Çelebi, Hayatı ve Eserleri Hakkında İncelemeler* (Ankara: Türk Tarih Kurumu).

Combe, Sonia (1994). *Archives interdites, Les peurs françaises face à l'Histoire contemporaine* (Paris: Albin Michel).

Cook, Michael A. *Population Pressure in Rural Anatolia 1450–1600* (London, New York, Toronto: Oxford University Press).

Curtin, Philip D. (1984). *Cross-Cultural Trade in World History* (Cambridge: Cambridge University Press).

Cvetkova, Bistra A. (1976). 'Les régistres des celepkeşan en tant que sources pour l'histoire de la Bulgarie et des pays Balkaniques', in *Hungaro-Turcica, Studies in Honour of Julius Németh*, ed. Gyula Káldy-Nagy (Budapest: Loránd Eötvös University), pp. 325–336.

Çakır, Serpil (1994). *Osmanlı Kadın Hareketi* (Istanbul: Metis Kadın Araştırmaları).

Çelik, Zeynep (1986). *The Remaking of Istanbul, Portrait of an Ottoman City in the Nineteenth Century* (Seattle, London: University of Washington Press).

Çizakça, Murat (1985). 'Incorporation of the Middle East into the European World Economy', *Review*, 8, 3, 353–78.

   (1996). *A Comparative Evolution of Business Partnerships, The Islamic World and Europe, with Specific Reference to the Ottoman Archives* (Leiden, New York: E. J. Brill).

Daniel, Norman (2nd edn, 1993). *Islam and the West, the Making of an Image* (Oxford: Oneworld).

Darling, Linda (1996). *Revenue-Raising and Legitimacy, Tax Collection and Finance Administration in the Ottoman Empire 1560–1660* (Leiden: E. J. Brill).

Davis, Ralph (1967). *Aleppo and Devonshire Square, English Traders in the Levant in the Eighteenth Century* (London, Melbourne, Toronto: Macmillan).

Davison, Roderic H. (2nd printing 1973). *Reform in the Ottoman Empire, 1856–1876* (New York: Gordian Press).

   (1990) *Essays in Ottoman and Turkish History, 1774–1923, The Impact of the West* (Austin: University of Texas Press).

   (1995). 'The Beginning of Published Biographies of Ottoman Statesmen: the Case of Midhat Pasha', in *Türkische Wirtschafts- und Sozialgeschichte von 1071 bis 1920*, ed. Hans Georg Majer and Raoul Motika (Wiesbaden: Harrassowitz), pp. 59–80.

Davison, Roderic H. with Dodd, Clement (1998). *Turkey, A Short History* (3rd revised edn) (Huntingdon: University of Texas Press).

Deguilhem, Randi (1991). 'Waqf Documents; A Multi-purpose Historical Source – the Case of 19th Century Damascus', in *Les villes dans l'Empire ottoman, activités et sociétés*, 2 vols. (Paris: Editions du CNRS), I, pp. 67–96.

Deny, Jean (1930). *Sommaire des archives turques du Caire* (Cairo: Société de Géographie d'Egypte).

Deringil, Selim (1998). *The Well-Protected Domains, Ideology and the Legitimation of Power in the Ottoman Empire, 1876–1909* (London: I. B. Tauris).

Derman, Uğur (1988). 'Celî Dîvânînin Tekâmülüne Dair', in *Tarih Boyunca Paleografya ve Diplomatik Semineri*, ed. Mübahat Kütükoğlu (İstanbul: Istanbul Üniversitesi Edebiyat Fakültesi), pp. 15–18.

Dernschwam, Hans (1923). *Hans Dernschwams Tagebuch einer Reise nach Konstantinopel und Kleinasien (1553–1555)*, ed. Franz Babinger (Munich, Leipzig: Duncker und Humblot).

Devrim, Şirin (1994). *A Turkish Tapestry, The Shakirs of Istanbul* (London: Quartet Books).

Dimitradis, Vassilis (1989). 'Ottoman Archive Materials in Greece', in *Die Staaten Südosteuropas und die Osmanen*, ed. Hans Georg Majer (Munich: Südosteuropa-Geselschaft), pp. 179–86)

Divitçioğlu, Sencer (1967). *Asya Tipi Üretim Tarzı ve Osmanlı Toplumu* (Istanbul: İstanbul Üniversitesi Yayınları).

Doughty, Charles M. (1979). *Travels in Arabia Deserta*, 2 vols. (New York: Dover Publications).

Doumani, Beshara (1995). *Rediscovering Palestine, Merchants and Peasants in Jabal Nablus, 1700–1900* (Berkeley, Los Angeles, London: University of California Press).

Duben, Alan and Cem Behar (1991). *Istanbul Households, Marriage, Family and Fertility, 1880–1940* (Cambridge: Cambridge University Press).

Duda, Herbert W. and Galab D. Galabov (eds.) (1960). *Die Protokollbücher des Kadiamtes Sofia* (Munich: R. Oldenbourg).

Dumont, Paul (1980). 'Une source pour l'étude des communautés juives de Turquie: les archives de l'Alliance Israélite Universelle', *Prilozi za Orientalnu Filologiju*, 36, 75–106.

Ebû'l-Ḥayr Rûmî. *Saltuk-nâme, Ebû'l-Ḥayr Rûmî'nin sözlü rivayetlerden topladığı Sarı Saltuk menakıbı*, ed. Fahir Iz (Cambridge: Harvard University).

Eldem, Edhem (1999). *French Trade in Istanbul in the Eighteenth Century* (Leiden: E. J. Brill).

Elifoğlu, Eugénie (1984). 'Ottoman *defters* Containing Ages of Children: A New Source for Demographic Research', *Archivum Ottomanicum*, IX, 321–8.

Elvan Çelebi. *Menâkıbu'l-Kudsiyye fî Menâsıbî'l Ünsiyye (Baba İlyas-ı Horasânî ve Sülâlesinin Menkabevî Tarihi)*, ed. Ismail Erünsal and Ahmet Yaşar Ocak (Istanbul: İstanbul Üniversitesi Edebiyat Fakültesi).

Enginün, Inci (2nd ed. 1995). *Halide Edip Adıvar'ın Eserlerinde Doğu ve Batı Meselesi* (Istanbul: Milli Eğitim Bakanlığı).

Erder, Leila (1975). 'The Measurement of Preindustrial Population Changes: The Ottoman Empire from the 15th to the 17th Century', *Middle Eastern Studies*, II, 3, 284–301.

Eren, Meşkûre (1960). *Evliya Çelebi Seyahatnâmesi Birinci Cildinin Kaynakları Üzerinde bir Araştırma* (Istanbul: n.p.).

Ergenç, Özer (1978–79). 'XVI. Yüzyılın Sonlarında Osmanlı Parası Üzerinde Yapılan İşlemlere İlişkin Bazı Bilgiler', *Türkiye İktisat Tarihi Üzerinde Araştırmalar, Gelişme Dergisi*, Özel sayısı, 86–97.

—— (1980). 'XVII. Yüzyıl Başlarında Ankara'nın Yerleşim Durumu Üzerine Bazı Bilgiler', *Osmanlı Araştırmaları*, 1, 85–108.

Erim, Neşe (1991). 'Trade, Traders and the State in Eighteenth-Century Erzurum', *New Perspectives on Turkey*, 5–6, 123–50.

Erünsal, Ismail E. (1977–79). 'Türk Edebiyatı Tarihine Kaynak Olarak Arşivlerin Değeri', *Türkiyat Mecmuası*, XIX, 213–22.

Esenbel, Selçuk (1994). 'The Anguish of Civilized Behaviour: The Use of Western Cultural Forms in the Everyday Lives of the Meiji Japanese and the Ottoman Turks During the Nineteenth Century', *Japan Review*, 5, 145–85.

—— (1995). 'İslam dünyasında Japonya İmgesi: Abdürreşid İbrahim ve Geç Meiji Dönemi Japonları', *Toplumsal Tarih*, 19 (1995), 18–26.

—— (1996). 'A *fin de siècle* Japanese Romantic in Istanbul: The Life of Yamada Torajiro and his Toruko Gakan', *Bulletin of the School of Oriental and African Studies, University of London*, 59, 2, 237–52.

Evans, Richard J. (1997). *In Defence of History* (London: Granta Books).

Evliya Çelebi (1314/1896/97 to 1938). *Seyahatnamesi*, 10 vols. (Istanbul, Ankara: İkdam and others).

[Evliya Çelebi] (2nd edn, 1987). *Im Reiche des Goldenen Apfels, des türkischen Weltenbummlers Evliya Çelebi denkwürdige Reise in das Giaurenland und in die Stadt und Festung Wien anno 1665*, trans. and annotated Richard F. Kreutel, Erich Prokosch and Karl Teply (Vienna: Verlag Styria).

—— (1988). *Evliya Çelebi in Diyarbekir, The Relevant Section of the Seyahatname edited with Translation, Commentary and Introduction*, ed. and trans. Martin van Bruinessen and Hendrik Boeschoten (Leiden: E.J. Brill).

Evliya Çelebi Seyahatnamesi, 1. Kitap: Istanbul (1989) ed. Şinasi Tekin, Gönül Alpay Tekin and Fahir Iz, 2 vols. (Cambridge MA: Harvard University Press).

—— (1990). *Evliya Çelebi in Bitlis, The Relevant Section of the Seyahatname edited with Translation, Commentary and Introduction*, ed. and trans. Robert Dankoff (Leiden: E. J. Brill).

—— (1991). *The Intimate Life of an Ottoman Statesman, Melek Ahmed Pasha (1588–1662) as Portrayed in Evliya Çelebi's Book of Travels*, trans. and annotated Robert Dankoff and Rhoads Murphey (Albany: SUNY Press).

—— (1994). *Ins Land der geheimnisvollen Func, des türkischen Weltenbummlers Evliyā*

Çelebi Reise durch Oberägypten und den Sudan nebst der Provinz Habeş in den Jahren 1672/73, trans. and annotated Erich Prokosch (Vienna: Verlag Styria).

Evliya Çelebi (1995) *Seyahatnamesi, 1. Kitap Istanbul.* Topkapı Sarayı Bağdat 30 Yazmasının Transkripsyonu-Dizini, ed. Orhan Şaik Gökyay (Istanbul: Yapı ve Kredi Bankası).

Farooqi, Naim R. (1986). 'Mughal-Ottoman Relations: a Study of Political and Diplomatic Relations between Mughal India and the Ottoman Empire, 1556–1748', unpubl. PhD dissertation (Madison, Wisc.: University Microfilms).

Faroqhi, Suraiya (1976). 'Agricultural Activities in a Bektashi Center 1750–1826: the *tekke* of Kızıldeli', *Südost-Forschungen*, 35, 69–96.

(1979). 'Sixteenth-Century Periodic Markets in Various Anatolian *sancaks*', *JESHO*, XXII, 1, 32–80.

(1981). *Der Bektaschi-Orden in Anatolien (vom späten fünfzehnten Jahrhundert bis 1826)* (Vienna: Verlag des Instituts für Orientalistik).

(1984). *Towns and Townsmen of Ottoman Anatolia, Trade, Crafts and Food Production in an Urban Setting* (Cambridge: Cambridge University Press).

(1987). *Men of Modest Substance, House Owners and House Property in Seventeenth-Century Ankara and Kayseri* (Cambridge: Cambridge University Press).

(1991). 'Wealth and Power in the Land of Olives: The Economic and Political Activities of Muridoğlu Hacı Mehmed Ağa, Notable of Edremit (died in or before 1823)', in *Landholding and Commercial Agriculture in the Middle East*, ed. Çağlar Keyder and Faruk Tabak (Albany: SUNY Press), pp. 77–96.

(1992) 'Two Women of Substance', in *Festgabe an Josef Matuz, Osmanistik, Turkologie, Diplomatik*, ed. Christa Fragner and Klaus Schwarz (Berlin: Klaus Schwarz Verlag), pp. 37–56.

(1995). *Kultur und Alltag im Osmanischen Reich, Vom Mittelalter bis zum Anfang des 20. Jahrhunderts* (Munich: C. H. Beck).

Fawaz, Leila Tarazi (1983). *Merchants and Migrants in Nineteenth-Century Beirut* (Cambridge Mass, London: Harvard University Press).

Fekete, L. (1926). *Einführung in die osmanisch-türkische Diplomatik der türkischen Botmäßigkeit zu Ungarn* (Budapest: Royal Hungarian State Archive).

Ferrier, R. W. (1973). 'The Armenians and the East India Company in the Seventeenth and Early Eighteenth Centuries', in *Economic History Review*, 26, 38–62.

Findley, Carter V. (1980). *Bureaucratic Reform in the Ottoman Empire, The Sublime Porte 1789–1922* (Princeton: Princeton University Press).

(1983). 'Social Dimensions of Dervish Life, as Seen in the Memoirs of Aşçı Dede Halil Ibrahim', in *Economies et societés dans l'Empire ottoman (fin du XVIIIe – début du XXe siècle)* (Paris: Editions du CNRS), pp. 129–44.

(1989). *Ottoman Civil Officialdom, A Social History* (Princeton: Princeton University Press).

(1995a). 'Fatma Aliye: first Ottoman Novelist, Pioneer Feminist', in *Histoire économique et sociale de l'Empire Ottoman et de la Turquie (1326–1960)*, ed. Daniel Panzac (Louvain: Peeters), pp. 783–94.

(1995b). 'La soumise, la subversive: Fatma Aliye, romancière et féministe', *Turcica*, 27, 153–72.

(1998). 'Mouradgea D'Ohsson (1740–1807): Liminality and Cosmopolitanism in the Author of the *Tableau Général de l'empire Othoman'*, *Turkish Studies Association Bulletin*, 22, 1, 21–36.

Finkel, Caroline (1988). *The Administration of Warfare: the Ottoman Military Campaigns in Hungary, 1593–1606*, 2 vols. (Vienna: VWGÖ)

Fleischer, Cornell H. (1986). *Bureaucrat and Intellectual in the Ottoman Empire, The Historian Mustafa Âli (1541–1600)* (Princeton: Princeton University Press).

(1990). 'From Şehzade Korkud to Mustafa Âli: Cultural Origins of the Ottoman Nasîhatname', in *Congress on the Economic and Social History of Turkey*, ed. Heath Lowry and Ralph Hattox (Istanbul: ISIS), pp. 67–78.

Frangakis-Syrett, Elena (1992). *The Commerce of Smyrna in the Eighteenth Century (1700–1820)* (Athens: Centre for Asia Minor Studies).

Fukasawa, Katsumi (1987). *Toilerie et commerce du Levant d'Alep à Marseille* (Paris: Editions du CNRS).

Gara, Eleni (1998). 'In Search of Communities in Seventeenth-Century Ottoman Sources: The Case of the Kara Ferye District', *Turcica*, 30, 135–62.

Genç, Mehmet (1975). 'Osmanlı Maliyesinde Malikâne Sistemi', in *Türkiye İktisat Tarihi Semineri, Metinler–Tartışmalar . . .*, ed. Osman Okyar and Ünal Nabantoğlu (Ankara: Hacettepe Üniversitesi).

(1987). 'A Study of the Feasibility of Using Eighteenth-Century Ottoman Financial Records as an Indication of Economic Activity', in *The Ottoman Empire and the World Economy*, ed. Huri Islamoğlu-Inan (Cambridge, Paris: Cambridge University Press and Maison des Sciences de l'Homme), pp. 345–73.

Georgeon, François and Dumont, Paul (eds.) (1997). *Vivre dans l'Empire ottoman, Sociabilités et relations intercommunautaires (XVIIIe–XXe siècles)* (Paris: L'Harmattan).

Gibb, H. A. R. and Harold Bowen (1950–57). *Islamic Society and the West, A Study of the Impact of Western Civilization on Moslem Culture in the Near East*, 2 vols. as one: *Islamic Society in the Eighteenth Century* (London, New York, Toronto: Oxford University Press).

Gilles, Pierre (1988). *The Antiquities of Constantinople*, trans. John Ball and ed. Ronald G. Musto (New York: Italica Press).

Gyllius, Petrus (1997). *Istanbul'un Tarihi Eserleri*, trans. from the Latin original and intro. by Erendiz Özbayoğlu (Istanbul: Eren).

Glaß, Dagmar (1995). 'Die Masāil-Kolumne in *al-Muqtataf*. Ein Indikator für die Rezeption einer arabischen Wissenschaftszeitschrift des 19. Jahrhunderts?' in *Presse und Öffentlichkeit im Nahen Osten*, ed. Christoph Herzog, Raoul Motika and Anja Pistor-Hatam (Heidelberg: Heidelberger Orientverlag), pp. 59–82.

Goffman, Daniel (1990). *Izmir and the Levantine World, 1550–1650* (Seattle: University of Washington Press).

(1998). *Britons in the Ottoman Empire 1642–1660* (Seattle, London: University of Washington Press).

Gökbilgin, M. Tayyip (1964). 'Venedik Devlet Arşivindeki Vesikalar Külliyatında Kanunî Sultan Süleyman Devri Belgeleri', *Belgeler*, 1, 2, 119–220.

(1979, 2nd printing 1992). *Osmanlı Paleografya ve Diplomatik İlmi* (İstanbul: Enderun).

Goldstone, Jack A. (1991). *Revolution and Rebellion in the Early Modern World* (Los Angeles, Berkeley: University of California Press).

Gölpınarlı, Abdülbaki (1953). *Mevlânâ'dan Sonra Mevlevîlik* (İstanbul: İnkılâp).

(1955–56). 'Konya'da Mevlânâ Dergâhının Arşivi', *İstanbul Üniversitesi İktisat Fakültesi Mecmuası*, 17, 1–4, 156–78.

Göyünç, Nejat (1962–63). 'Salomon Schweigger ve Seyahatnamesi', *Tarih Dergisi*, 13, 17/18, 119–40.

Griswold, William J. (1983). *The Great Anatolian Rebellion, 1000–1020/1591–1611* (Berlin: Klaus Schwarz).

Groot, Alexander de (1978). *The Ottoman Empire and the Dutch Republic, A History of the Earliest Diplomatic Relations 1610–1630* (Leiden, Istanbul: Nederlands Historisch-Archaelogisch Instituut voor het Nabije Oosten).

Guboglu, Mihail (1958). *Paleografia şi Diplomatica Turco-Osmana, Studiu şi Album* (Bucarest: Editura Academiei Republicii Populare Romine).

Haarmann, Ulrich (1976). 'Evliya čelebīs Bericht über die Altertümer von Gize', *Turcica*, 8, 157–230.

Halasi-Kun, Tibor (1964). 'Sixteenth-century Turkish Settlements in Southern Hungary', *Belleten*, 28, 109, 1–72.

Haldon, John (1992). 'The Ottoman State and the Question of State Autonomy', in *New Approaches to State and Peasant in Ottoman History*, ed. Halil Berktay and Suraiya Faroqhi (London: Frank Cass), pp. 18–108.

(1993). *The State and the Tributary Mode of Production* (London, New York: Verso).

Hanna, Nelly (1991). *Habiter au Caire aux XVIIᵉ et XVIIIᵉ siècles* (Cairo: Institut Français d'Archéologie Orientale).

Har-El, Shai (1995). *Struggle for Domination in the Middle East, The Ottoman-Mamluk War 1485–1491* (Leiden: E. T. Brill).

Hasluck, F. W. (1929). *Christianity and Islam under the Sultans*, ed. Margaret Hasluck, 2 vols. (Oxford: The Clarendon Press).

Heeringa, K. and G. Nanninga (eds.) (1910–17). *Bronnen tot de Geschiedenis van den Levantschen Handel*, I, 2 parts: *1590–1660, 1561–1726* (The Hague: Martinus Nijhoff).

Hellie, Richard (1971). *Enserfment and Military Change in Muscovy* (Chicago, London: University of Chicago Press).

Hering, Gunnar (1989). 'Die Osmanenzeit im Selbstverständnis der Völker Südosteuropas', in *Die Staaten Südosteuropas und die Osmanen*, ed. Hans Georg Majer (Munich: Südosteuropa Gesellschaft), pp. 355–380.

Herzog, Christoph, Raoul Motika and Anja Pistor-Hatam (eds.) (1995). *Presse und Öffentlichkeit im Nahen Osten* (Heidelberg: Heidelberger Orientverlag).

Hess, Andrew (1978). *The Forgotten Frontier, A History of the Sixteenth-century Ibero-African Frontier* (Chicago, London: Chicago University Press).

Hickok, Michael R. (1997). *Ottoman Military Administration in Eighteenth-Century Bosnia* (Leiden: E. J. Brill).

Hitzel, Frédéric ed. (1997). *Istanbul et les langues orientales* (Paris: IFEA, L'Harmattan, INALCO).

Hobsbawm, E.J. (1990). *Echoes of the Marseillaise, Two Centuries Look Back on the French Revolution* (London, New York: Verso).

Hodgson, Marshall G. S. (1973–74). *The Venture of Islam, Conscience and History in a World Civilization*, vol. 3: *The Gunpowder Empires and Modern Times* (Chicago, London: Chicago University Press).

Holbrook, Victoria Rowe (1994). *The Unreadable Shores of Love, Turkish Modernity and Mystic Romance* (Austin: University of Texas Press).

Holt, Peter, Ann K. S. Lambton and Bernhard Lewis (1970). *The Cambridge History of Islam*, 2 vols. (Cambridge University Press).

Hourani, Albert (1992). *A History of the Arab Peoples* (New York: Warner Books).

Howard, Douglas (1988). 'Ottoman Historiography and the Literature of "Decline" in the Sixteenth and Seventeenth Centuries', *Journal of Asian History*, 22, 1, 52–76.

Humphreys, R. Stephen (revised edn 1995). *Islamic History, a Framework for Inquiry* (London, New York: I. B. Tauris).

Hütteroth, Wolf D. (1968). *Ländliche Siedlungen im südlichen Inneranatolien in den letzten vierhundert Jahren* (Göttingen: Geographisches Institut der Universität Göttingen).

Hütteroth, Wolf Dieter and Kamal Abdulfattah (1977). *Historical Geography of Palestine, Transjordan and Southern Syria in the Late 16th Century* (Erlangen/ Germany: Fränkische Geographische Gesellschaft).

Ihsanoğlu, Ekmeleddin (ed.) (1994, 1998). *Osmanlı Devleti ve Medeniyeti Tarihi* 2 vols. (Istanbul: IRSICA).

Ilbert, Robert (1996). *Alexandrie, 1830–1930, Histoire d'une communauté cittadine*, 2 vols. (Cairo: Institut Français d'Archéologie Orientale).

Imber, Colin (1990). *The Ottoman Empire 1300–1481* (Istanbul: ISIS).

Inalcık, Halil (1948). 'Osmanlı-Rus Rekabetinin Menşei ve Don-Volga Kanalı Teşebbüsü', *Belleten*, 12, 46, 349–402.

   (1954a). *Hicrî 835 Tarihli Sûret-i Defter-i Sancak-i Arvanid* (Ankara: Türk Tarih Kurumu).

   (1954b). 'Ottoman Methods of Conquest', *Studia Islamica*, III, 103–29.

   (1958). 'The Problem of the Relationship between Byzantine and Ottoman Taxation', in *Akten des XI. Internationalen Byzantinistenkongresses* (Munich), pp.

237–242.

(1959). 'Osmanlılarda Raiyyet Rusûmu', *Belleten*, 23, 575–610.

(1960a). 'Bursa and the Commerce of the Levant', *Journal of the Economic and Social History of the Levant*, 3, 131–47.

(1960b). 'Bursa, XV. Asır Sanayi ve Ticaret Tarihine Dair Vesikalar', *Belleten*, 24 (1960), 45–102.

(1964). 'The Nature of Traditional Society: Turkey', in *Political Modernization in Japan and Turkey*, ed. Robert E. Ward and Dankwart A. Rustow (Princeton NJ: Princeton University Press), pp. 42–63.

(1973). *The Ottoman Empire, The Classical Age, 1300–1600* (Weidenfeld & Nicholson).

(1975). 'The Socio-Political Effects of the Diffusion of Firearms in the Middle East', in *War, Technology and Society in the Middle East*, ed. M.E. Yapp (London, Oxford: Oxford University Press).

(1984). 'The Emergence of Big Farms, *çiftliks*: State, Landlords and Tenants', in *Contributions à l'histoire économique et sociale de l'Empire ottoman*, Collection Turcica III (Louvain: Editions Peeters), pp. 105–26

(1986). 'The Appointment Procedure of a Guild Warden (Kethudā)', *Wiener Zeitschrift für die Kunde des Morgenlandes, Festschrift Andreas Tietze*, 76, 135–42.

(1994). 'The Ottoman State: Economy and Society, 1300–1600', in *An Economic and Social History of the Ottoman Empire, 1300–1914*, ed. Halil Inalcık with Donald Quataert (Cambridge: Cambridge University Press) (paperback version 1997, Inalcık's work appears as vol. 1).

Inuğur, Nuri (1992). 'Naissance et développement de la presse dans l'Empire ottoman', in *Presse turque et presse de Turquie, Actes des Colloques d'Istanbul*, ed. Nathalie Clayer, Alexandre Popovic and Thierry Zarcone (Istanbul, Paris: ISIS), pp. 83–92.

Islamoğlu-Inan, Huri (1987). 'Oriental Despotism in World System Perspective', in *The Ottoman Empire and the World Economy*, ed. Huri Islamoğlu-Inan (Cambridge, Paris: Cambridge University Press and Maison des Sciences de l'Homme), pp. 1–26.

(1994). *State and Peasant in the Ottoman Empire, Agrarian Power Relations and Regional Economic Development in Ottoman Anatolia During the Sixteenth Century* (Leiden: E. J. Brill).

Islamoğlu, Huri and Suraiya Faroqhi (1979). 'Crop Patterns and Agricultural Production Trends in Sixteenth-Century Anatolia', *Review*, II, 3, 401–36.

Israel, Jonathan (1989). *Dutch Primacy in World Trade, 1585–1740* (Oxford: The Clarendon Press).

Issawi, Charles (1966). *The Economic History of the Middle East, 1800–1914, A Book of Readings* (Chicago and London: The University of Chicago Press).

Itzkowitz, Norman (1962). 'Eighteenth-Century Ottoman Realities', *Studia Islamica*, 16, 73–94.

Iz, Fahir (1970). 'Turkish Literature', in *The Cambridge History of Islam*, ed. Peter

Holt, Ann K. S. Lambton and Bernard Lewis (Cambridge: Cambridge University Press), II, 2, pp. 682–94.

Jelavich, Charles and Barbara (1977). *The Establishment of the Balkan National States, 1804–1920* (Seattle, London: University of Washington Press).

Jelavich, Barbara (1983). *History of the Balkans*, vol. 1: *Eighteenth and Nineteenth Centuries*, vol. 2: *The Twentieth Century* (Cambridge: Cambridge University Press).

Jennings, Ronald (1975). 'Women in early 17th Century Ottoman Judicial Records – The Sharia Court of Anatolian Kayseri', *Journal of the Economic and Social History of the Orient*, 17,2, 53–114.

Jolles, André (2nd printing 1958). *Einfache Formen, Legende/ Sage/ Mythe/ Rätsel/ Spruch/ Kasus/ Memorabile/ Märchen/ Witz* (Tübingen / Germany: Max Niemeyer).

Kafadar, Cemal (1986). 'When Coins Turned into Drops of Dew and Bankers Became Robbers of Shadows: the Boundaries of Ottoman Economic Imagination at the End of the Sixteenth Century' (unpubl. PhD dissertation, McGill University, Montréal.)

(1989). 'Self and Others: The Diary of a Dervish in Seventeenth-Century Istanbul and First-Person Narratives in Ottoman Literature', *Studia Islamica*, 69, 121–50.

(1992). 'Mütereddit bir Mutasavvıf: Üsküp'lü Asiye Hatun'un Rüya Defteri 1641–43', *Topkapı Sarayı Müzesi, Yıllık* 5, 168–222.

(1995). *Between Two Worlds, The Construction of the Ottoman State* (Berkeley, Los Angeles: University of California Press).

Kal'a, Ahmet et al. (eds.) (1997–). *Istanbul Külliyatı I, Istanbul Ahkâm Defterleri . . .* (Istanbul: Istanbul Büyükşehir Belediyesi).

Karamustafa, Ahmet T. (1993). *Vâhîdî's Menâkıb-ı Hvoca-i Cihân ve Netîce-i Cân: Critical Edition and Analysis* (Cambridge MA: Harvard).

Kaser, Karl (1990). *Südosteuropäische Geschichte und Geschichtswissenschaft, eine Einführung* (Vienna, Cologne: Böhlau).

Katip Çelebi'den Seçmeler (1968), ed. and trans. Orhan Şaik Gökyay (Istanbul: Milli Eğitim Bakanlığı).

Kévonian, Keram (1975). 'Marchands arméniens au XVIIe siècle, à propos d'un livre arménien publié à Amsterdam en 1699', *Cahiers du monde russe et soviétique*, 162, 199–244.

Keyder, Çağlar (1987). *State and Class in Turkey, a Study in Capitalist Development* (London, New York: Verso).

Kolodziejczyk, Dariusz (forthcoming). *Ottoman-Polish Diplomatic Relations: the 'ahdnames (15th–18th c.)* (Leiden: E. J. Brill).

Kologlu, Orhan (1992a). 'Le premier journal officiel en français à Istanbul et ses repercussions en Europe', in *Presse turque et presse de Turquie, Actes des Colloques d'Istanbul*, ed. Nathalie Clayer, Alexandre Popovic and Thierry Zarcone (Istanbul, Paris: ISIS), pp. 3–14.

(992b). 'La formation des intellectuels à la culture journalistique dans l'Empire ottoman et l'influence de la presse étrangère', in *Presse turque et presse de Turquie, Actes des Colloques d'Istanbul*, ed. Nathalie Clayer, Alexandre Popovic and Thierry Zarcone (Istanbul, Paris: ISIS), pp. 123–42.

Köprülü, M. Fuad (1935). *Türk Halk Edebiyatı Ansiklopedisi . . .*, fasc. 1 Aba-Abdal Musa (no more publ.) (Istanbul).

(1959). *Osmanlı Devleti'nin Kuruluşu* (Ankara: Türk Tarih Kurumu).

(1966). *Türk Edebiyatı'nda İlk Mutasavvıflar*, 2nd ed. (Ankara: Diyanet İşleri Başkanlığı Yayınları).

(reprint 1981). *Bizans Müesseselerinin Osmanlı Müesseselerine Tesiri* (Istanbul: Ötüken).

Kraelitz, Friedrich (1992). *Osmanische Urkunden in türkischer Sprache aus der zweiten Hälfte des 15. Jahrhunderts* (Vienna: Alfred Hölder).

Kreiser, Klaus (1995). '*Servet-i Fünûn* und seine Leser im Spiegel der tausendsten Nummer', in *Presse und Öffentlichkeit im Nahen Osten*, ed. Christoph Herzog, Raoul Motika and Anja Pistor-Hatam (Heidelberg: Heidelberger Orientverlag), pp. 93–100.

Kuban, Doğan (1996). *Istanbul, an Urban History, Byzantion, Constantinopolis, Istanbul* (Istanbul: Habitat II, Türkiye Ekonomik ve Toplumsal Tarih Vakfı).

Kuniholm, Peter I. (1989). 'Archaeological Evidence and Non- Evidence for Climatic Change', *Philosophical Transactions of the Royal Society*, A330, 645–655.

Kunt, I. Metin (1974). 'Ethnic-Regional (*Cins*) Solidarity in the Seventeenth-Century Ottoman Establishment', *International Journal of Middle East Studies*, 5, 233–9.

(1983). *The Sultan's Servants, The Transformation of Ottoman Provincial Government 1550–1650* (New York: Columbia University Press).

Kütükoğlu, Bekir (1962). *Osmanlı-İran Siyâsî Münasebetleri, I 1578–1590* (Istanbul: İstanbul Üniversitesi Edebiyat Fakültesi).

(1974). *Kâtib Çelebi 'Fezleke'sinin Kaynakları* (Istanbul: Istanbul Üniversitesi Edebiyat Fakültesi).

Kütükoğlu, Mübahat (1991). *Tarih Araştırmalarında Usûl* (Istanbul: Kubbealtı).

(1994). *Osmanlı Belgelerinin Dili (Diplomatik)* (Istanbul: Kubbealtı Akademisi Kültür ve Sanat Vakfı).

Kütukoğlu, Mübahat (ed.) (1983). *Osmanlılarda Narh Müessesesi ve 1640 Tarihli Narh Defteri* (Istanbul: Enderun Kitabevi).

(1988) Tarih Boyunca Paleografya ve Diplomatik Semineri (Istanbul: Istanbul Universitesi Edebiyat Fakültesi).

Lamers, Hanneke (1988). 'On Evliya's Style', in M. van Bruinessen and H. Boeschoten (eds.), *Evliya Çelebi in Diyarbekir . . .* (Leiden: E. J. Brill), pp. 64–70.

Lampe, John R. and Marvin R. Jackson (1982). *Balkan Economic History, 1550–1950, From Imperial Borderlands to Developing Nations* (Bloomington/ Indiana: Indiana University Press).

Lapidus, Ira M. (1998). *A History of Islamic Societies* (Cambridge: Cambridge University Press).

van Leeuwen, Richard (1994). *Notables and Clergy in Mount Lebanon, The Khazin Sheiks and the Maronite Church (1736–1840)* (Leiden: E. J. Brill), pp. 64–70.

Leila Hanoum (1991). *Le Harem impérial et les sultanes au XIXe siècle*, trans. and ed. Youssouf Razi, preface by Sophie Basch (Brussels: Editions Complexe).

Le Roy Ladurie, Emmanuel (1974). *The Peasants of Languedoc*, trans. John Day (Urbana Illinois: University of Illinois Press).

Le Roy Ladurie, Emmanuel (1983). *Histoire du climat depuis l'an mil*, 2 vols. (Paris: Champs-Flammarion).

Lewis, Bernard (1954). 'Studies in the Ottoman Archives – I', *Bulletin of the School of Oriental and African Studies*, 16, 469–501.

(2nd edn 1968). *The Emergence of Modern Turkey* (London, Oxford, New York: Oxford University Press).

Lewis, Geoffrey (3rd edn, 1965). *Turkey* (London: Ernest Benn Ltd.).

Lindner, Rudi Paul (1983). *Nomads and Ottomans in Medieval Anatolia* (Bloomington/Indiana: Indiana University Press).

Lory, Bernard (1985). *Le sort de l'héritage ottoman en Bulgarie, l'exemple des villes bulgares 1878–1900* (Istanbul: ISIS).

Lowry, Heath (1992). 'The Ottoman *Tahrir Defterleri* as a Source for Social and Economic History: Pitfalls and Limitations', in *Studies in Defterology, Ottoman Society in the Fifteenth and Sixteenth Centuries* (Istanbul: ISIS), pp. 3–18.

Ludden, David (1989). *Peasant History in South India* (Delhi: Oxford University Press).

Luther, Usha M. (1989). *Historical Route Network of Anatolia (Istanbul – Izmir – Konya) 1550's to 1850's: A Methodological Study* (Ankara: Türk Tarih Kurumu).

van Luttervelt, R. (1958). *De 'Turkse' Schilderijen van J. B. Vanmour en zijn School, De verzameling van Cornelis Calkoen, Ambassadeur bij de Hoge Porte 1725–1743* (Istanbul: Nederlands Historisch-Archaeologisch Instituut vor het Nabije Osten).

Lybyer, Albert Howe (1913, reprint 1966). *The Government of the Ottoman Empire in the Time of Suleiman the Magnificent* (New York: Russel & Russel).

Majer, Hans Georg (1978). *Vorstudien zur Geschichte der Ilmiye im Osmanischen Reich*, 1. *Zu Uşakîzade, seiner Familie und seinem Zeyl-i Şakayık* (Munich: Dr. Dr. Rudolf Trofenik).

(1989). 'Der Tod im Mörser: eine Strafe für osmanische Schejchülislame?' in *Von der Pruth-Ebene bis zum Gipfel des Ida . . . Festschrift zum 70. Geburtstag von Emanuel Turczynski*, ed. Gerhart Grimm (Munich: Südosteuropa-Gesellschaft), pp. 141–152.

Mantran, Robert (1962). *Istanbul dans la seconde moitié du XVIIe siècle, Essai d'histoire institutionelle, économique et sociale* (Paris, Istanbul: Institut Français d'Archéologie d'Istanbul and Adrien Maisonneuve).

Mantran, Robert (ed.) (1989). *Histoire de l'Empire Ottoman* (Paris: Fayard).

Marcus, Abraham (1989). *The Middle East on the Eve of Modernity, Aleppo in the Eighteenth Century* (New York: Columbia University Press).

Mardin, Şerif (1962). *The Genesis of Young Ottoman Thought, A Study in the Modernization of Turkish Political Ideas* (Princeton: Princeton University Press).

(1971). 'Tanzimattan Sonra Aşırı Batılılaşma', in *Türkiye, Coğrafi ve Sosyal Araştırmalar*, ed. E. Tümertekin, F. Mansur and P. Benedict (Istanbul: Istanbul Üniversitesi Edebiyat Fakültesi, Coğrafya Enstitüsü), pp. 411–58.

Marsot, Afaf Lutfi al-Sayyid (1984). *Egypt in the Reign of Muhammad Ali* (Cambridge: Cambridge University Press).

Masson, Paul (1896). *Histoire du commerce français dans le Levant au XVIIe siècle* (Paris: Hachette).

(1911). *Histoire du commerce français dans le Levant au XVIIe siècle* (Paris: Hachette).

Masters, Bruce (1994). 'The View from the Province: Syrian Chronicles of the Eighteenth Century', *Journal of the American Oriental Society*, 114,3, 353–62.

(forthcoming). 'The Evolution of an Imagined Community: Aleppo's Catholics in the 18th and 19th Centuries'.

Maundrell, Henry (reprint, 1963). *A Journey from Aleppo to Jerusalem in 1697*, ed. David Howell (Beirut: Khayat).

McCarthy, Justin (1997). *The Ottoman Turks, an Introductory History to 1923* (London: Addison Wesley Longman Ltd.).

McGowan, Bruce (1969). 'Food Supply and Taxation on the Middle Danube (1568–1579)', *Archivum Ottomanicum* 1, 139–196.

(1981). *Economic Life in Ottoman Europe, Taxation, Trade and the Struggle for Land, 1600–1800* (Cambridge, Paris: Cambridge University Press and Maison des Sciences de l'Homme).

(1987). 'The Middle Danube cul-de sac', in *The Ottoman Empire and the World Economy*, ed. by Huri Islamoğlu-Inan (Cambridge, Paris: Cambridge University Press and Maison des Sciences de l'Homme), pp. 170–77.

(1994). 'The Age of the *Ayan*s, 1699–1819', in *An Economic and Social History of the Ottoman Empire 1300–1914*, ed. Halil Inalcık with Donald Quataert (Cambridge: Cambridge University Press), pp. 637–758.

McNeill, William (1964). *Europe's Steppe Frontier, 1500–1800* (Chicago, London: The University of Chicago Press).

Mélikoff, Irène (1975). 'Le problème kızılbaş', *Turcica*, 6, 49–67.

Melman, Billie (1992). *Women's Orients, English Women and the Middle East 1718–1918, Sexuality, Religion and Work* (London, Basingstoke: Macmillan).

Ménage, Victor (1978). Review of *History of the Ottoman Empire and Modern Turkey*, vol. I: *Bulletin of the School of Oriental and African Studies*, 41, 160–2.

Meriç, Rıfkı Melul (1965). *Mimar Sinan, Hayatı, Eseri I: Mimar Sinan'ın Hayatına Eserlerine dair Metinler* (Ankara: Türk Tarih Kurumu).

Meriç, Ümit (2nd printing, 1979). *Cevdet Paşa'nın Cemiyet ve Devlet Görüşü* (Istanbul: Ötüken Yayınevi).

Micklewright, Nancy (1990). 'Late-Nineteenth-Century Ottoman Wedding Costumes as Indicators of Social Change', *Muqarnas*, 6, 164–74.

Montague, Lady Mary Wortley (1993). *Turkish Embassy Letters*, ed. Anita Desai and Malcolm Jack (London: Pickering).

Moran, Berna (1983–1994). *Türk Romanına Eleştirel bir Bakış*, 3 vols. (Istanbul: Ileştim), vol. 1: *Ahmet Mithat'tan A.H. Tanpınar'a*.

Mordtmann, A. J. Sen. (1925). *Anatolien, Skizzen und Reisebriefe aus Kleinasien (1850–1859)*, ed. and annotated by Franz Babinger (Hannover/Germany: Heinz Lafaire).

Mukerji, Chandra (1993). 'Reading and Writing with Nature: A Materialist Approach to French Formal Gardens', in *Consumption and the World of Goods*, ed. John Brewer and Roy Porter (London, New York: Routledge), pp. 439–61.

Murphey, Rhoads ed. (1985). *Kanûn-nâme-i Sultânî li ʿAzîz Efendi: Aziz Efendi's Book of Sultanic Laws and Regulations: An Agenda for Reform by a Seventeenth-Century Ottoman Statesman* (Cambridge MA: Harvard).

[Mustafa Âlî] (1975). *Muṣṭafâ ʿÂlî's Description of Cairo of 1599*, trans. and ed. Andreas Tietze (Vienna: Österreichische Akademie der Wissenschaften).

   (1979, 1982). *Muṣṭafâ ʿAlî's Counsel for Sultans of 1581*, 2 vols., ed. and trans. by Andreas Tietze (Vienna: Österreichische Akademie der Wissenschaften).

Necipoğlu, Gülru (1989). 'Süleyman the Magnificent and the Representation of Power in the Context of Ottoman-Habsburg-Papal Rivalry', *The Art Bulletin*, 71, 3, 401–27.

   (1991). *Architecture, Ceremonial and Power, The Topkapı Palace in the Fifteenth and Sixteenth Centuries* (Cambridge MA: The Architectural History Foundation and MIT Press).

Neumann, Christoph (1994). *Das indirekte Argument, Ein Plädoyer für die Tanzimat vermittels der Historie, Die geschichtliche Bedeutung von Ahmed Cevdet Paşas Ta'rih* (Münster, Hamburg: Lit Verlag).

Nicolay, Nicolas de (1989). *Dans l'Empire de Soliman le Magnifique*, ed. Marie-Christine Gomez-Géraud and Stéphane Yérasimos (Paris: Presses du CNRS).

Ocak, Ahmet Yaşar (1978). 'Emirci Sultan ve Zaviyesi', *Tarih Enstitüsü Dergisi*, 9, 129–208.

   (1989). *La révolte de Baba Resul ou la la formation de l'hétérodoxie musulmane en Anatolie au XIIIe siècle* (Ankara: Türk Tarih Kurumu).

Odorico, Paolo, with S. Asdrachas, T. Karanastassis, K. Kostis and S. Petmézas (1996). *Conseils et mémoires de Synadinos prêtre de Serrès en Macédoine (XVIIe siècle)* (Paris: Association 'Pierre Belon').

Okay, M. Orhan (n.d.). *İlk Türk Positivist ve Natüralisti Beşir Fuad* (Istanbul: Dergâh Yayınları).

Orhonlu, Cengiz (1963). *Osmanlı İmparatorluğunda Aşiretleri İskân Teşebbüsü (1691–1696)* (Istanbul: İstanbul Üniversitesi Edebiyat Fakültesi).

   (1967). *Osmanlı İmparatorluğunda Derbend Teşkilâtı* (Istanbul: İstanbul Üniversitesi Edebiyat Fakültesi).

(1974). *Osmanlı İmparatorluğunun Güney Siyaseti, Habeş Eyaleti* (Istanbul: I.Ü. Edebiyat Fakültesi).

Ortaylı, Ilber, (1983). *İmparatorluğun en Uzun Yüzyılı* (Istanbul: Hil Yayın).

(1986). *Istanbul'dan Sayfalar* (Istanbul: Hil Yayınları).

[Osman Ağa] (1962). *Der Gefangene der Giauren, Die abenteuerlichen Schicksale des Dolmetschers Osman Ağa aus Temeschwar, von ihm selbst erzählt*, trans. and annotated Richard Kreutel and Otto Spies (Vienna: Verlag Styria).

(1980). *Die Autobiographie des Dolmetschers ʿOsmān Ağa aus Temeschvar*, ed. Richard Kreutel (Cambridge: Gibb Memorial Trust).

Owen, E. R[oger] J. (1969). *Cotton and the Egyptian Economy 1820–1914* (Oxford: The Clarendon Press).

Roger (1981). *The Middle East in the World Economy 1800–1914* (London: Methuen).

Özbaran, Salih (1997). 'Osmanlı İmparatorluğu ve Hindistan Yolu:, *Tarih Dergisi*, 31, 65–146.

(1994). *The Ottoman Response to European Expansion, Studies on Ottoman Portuguese Relations in the Indian Ocean and Ottoman Administration in the Arab Lands During the Sixteenth Century* (Istanbul: The ISIS Press).

Pamuk, Şevket (1987). *The Ottoman Empire and European Capitalism, 1820–1913, Trade, Investment and Production* (Cambridge: Cambridge University Press).

(1988). *100 Soruda Osmanlı-Türkiye İktisadî Tarihi 1500–1914* (Istanbul: Gerçek Yayınevi).

(1994). 'A History of Ottoman Money', in *An Economic and Social History of the Ottoman Empire, 1300–1914*, ed. Halil Inalcık with Donald Quataert (Cambridge: Cambridge University Press), pp. 947–80.

Panzac, Daniel (1982). 'Affréteurs ottomans et capitaines français à Alexandrie: la caravane maritime en Méditerranée', *Revue de l'Occident Musulman et de la Méditerranée*, 34, 2, 23–38.

(1985). *La peste dans l'Empire Ottoman 1700–1850* (Louvain: Editions Peeters).

(1992). 'International and Domestic Maritime Trade in the Ottoman Empire During the 18th Century', *International Journal of Middle East Studies*, 14, 189–206.

(1996a). *Commerce et navigation dans l'Empire ottoman au XVIIIᵉ siècle* (Istanbul: ISIS).

(1996b). *Population et santé dans l'Empire ottoman (XVIIIᵉ-XXᵉ siècles)* (Istanbul: ISIS).

Papoulia, Basilike (1989). 'Die Osmanenzeit in der griechischen Geschichtsforschung seit der Unabhängigkeit', in *Die Staaten Südosteuropas und die Osmanen*, ed. Hans Georg Majer (Munich: Südosteuropa-Gesellschaft), pp. 113–26.

Parker, Geoffrey (1985). *The Dutch Revolt* Harmondsworth: Penguin Books).

Parry, Vernon J. *et al.* (eds.) (1976). *A History of the Ottoman Empire to 1730, Chapters from the Cambridge History of Islam and the New Cambridge Modern History* (Cambridge: Cambridge University Press).

Pedani, Maria Pia (1994b). *Il nome del Gran Signore, Inviati Ottomani a Venezia dalla caduta di Costantinopoli alla guerra di Candia* (Venezia: Deputazione Editrice).

Peirce, Leslie P. (1993). *The Imperial Harem, Women and Sovereignty in the Ottoman Empire* (Oxford, New York: Oxford University Press).

Pegolotti, Francesco Balducci (1936). *La pratica della mercatura*, ed. Alan Evans (Cambridge MA: The Medieval Academy of America).

Pitts, Joseph (1949). 'An Account by Joseph Pitts of his Journey from Algiers to Mecca and Medina and back', in *The Red Sea and Adjacent Countries at the Close of the Seventeenth Century, as described by Joseph Pitts, William Daniel and Charles Jacques Poncet*, ed. Sir William Foster CIE (London), pp. 3–49.

Planhol, Xavier de (1968). *Les fondements géographiques de l'histoire de l'Islam* (Paris: Flammarion).

Popovic, Alexandre and Gilles Veinstein (eds.) (1996). *Les voies d'Allah, Les ordres mystiques dans le monde musulman des origines à aujourd'hui* (Paris: Fayard).

Prätor, Sabine (1995). 'Arabische Stimmen in der Istanbuler Presse der Jungtürkenzeit', in *Presse und Öffentlichkeit im Nahen Osten*, ed. Christoph Herzog, Raoul Motika and Anja Pistor-Hatam (Heidelberg: Heidelberger Orientverlag), pp. 121–30.

(1997). 'Şehbal – ein herausragendes Beispiel früher türkischer Magazinpresse', *Turcica*, 29, 433–45.

(1998). 'Zum Stand der Forschung über die osmanische Presse', in *Turkologie heute – Tradition und Perspektive, Materialien der dritten Deutschen Turkologen Konferenz, Leipzig, 4.-7. Oktober 1994* (Wiesbaden: Harrasowitz), pp. 225–38.

Quataert, Donald (1983). *Social Disintegration and Popular Resistance in the Ottoman Empire, 1881–1908* (New York: New York University Press).

(1993). *Ottoman Manufacturing in the Age of the Industrial Revolution* (Cambridge: Cambridge University Press).

(1994). "The Age of Reforms, 1812–1914," in *An Ecomomic and Social History of the Ottoman Empire*, ed. Halil Inalcik with Donald Quataert (Cambridge: Cambridge University Press), pp. 759–946.

Queller, Donald E. (1973). 'The Development of Ambassadorial Relazioni', in *Renaissance Venice*, ed. J. R. Hale (London: Faber & Faber), pp. 174–96.

Quirin, Heinz (1991). *Einführung in das Studium der mittelalterlichen Geschichte* (Stuttgart: Franz Steiner).

Raby, Julian (1980). 'Cyriacus of Ancona and the Ottoman Sultan Mehmed II', *Journal of the Warburg and Courtauld Institutes*, 43, 242–6.

Rafeq, Abdul-Karim (1976). 'The Law Court Registers of Damascus, with Special Reference to Craft Corporations during the First Half of the Eighteenth Century', in *Les Arabes par leurs archives (XVIe-XXe siècles)*, ed. Jacques Berque and Dominique Chevallier (Paris: Editions du CNRS), pp. 141–59.

Rambert, Gaston (ed.) (1951, 1954, 1957). *Histoire du commerce de Marseille, publiée par la Chambre de Commerce de Marseille*, vol. III: *De 1480 à 1515, de 1515 à 1599*; vol. IV: *De 1599 à 1660, de 1660 à 1789*; vol. V: *De 1660 à 1789, Le*

Levant (every volume has a different author) (Paris: Plon).

Raymond, André (1973–74). *Artisans et commerçants au Caire, au XVIIIe siècle*, 2 vols. (Damascus: Institut Français de Damas).

Richter, Otto F. von (1822). *Wallfahrten im Morgenlande, Aus seinen Tagebüchern und Briefen dargestellt* von Johann Philipp Gustav Ewers . . . (Berlin: Reimer).

Ritter, Carl (1843–). *Die Erdkunde Westasiens*, (Berlin: G. Reimer).

Saatçı, Suphi (1990). 'Tezkiret-ül Bünyan'ın Topkapı Sarayı Revan Kitaplığındaki Yazma Nüshası', *Topkapı Sarayı Yıllığı*, 4, 55–102.

Sabatier, Daniel (1976). 'Les relations commerciales entre Marseille et la Crète dans la première moitié du XVIIIe siècle', in Jean-Pierre Filippini *et al.*, *Dossiers sur le commerce français en Méditerranée orientale au XVIII siècle* (Paris: Presses Universitaires de France), pp. 151–234.

Sadok, Boubaker (1987). *La Régence de Tunis au XVIIe siècle: ses relations commerciales avec les ports de l'Europe méditerranéenne, Marseille et Livourne* (Zaghouan: CEROMA).

Sagaster, Börte (1989). *Im Harem von Istanbul: osmanisch-türkische Frauenkultur im 19. Jahrhundert* (Rissen, Hamburg: E.B.-Verlag).

Sahillioğlu, Halil (1962–63). 'Bir Mültezim Zimem Defterine göre XV. Yüzyıl Sonunda Osmanlı Darphane Mukataaları', *İstanbul Üniversitesi İktisat Fakültesi Mecmuası*, 23, 1–2, 145–218.

——— (1985), 'Yemen'in 1599–1600 Yılı Bütçesi', in *Yusuf Hikmet Bayur Armağanı* (Ankara: Türk Tarih Kurumu), pp. 287–319.

Said, Edward W. (1978). *Orientalism* (New York: Vintage Books).

Salzmann, Ariel (1993). 'An Ancien Régime Revisited: "Privatization" and Political Economy in the Eighteenth-century Ottoman Empire', *Politics and Society*, 21, 4, 393–423.

——— (1995). Measures of Empire: Tax Farmers and the Ottoman Ancien Régime, 1695–1807', unpublished PhD diss., Columbia University, New York.

Schaendlinger, Anton (1983). *Die Schreiben Süleymāns des Prächtigen an Karl V., Ferdinand I. und Maximilian II. aus dem Haus-, Hof- und Staatsarchiv zu Wien*, 2 vols. (Vienna: Österreichische Akademie der Wissenschaften).

Schaendlinger, Anton (1986). *Die Schreiben Süleymāns des Prächtigen an Vasallen, Militärbeamte, Beamte und Richter aus dem Haus-, Hof- und Staatsarchiv zu Wien*, 2 vols. (Vienna: Österreichische Akademie der Wissenschaften).

Schiltberger, Johannes (1983). *Als Sklave im Osmanischen Reich und bei den Tataren 1394–1427*, trans. and ed. Ulrich Schlemmer (Stuttgart: Erdmann-Thienemann).

Schweigger, Salomon (1986). *Zum Hofe des türkischen Sultans* (Leipzig: VEB F.A. Brockhaus).

Sehī Beg (1978). *Heşt Bihişt, The tezkire by Sehi Beg . . .*, ed. Günay Kut (Duxbury, Cambridge MA: Orient Press).

Sertel, Yıldız (1993). *Annem Sabiha Sertel Kimdi Neler Yazdı, Yaşantı* (Istanbul: Yapı ve Kredi Bankası).

Shaw, Stanford J. (1962). *The Financial and Administrative Development of Ottoman Egypt 1517–1798* (Princeton NJ: Princeton University Press).

(1977). *History of the Ottoman Empire and Modern Turkey*, 2 vols. vol. II coauthored with Ezel Kural Shaw (Cambridge: Cambridge University Press).

Shaw, Stanford J. (ed.) (1968). *The Budget of Ottoman Egypt 1005–1006/1596–97* (The Hague, Paris: Mouton).

Singer, Amy (1990). 'Tapu Tahrir Defterleri and Kadı Sicilleri: A Happy Marriage of Sources,' *Târîh*, I, 95–125.

(1994). *Palestinian Peasants and Ottoman Officials, Rural Administration around Sixteenth-Century Jerusalem* (Cambridge: Cambridge University Press).

Skilliter, Susan (1976). 'The Sultan's Messenger, Gabriel Defrens; An Ottoman Master-Spy of the Sixteenth Century', *Wiener Zeitschrift für die Kunde des Morgenlandes*, 68, 47–60.

Snouck Hurgronje, Christian (1931). *Mekka in the Latter Part of the 19th Century, Daily Life, Customs and Learning, the Moslims of the East-Indian-Archipelago*, trans. J.H. Monahan (Leiden, London: E. J. Brill and Luzac).

Stavrianos, Leften S. (1958). *The Balkans since 1453* (New York: Rinehart & Company).

Steensgaard, Niels (1968). 'Consuls and Nations in the Levant from 1570 to 1650', in *The Scandinavian Economic History Review*, XV, 1–2, 13–55.

Stewart-Robinson, J. (1965). 'The Ottoman Biographies of Poets', *Journal of Near Eastern Studies*, 24, 57–74.

Stirling, Paul (ed.) (1993). *Culture and Economy, Changes in Turkish Villages* (Huntingdon: The Eothen Press).

St. Martin, M. Vivien de (1852). *Description historique et géographique de l'Asie mineure*, 2 vols. (Paris: A. Bertrand).

Stoianovich, Traian (1953). 'Land Tenure and Related Sectors of the Balkan Economy, 1600–1800', *The Journal of Economic History* 13, 398–411.

Stoianovich, Traian (1970). 'Model and Mirror of the Pre-Modern Balkan City,' in *La ville balkanique, XVe-XIVe siècles, Studia Balkanica*, vol. 3 (Sofia: Académie Bulgare des Sciences, Institut d'Etudes balkaniques), 83–110.

(1994). *Balkan Worlds. The First and Last Europe* (Armonk NY, London: M. S. Sharpe).

Stojanov, Valery (1983). *Die Entstehung und Entwicklung der osmanisch-türkischen Paläographie und Diplomatik, mit einer Bibliographie* (Berlin: Klaus Schwarz).

Stoye, John (1994). *Marsigli's Europe 1680–1730, The Life and Times of Luigi Fernando Marsigli, Soldier and Virtuoso* (London, New Haven: Yale University Press).

Strauß, Johann (1995). 'Probleme der Öffentlichkeitswirkung der muslimischen Presse Kretas,' in *Presse und Öffentlichkeit im Nahen Osten*, ed. by Christoph Herzog, Raoul Motika and Anja Pistor-Hatam (Heidelberg: Heidelberger Orientverlag), pp. 155–74.

(forthcoming). 'Ottoman Rule Experienced and Remembered. Remarks on

Some Local Greek Chronicles of the *Tourkokratia.*'

Subrahmanyam, Sanjay (1990). *The Political Economy of Commerce: India, 1500–1650* (Cambridge: Cambridge University Press).

Sugar, Peter F. (1997). *Southeastern Europe under Ottoman Rule 1354–1805* (Seattle, London: Universiy of Washington Press).

Sümer, Faruk (3rd edn. 1980). *Oğuzlar (Türkmenler), Tarihleri, Boy Teşkilatı, Destanları* (n.p.: Ana Yayınları).

Svoronos, N. (1956). *Le commerce de Salonique au XVIIIe siècle* (Paris: PUF).

Tabakoğlu, Ahmet (1985). *Gerileme Dönemine Girerken Osmanlı Maliyesi* (Istanbul: Dergâh Yayınları).

Ṭašköprüzāde (1927). *Eš-šaqā'iq en-nomānijje von Ṭašköprüzāde, enthaltend die Biographien der türkischen und im osmanischen Reiche wirkenden Gelehrten, Derwisch-Scheih's und Ärzte von der Regierung Sultan 'Otmān's bis zu der Sülaimāns des Großen*, trans. O. Rescher (Istanbul: Phoenix).

Tavernier, Jean Baptiste (1981). *Les six voyages en Turquie et en Perse*, 2 vols., abridged and annoted Stéphane Yérasimos (Paris: François Maspéro/La Découverte).

Thévenot, Jean (1980). *Voyage du Levant*, ed. Stéphane Yérasimos (Paris: François Maspéro / La Découverte).

Thomas, Lewis (1972). *A Study of Naima*, ed. Norman Itzkowitz (New York: New York University Press).

Tilly, Charles (1985). 'War Making and State Making as Organized Crime', in *Bringing the State Back In*, ed. Peter Evans, Dietrich Rueschemeyer and Theda Skocpol (Cambridge: Cambridge University Press), pp. 169–91.

Todorova, Maria N. (1993). *Balkan Family Structure and the European Pattern, Demographic Developments in Ottoman Bulgaria* (Washington: The American University Press).

—— (1996). 'The Ottoman Legacy and the Balkans', in *Imperial Legacy, The Ottoman Imprint on the Balkans and the Middle East*, ed. L. Carl Brown (New York: Columbia University Press), pp. 45–77.

Togan, Isenbike (1992). 'Ottoman History by Inner Asian Norms', in *New Approaches to State and Peasant in Ottoman History*, ed. Halil Berktay and Suraiya Faroqhi (London: Frank Cass), pp. 185–210.

Tournefort, Joseph Pitton de (1982). *Voyage d'un botaniste*, 2 vols., abridged and annotated Stéphane Yérasimos (Paris: François Maspéro/La Découverte).

Tucker, Judith (1985) *Women in Nineteenth-Century Egypt* (Cambridge: Cambridge University Press).

Tulum, Mertol *et al.* (eds.) (1993). *Mühimme Defteri 90* (Istanbul: Türk Dünyası Araştırmaları Vakfı).

Türek, Fahri and Çetin Derin (trans.) (1969). 'Feyzullah Efendi'nin kendi Kaleminden Hal Tercümesi', *Tarih Dergisi*, 23, 205–18; 24, 69–93.

Ünal, Mehmet Ali (ed.) (1995) *Mühimme Defteri 44* (Izmir: Akademi Kitabevi).

Ünver, Süheyl (1960). 'XVinci Asırda Kullandığımız Filigranlı Kağıtlar Üzerine', in

V. *Türk Tarih Kongresi (Ankara 12–17 Nisan 1956) Kongreye Sunulan Tebliğler* (Ankara: Türk Tarih Kurumu), pp. 338–91.

(1962). 'XV. Yüzyılda Türkiye'de Kâgitlar ve Su Damgaları', *Belleten*, 26, 104, 739–62.

Uzluk, Feridun Nâfiz (1958). *Fâtih Devrinde Karaman Eyâleti Vakıfları Fihristi, Tapu ve Kadastro Umum Müdürlüğü Arşivindeki Deftere Göre* (Ankara: Vakıflar Umum Müdürlüğü).

Uzunçarşılı, İsmail Hakkı (1941a). 'Buyruldı', *Belleten*, 5,19, 289–318.

(1941b). 'Tuğra ve Pençelerle Ferman ve Buyuruldulara Dair', *Belleten*, 5,/ 17–18, 101–57.

(1941c). *Osmanlı Devleti Teşkilâtına Medhal* . . . (Istanbul: Maarif Matbaası).

(1943, 1944). *Osmanlı Devleti Teşkilâtından Kapukulu Ocakları*, 2 vols. (Ankara: Türk Tarih Kurumu).

(1945). *Osmanlı Devletinin Saray Teşkilâtı* (Ankara: Türk Tarih Kurumu).

(1948). *Osmanlı Devletinin Merkez ve Bahriye Teşkilâtı* (Ankara: Türk Tarih Kurumu).

(1965). *Osmanlı Devletinin İlmiye Teşkilâtı* (Ankara: Türk Tarih Kurumu).

(2nd printing 1974). *Çandarlı Vezir Ailesi* (Ankara: Türk Tarih Kurumu).

(reprint 1977, 1982, 1983). *Osmanlı Tarihi*, 4 vols.; vol. 1: *Anadolu Selçukluları ve Anadolu Beylikleri hakkında bir Mukaddime ile Osmanlı Devleti'nin Kuruluşundan Istanbul'un Fethine kadar;* vol. 2: *Istanbul'un Fethinden Kanunî Sultan Süleyman'ın Ölümüne kadar;* vol. 3, part 1: *II Selim'in Tahta Çıkışından 1699 Karlofça Andlaşmasına kadar.* vol. 3, part 2: *XVI. Yüzyıl Ortalarından XVII. Yüzyıl Sonuna Kadar;* vol. 4, part 1: *Karlofça Anlaşmasından (sic) XVIII. Yüzyılın Sonuna kadar;* vol. 4, part 2: *XVIII. Yüzyıl* (Ankara: Türk Tarih Kurumu).

(1981–86). 'Osmanlı Sarayı'nda Ehl-i Hiref (Sanatkârlar) Defteri', *Belgeler*, 11, 15, 23–76.

Valensi, Lucette (1987). *Venise et la Sublime Porte, La naissance du despote* (Paris: Hachette).

Veinstein, Gilles (1975). 'Ayân de la région d'Izmir et le commerce du Levant (deuxième moitié du XVIIIe siècle)', *Revue de l'Occident musulman et de la Méditerranée* 20, 131–46.

Veinstein, Gilles (1996). 'L'oralité dans les documents d'archives ottomans: paroles rapportés ou imaginées?' *Oral et écrit dans le monde turco-ottoman*, special issue of *Revue du monde musulman et de la Méditerranée* (Aix-en-Provence: Edisud), 75–6, 133–42.

Vries, Jan de (1993). 'Between Purchasing Power and the World of Goods: Understanding the Household Economy in Early Modern Europe', in *Consumption and the World of Goods*, ed. John Brewer and Roy Porter (London: Routledge), pp. 85–132.

Vryonis Jr., Speros (1971). *The Decline of Medieval Hellenism in Asia Minor and the Process of Islamization from the Eleventh through the Fifteenth Century* (Berkeley, Los Angeles, London: University of California Press).

Wallerstein, Immanuel (1974, 1980, 1989). *The Modern World-System*, 3 vols. (New York etc.: Academic Press).

White, Hayden (1978). 'Historical Texts as Literary Artefacts', in *The Writing of History: Literary Form and Historical Understanding*, ed. R. Canary and H. Kosicki (Madison, Wisc. University of Wisconsin Press), pp. 41–62.

Wild, Johann (1964). *Reysbeschreibung eines Gefangenen Christen Anno 1604*, ed. Georg A. Narciß and Karl Teply (Stuttgart: Steingrüben).

Williams, Gerhild Scholz (1989). 'Geschichte und die literarische Dimension, Narrativik und Historiographie in der anglo-amerikanischen Forschung der letzten Jahrzehnte', *Deutsche Vierteljahrsschrift für Literaturwissenschaft und Geistesgeschichte*, 63, 315–392.

Wirth, Eugen (1986). 'Aleppo im 19. Jahrhundert – ein Beispiel für Stabilität und Dynamik spätosmanischer Wirtschaft', in *Osmanistische Studien zur Wirtschafts- und Sozialgeschichte: in memoriam Vančo Boškov*, ed. Hans Georg Majer (Wiesbaden: Harrassowitz), pp. 106–206. There is a corrected reprint, also dated 1986, available from the author.

Wittek, Paul (1938, reprint 1966). *The Rise of the Ottoman Empire* (London: The Royal Asiatic Society of Great Britain and Ireland).

Wittmann, Reinhard (1991). *Geschichte des deutschen Buchhandels* (Munich: C. H. Beck).

Wolf, Eric R. (1966). *Peasants* (Englewood Cliffs, NJ: Prentice-Hall).

Woodhead, Christine (1983). *Ta'līkī-zāde's şehnāme-i hümāyun, A History of the Ottoman Campaign into Hungary 1593–94* (Berlin: Klaus Schwarz).

Wurm, Heidrun (1971). *Der osmanische Historiker Hüseyin b. Ğa'fer, genannt Hezārfenn, und die Istanbuler Gesellschaft in der zweiten Hälfte des 17. Jahrhunderts* (Freiburg i.B.: Klaus Schwarz).

Yérasimos, Stéphane (1990). *La Fondation de Constantinople et de Sainte-Sophie dans les traditions turques* (Istanbul, Paris: Institut français d'études anatoliennes and Librairie d'Amérique et d'Orient).

(1991). *Les voyageurs dans l'empire ottoman (XIVᵉ-XVIᵉ siècles), Bibliographie, itinéraires et inventaire des lieux habités* (Ankara: Türk Tarih Kurumu).

Zachariadou, Elizabeth A. (1985). *Romania and the Turks (c. 1300 – c. 1500)* (London: Variorum).

Zilfi, Madeline (1986). 'Discordant Revivalism in Seventeenth-Century Istanbul', *The Journal of Near Eastern Studies*, 45, 4, 251–69.

(ed.) (1997). *Women in the Ottoman Empire* (Leiden: E. J. Brill).

Zirojević, Olga (1989). 'Die Bewahrung und Erforschung der osmanischen Hinterlassenschaft in Jugoslawien: Archive und Forschungseinrichtungen', in *Die Staaten Südosteuropas und die Osmanen*, ed. Hans Georg Majer (Munich: Südosteuropa Gesellschaft), pp. 187–204.

Zürcher, Erik J. (1993). *Turkey, a Modern History* (London, New York: I.B. Tauris).

INDEX

251

household, as a non-capitalist undertaking
    104, 196
households 97, 99
landholding 102
lands, not expropriated 106
lands, taken over by non-peasants 102, 103
soldier: see *müsellem*, see *yaya*
peasantry 106, 192
peasants 21, 84, 100, 101, 192, 196, 201, 206,
    220
    European 86
Peçevi, Ibrahim 152, 153
Peçin 83
Pegolotti 118
pençe 70
pen(s) 70
Pera *see* Beyoğlu
periodical press 168, 170
perspectives, contrasting, brought together by
    historians 140
Peysonnel, French consular family 64
photography 204
pilgrimage, to Jerusalem and the Holy Land
    113
pilgrimage account 22
pilgrims, pilgrimage to Mecca 8, 16, 114–117,
    133
Pitts, Joseph 117
Planhol, Xavier de 100
pluralism, of research methods 106
Poland, Poles, Polish 2, 73, 80, 102, 141, 179,
    196
poll tax *see cizye*
Pope, Alexander 126
population 194
    density 107
    exchange, Greco-Turkish 187
    growth 90, 104, 105
    growth, as an economic stimulant 105
    increase, spurious 91
    pressure 105
    size, Ottoman 88, 89
port 137
port cities/towns 110, 136, 138, 140
Portugal, Portuguese 8, 67, 68, 187
power of capital 98
power sharing, between centre and provincial
    elites 213–215
Prague 48
press, periodical 145
price revolution 98
Prime Minister's Archive: see Başbakanlık Arşivi
printing 46
prisoners of war 116
private lands *see mülk*
problématique 38, 39, 206
problem-oriented studies 38

Prokosch, Erich 33
Protestants, Hungarian 185
protoindustries 201
province *see vilayet*
provincial culture, of Ottoman Christians 158,
    159, 201, 202
provisioning, Ottoman 196
Public Record Office (London) 65, 136, 190
publication of texts 144

Quataert, Donald 18, 137, 140, 195, 196

railway 138
rainfall 83, 84, 100
Ranke, Leopold von 114
Raid 150
Raymond, André 9, 213
reaya çiftliği 102
Registers of Important Affairs *see* Mühimme
    Registers
rehabilitation, historiographical, of the Ottoman
    eighteenth century 213
relazioni 114
reports, consular 64, 141, 142
Resmi, Ahmed 154, 155, 156
Revan see Eriwan
Revan Köşkü 47
revenue collector 82
revisions, of texts 147, 148
Reychman, Jan 73
rice 106
Richter, Otto von 116
rik'a 50
Ritter, Carl 112
robberies 95
Rome 123, 154
Roumania, Roumanian 59, 73, 178, 185, 196
Rousseau, French consul in Aleppo 64
routes 111, 119, 133, 159, 160, 161
Rum Mehmed Paa 148
Rumeli 156
Rumelia 150
rural life 82
    neglected by both Evliya Çelebi and J.B.
        Tavernier 134
rural settlement 100
Ruse 59
Russia, Russian 5, 15, 53, 175, 179, 186, 190,
    196, 219, 220
ruzname 74
Rüstem Pasha 112

Sacra Congregatio de Propaganda Fide (Vatican
    City) 67
Sadeddin (Arel) 169
Sadok, Boubaker 63
Sadreddin-i Konevi 46